GRANDMOTHER BROWN'S
HUNDRED YEARS

GRANDMOTHER BROWN IN HER THIRTIES

GRANDMOTHER BROWN'S HUNDRED YEARS

1827—1927

BY

HARRIET CONNOR BROWN

WITH DECORATIVE HEADINGS BY
STANLEY SCOTT

BLUE RIBBON BOOKS
New York

Copyright, 1929,
By Harriet Connor Brown

All rights reserved

Published October, 1929
Reprinted December, 1929 (three times)
Reprinted February, 1930
Reprinted May, 1930
Reprinted October, 1930
Reprinted April, 1931
Reprinted January, 1932

PRINTED IN THE UNITED STATES OF AMERICA
PRINTED BY THE CORNWALL PRESS, INC.
CORNWALL, N. Y.

To
My Husband and My Daughter

FOREWORD

THE older our country becomes, the larger its population, the greater its diversification of industry, of blood, and of culture, the more our calm judgment acknowledges the debt this people and nation owe to its early settlers. It was they who laid the foundation and fashioned the shape of the governmental, social, and industrial edifice, to which we of this generation make only additions or subtractions.

The first settlers in New England were differentiated from the first settlers of any number in Western North America by the fact that religious intolerance in England at the time of their emigration was a compelling force in causing it. This gave the movement and settlement a somewhat religious character. Unquestionably the New England settler who had fled from religious oppression and his descendants were a great influence in the formation of what may be called our American institutions, which so effectively guard man in his freedom of worship, freedom of speech, his choice of religion, his right of trial by jury, his right to property, and those other inalienable rights upon which no other individual or even government itself can encroach, the statement of which was finally permanently embodied in the Constitution of the United States.

This book is a record of the descendants of that stock in another and later development of our national life. It was one hundred and sixty-seven years after the landing of the Pilgrims and shortly after the Revolutionary War, in April,

1788, when there occurred the great emigration to the "Territory Northwest of the River Ohio," to be governed under the ordinance passed by Congress in 1787 with its antislavery provision. During this period of one hundred and sixty-seven years American institutions may be said in general to have been defined, although the antislavery provisions of the Ordinance of 1787 were not included in the Constitution of the United States until after the Civil War.

It is fortunate for America that her institutions had this long evolution in a population the character of which did not greatly change, either through emigration or incongruous immigration, and which developed its strong characteristics largely because of a difficult environment. From no other kind of people or conditions could such institutions have been evolved.

It is not too much to say that had the transportation facilities of the early days in America been what they are now, to say nothing of other great differences between past and modern environment, our institutions would have developed along far different lines. Principles do not take root in rapidly changing or moving populations. But once our institutions were firmly established and become the heritage of all our people, the easy transportation which in the old days would have prevented their development became in later days the means of establishing them in all parts of our country.

A study of the development of the spirit of the Middle West is simply the study of the reaction of the oldest American stock imbued with the old American traditions and the spirit of its institutions to a new environment different in some respects from that in which the same stock evolved those institutions and traditions.

This book — *Grandmother Brown's Hundred Years* — will

FOREWORD

be for a student of American human nature a classic textbook. This wonderful woman tells in a simple and natural way the story of her life. If her purpose was any other than to tell her story exactly as it was, the book would have lost its value. As one reads these pages, he realizes that Grandmother Brown gives facts as she sees them and opinions formed without the handicap of a preconceived philosophy which often warps the statements of historical writers.

The author of the book, her daughter-in-law, has succeeded in transferring to its pages a fine picture of the New England character as it reacted two hundred years after the landing of the Pilgrim Fathers to a new environment. The book is more than that. It is an epic of American life in the early and later days of the Middle West.

No one can read the story without the continuing sense of its inherent truthfulness, without added reverence for the old American stock, transplanted but unchanged, without an added realization of the fact that the important things of life are the simple ones, and that small duties, faithfully performed, sum themselves up finally in the creation of high character commanding universal respect and interest, and becoming an influence for unbounded good to our citizenship.

CHARLES G. DAWES.

CONTENTS

FOREWORD BY THE HONORABLE CHARLES G. DAWES . . vii
INTRODUCTION xv

YOUTH

I	THE NORTHWEST TERRITORY	. . . .	3
II	MARIA FOSTER	. . . . .	26
III	THE BROWNS	. . . . . .	81
IV	EARLY MARRIED LIFE	. . . .	91

MIDDLE AGE

| V | AN IOWA FARM | . . . . . . | 111 |
| VI | AN IOWA VILLAGE | . . . . . | 180 |

OLD AGE

VII	INDIAN SUMMER	. . . . .	217
VIII	DAN'L'S DEATH	. . . . .	238
IX	GRANDMOTHER BROWN'S TRAVELS	. .	270
X	SHUT-IN	. . . .	304
XI	THE CENTENNIAL	. . . . .	344
	EPILOGUE	. . . . . .	363

INTRODUCTION

On April 9, 1926, the *Evening Democrat* of Fort Madison, Iowa, contained the following announcement: —

Mrs. Brown's Birthday

An unusual family party took place to-day when Mrs. Maria D. Brown celebrated her 99th birthday. Gathered about her at the dinner table were her widowed daughter and her five sons with their wives. The oldest son is 80 years old, the youngest 56. The combined age of the family group, mother and six children, is 521 years. All are in sound health, physically and mentally. The party took place at the Brown homestead, where Mrs. Brown has lived for more than a half century. She presided at the dinner table, asking the blessing in a strong voice and blowing out the candles on her birthday cake in one vigorous breath. Not the least among the achievements is the fact that she has kept to her extreme age a high degree of personal beauty and is still lovely to look at.

This family has on both sides a remarkable record of longevity.

INTRODUCTION

Mrs. Brown is the last survivor of a family of six sisters and one brother, all of whom lived to be over 70. She was born in Athens, Ohio, the daughter of Eben Foster, scion of Revolutionary ancestors who had migrated from Massachusetts. Her husband, Daniel Truesdell Brown, who was also born in Ohio, and was well known in Iowa as a paper manufacturer, died in 1906 at the age of 84. Considering him and his wife and their children as a family, there have been only three deaths in a family of 10 in 104 years, his own and those of two infant daughters. Aside from his death, there has been no death in the family for 60 years.

The oldest son, William E. Brown, 80 years old, is still actively engaged in business in Sioux Falls, South Dakota, where he is associated with his son, Knapp Brown, in the automobile business. The second son, Charles P. Brown, 78 years old, is a retired farmer living at Revere, Missouri. The third son, Augustus P. Brown, 72 years old, who lives in the old homestead at Fort Madison, was formerly mayor and president of the Brown Paper Company. He is now president of the Artesian Ice Company. The fourth son, Frank R. Brown, 62 years old, is manager of the Artesian Ice Company. The youngest son, Herbert D. Brown, 56 years old, lives in Washington, D. C., and is chief of the United States Bureau of Efficiency. The only daughter, Mrs. Elizabeth Davis, 74 years old, is the mother of Dan C. Davis, lubrication supervisor of the Santa Fe Railway system, and William Lynn Davis, efficiency engineer of the Staley Manufacturing Company of Decatur, Illinois.

Following the dinner with her children, Mrs. Brown received grandchildren, great-grandchildren, and numerous citizens of Fort Madison, who showered her with gifts and loving attention. It was an exciting day, which she experienced with great joy and without undue fatigue.

As the wife of the youngest son, I was present at this memorable birthday party. Many tender memories filled my mind as I looked over the company of people assembled to do honor to "Grandmother Brown." For nearly thirty years I myself had sat at her feet. Into my ear she had poured, from time to time, not only stories of her own childhood and the infancy of her children and grandchildren, but also stories handed down from her forebears of their remote childhood. I mused on the significance of many things she had told me.

Back almost a century her own clear memory stretched and, back beyond that, by hearsay, her traditions carried her another century or two into the very beginnings of English colonization upon this continent. It came upon me that she sat enthroned among us not merely as head of her family, a precious figure of maternity, but that, in some sense, she had become a historical personage, symbol of the pioneer age in the development of our great country. Of her like, few were now left on earth — not more than one in every twenty-five thousand of our population — who were alive when John Quincy Adams was president. Sprung from colonists who had settled the Atlantic seaboard, established its independence of Europe, and then pushed on into the Northwest Territory, claiming it too for freedom, she herself had joined in the great migration down the Ohio, helping to carry forward the customs and ideals of the English-speaking world into the wilderness that lay beyond the Mississippi.

I felt that, dearly as they loved her, greatly as they honored her, it had hardly occurred to her twoscore descendants that she represented, in her person, something bigger than her own family, a complete tradition of many families, which had significance for the whole nation. I was filled with a desire to take from her own lips her impressions of the stirring age of which she had been a part. And so, when the reunion was over, and others had returned to their homes, I lingered a little longer, sitting beside her every day for two weeks and taking down in her own vigorous language her memories of life in the past century. This book is, essentially, the record of that interview, prefaced by sufficient historical data to make clear the background of her life, and completed by selections from her letters. The result is not only a chronicle of typical experience in the life of Woman, but also a panoramic view of an age seen through the eyes of an individual.

Had Grandmother Brown been a woman of literary attainments, of wider reading and more varied acquaintance with the great world, her observation on life might be more interesting to the sophisticated. But the mass of men and women who have made America have not been literary or sophisticated. They have, however, been people of ideals, people of courage. What benefits we now enjoy in America have come to us as the result of the labors of people inspired by ideals such as Grandmother Brown has cherished, upheld by courage such as she has had. As we go forward into another period of our country's development, it is well for us to try to understand the forces that have created us and the world in which we find ourselves, even though we ourselves are driven by very different forces and are building up another kind of society based perhaps on a different philosophy of life. Many of the influences that have affected Grandmother Brown — religious, political, social — leave me unmoved, but I can understand how they wrought on her in her day, can understand and sympathize.

Recording her story in her own pungent speech, I have hoped to catch and preserve for Grandmother Brown's descendants some of the flavor of her personality; her aspirations, her achievements, even her limitations; her innocent vanities; her lovable animosities; her patient endeavors. Especially her summing up as she reviews it all. It is **not** merely that she has lived a hundred years — significant as is that fact alone in the history of poor, feeble mankind — which moves me. It is the fact that she is, after a century of wear and tear, still a vivid Person. I can see that, sitting on the edge of the world and peering over, she gets a thrill from that experience as from all others. A pity to let so much of intelligence and sweetness and gallantry at age ninety-nine go unsung! The reactions of Nineteen to life we have all heard about many times; those of Nine-and-ninety we have, as yet, merely divined. To the psychologist — if not to the poet and preacher — those reactions are, as yet, little known. Perhaps we may learn from Grandmother Brown the secret of growing old gracefully.

Chiefly, I think of her as a mother. In that experience she has found understanding of many things. A careful craftsman in all she does, and by nature proud, — though timid too, — she demands that her pride be satisfied in her children. It is impossible to tell her story and not refer constantly to her children, to her hopes and plans and work for them, and their reaction to her efforts. Otherwise, she has no "story." And, indeed, her story is the typical story of women. What is noteworthy about it is her attitude towards it. "Why, what has she ever done that is great?" is a question that nettled me when I told a friend that I was trying to write the history of my hundred-year-old mother-in-law. The general attitude of mind reflected by my friend's question is the thing that makes me want to see published the story of how one good mother has spent a hundred years. I want to honor a woman not esteemed "great," one who has had the common fate and will be consigned to oblivion, despite work well done throughout a full century of living, unless someone like myself can rescue her from it. To read of her may comfort other women who, passionately and devotedly, but more or less rebelliously, are doing the duty that Nature points them to, the kind of work which the man-world, despite all its fine talk about the glory of womanhood, holds so lightly.

As there is no escape from the fact that the first characteristic of motherhood is suffering, I find, beneath all Grandmother Brown's brave commentary on life, an undercurrent of sadness. To have lived a hundred years means that one must have stood often beside the portals of sorrow, must have heard many times the birth cry, many times the death rattle, must have been disillusioned and disappointed again and again. But, like proud old Hecuba, believing in the final triumph of Eternal Justice, Grandmother Brown clasps to her bosom all that makes up life, all the joy and anguish, the hope and despair, that have come her way; lives through it all, rises above it all, makes it all her own. And I thrill as I hear her echo, in her own words, that cry of Hecuba: —

> Thou deep Base of the World, and thou high Throne
> Above the World, whoe'er thou art, unknown
> And hard of surmise, Chain of Things that be,
> Or Reason of our Reason; God, to thee
> I lift my praise, seeing the silent road
> That bringeth *justice* ere the end be trod
> To all that breathes and dies.

WASHINGTON, D. C. H. C. B.
April 15, 1928.

YOUTH

I

THE NORTHWEST TERRITORY

GRANDMOTHER BROWN was born in Athens, Ohio, at ten o'clock in the morning, on April 9, 1827. She was the third child of Ebenezer Foster and Achsah Culver. They named the pretty baby "Maria Dean" after her father's sister Maria, who had married John Nicholson Dean and lived across the street.

"Tell me, Grandmother Brown," I began, drawing up my chair beside her on the morning of the day when she entered on her hundredth year, "how it was in Ohio when you were a little girl."

"It was n't like this," she mused, gazing out of the window into the Iowa sunshine. "I was born in an April shower. They used to say that was why I cried so easily. But I was born into a happy home, where there was little cause for crying. Two children were there before me — Brother John, five years old, and Sister Libbie, who was two. When I was three years old, Sister Kate came to join us. We lived in a commodious house surrounded by gardens and orchards. Our home occupied just one square block in the town of Athens. Oh, there never was any place that looked to me so beautiful as that did in my childhood days!"

To get a clear picture of that early home one must remember that, when little Maria first opened her observant blue eyes, she looked out on a cultural environment that had been developed by her parents and grandparents and their contemporaries in the short space of only forty years. Scarce four decades had elapsed since Congress had passed the famous Ordinance of 1787 under which the Government of the Northwest Territory had been established. Before that, the beautiful Hocking Valley where Maria was born had echoed to the tread of hardly any feet save those of red men and wild beasts. To be sure, French and British had passed that way, but only fleetingly.

None of Maria's forebears had been in that band of forty-eight heroes of the Revolution whom General Rufus Putnam had landed, on April 7, 1788, at the point on the Ohio River where now stands Marietta. But her grandfather, Zadoc Foster, — a resident, like Putnam, of Rutland, Massachusetts, — came to Marietta only eight years later. In his boyhood he had known General Putnam, who had dwelt in a house not far from the one built and occupied by Zadoc's father, Lieutenant Ebenezer Foster. The families were friends. Both houses are still standing. Both are substantial, dignified structures of the type occupied by the leading citizens of New England a century and a half ago.

Lieutenant Foster had come to Rutland in 1744. He was the third Ebenezer in direct descent from the John Foster who had come to Salem from England in the early part of the seventeenth century. Grandmother Brown had a pretty vanity in the doings of more or less mythical ancestors who lie back of that John and his beginnings in the Old World. At least, she was likely to tell you, primly, some day as she lifted her handsome white head from perusal of her *Foster Genealogy*,[1] that her kin, the Forester family, were "the principal chieftains in Northumberland and allied by marriage with all the eminent northern families of England." She could tell you about the part played by Foresters at the Battle of Hastings and at the Battle of Bannockburn, and how one Sir John Foster saved the life of Richard Lionheart at the Siege of Acre. Plenty of the name spawning over into other lands. To Ireland, Jamaica, Nova Scotia, they emigrated in large numbers. Along the coast of New England at Dorchester, Salem, Scituate, Chelmsford, Andover, they settled thickly.

It was about a hundred years after John Foster had landed in Salem that his great-grandson, Ebenezer, came with his parents to Rutland. He was then eleven years old. When he was twenty-two, he went on a military expedition sent by Massachusetts against Crown Point. At the age of twenty-four, he married Hannah Parlin of Concord. He had purchased, the year before, a tract of one hundred acres of land in

---

[1] The record of the posterity of Reginald Foster, an early inhabitant of Ipswich, in New England, whose genealogy is traced back to Anacher, Great Forester of Flanders, who died in 837 A.D.; also the record of all other American Fosters. By Frederick Clifton Pierce.

what was called Rutland West Wing, but is now known as Oakham, and there, about 1766, he built his comfortable home. He became prominent in local history and, according to the *Foster Genealogy*, "held most of the offices within the gift of the town." At the Lexington alarm in April 1775, he was one of the Minute Men who sprang to arms. With a company of his fellow citizens he marched toward the scene of the encounter, but he arrived too late to be of service in the fight. However, we know that he was an active officer in the militia. The record shows that he was commissioned on June 4, 1776, for the post of Adjutant of the Fourth Worcester County Regiment of the Massachusetts Militia. His family respected that connection sufficiently to have his title of lieutenant engraved on his tombstone in the old churchyard at Oakham. Grandmother Brown's patriotic soul thrilled at mention of his name.

To Rufus Putnam, his neighbor, distinguished honors had come during the war. Though he was poor and self-taught, Washington considered Putnam "the ablest engineer officer of the war, whether American or Frenchman." To him was due the success of the first great military operation of the Revolution, the defense of Boston. The war over, Putnam purchased the large farm and attractive dwelling house at Rutland. There he tilled his land, and, like his neighbor, Ebenezer Foster, held various public offices.

"When I visited Rutland in 1911," said Grandmother Brown, "I bought this picture of Putnam. It's a good face, but not very handsome. How I'd like to have a similar picture of my great-grandfather, Ebenezer Foster! I wonder if he wore his hair long, tied back like that, and if he wore ruffled shirts. I fancy that he did. My mother had an uncle — Uncle Rowley — who used to come to see her when I was a child. He wore a ruffled shirt, and his hair — it was white or powdered, I don't know which — was tied in a bag. When he got on his horse and rode away, that hair kept whacking at the back of his neck. We children always used to laugh, as we watched him ride away."

During the years following the war, Putnam's fertile mind was busy. Two pressing problems confronted the victorious leaders of the Revolution: how to pay the soldiers of the war, and how to settle up the West.

The soldiers had been paid in continental currency or certificates redeemable at the option of the colonial Congress. As the Treasury was bankrupt, these certificates had little value. Naturally, there was much dissatisfaction among war veterans, much suffering among their families. These men had staked "their lives, their fortunes, and their sacred honor" to gain independence for their country. Life and honor were left them, but those did not suffice, in the absence of fortune, to feed and clothe their families.

There was apprehension at this time lest some foreign power — Great Britain, Spain, France — should colonize the West and become a menace to the new nation that had been born of the Revolution. Gradually the idea took possession of certain thoughtful minds that the two problems might be solved together: the soldier's certificates might be exchanged for lands in the Ohio country. Thus, the new government might pay its debts to its defenders and at the same time promote colonization of the Western lands by its own loyal people.

General Putnam endorsed the scheme. He even helped to circulate a petition which officers of the Army presented to Congress, asking for a grant of lands north and northwest of the Ohio River to veterans of the army in redemption of the war certificates. He wrote to Washington about it, and Washington labored with Congress to honor the petition of his officers. But nothing happened until General Putnam and his friend, General Benjamin Tupper, — the latter just returned from surveying the Northwestern lands, — sat up all one January night in 1786 in Putnam's Rutland home and drew up a "Call" for a convention of veterans to form a company for the purchase and colonization of those Ohio lands. Walker, the historian,[1] draws a pretty picture of them sitting before a blazing fire in the open fireplace of the house at Rutland, hickory logs steaming and sparks flying up the chimney, Putnam's sword and spurs hanging, perhaps, on the wall.

Three months later, the Ohio Company was organized at the "Bunch of Grapes" tavern in Boston.

Numerous committees of Congress considered the plans presented by the Ohio Company for purchase of the Western lands and for government of the political bodies to be established there. But, notwithstanding the powerful support of Washington, no progress was made until July 6, 1787, when there came to the door of Congress a master diplomat in the modest person of Dr. Manasseh Cutler of Ipswich Hamlet, Massachusetts.

[1] *History of Athens County, Ohio*, by Charles M. Walker.

If General Putnam is honored as "the father of Ohio," surely Dr. Cutler should be remembered as its godfather. What Washington and Franklin were to the fate of the Thirteen Colonies, Putnam and Cutler were, respectively, to the development of the Northwest Territory. A lawyer, a minister, a physician, a statesman, a scholar, a scientist, — indeed, after Dr. Benjamin Franklin, the foremost scientist of the Western continent, — was Dr. Manasseh Cutler. All these he was and, at the same time, a man of consummate business ability and a master hand at diplomacy, a noble soul, a genial man, whose quiet activities had incalculable influence in shaping the destinies of our country. And with all his great dignity and serious aims, what endearing simplicity and sweetness of nature are revealed by his *Journal*,[1] are shown in the portrait of his handsome face!

In his *Journal* we see the careful steps by which Dr. Cutler, as director and agent of the Ohio Company, secured both lands and laws from Congress in accordance with his wise desires. How skillfully he ingratiated himself with the representatives of Massachusetts and Virginia and won their powerful endorsement of his plans! All in the short space too of two and twenty days! Never was there a speedier or more capable lobbyist than the good parson of Ipswich Hamlet. For three and a half million dollars he obtained a grant of nearly five million acres of land, one million and a half of which was for the Ohio Company, the remainder for other purchasers. "The greatest private contract ever made in America," noted Dr. Cutler with

[1] *Life, Journals and Correspondence of Reverend Manasseh Cutler, LL.D.*, by William Parker Cutler and Julia Perkins Cutler.

pardonable pride. Under its provisions, — drawn up by Dr. Cutler, — inhabitants of the Northwest Territory were guaranteed freedom from slavery and involuntary servitude. In such a soil it was that Grandmother Brown's life took root, a soil consecrated to the use of free men.

Before the year was out, Dr. Cutler had organized the first expedition to the lands of the Ohio Company. Under the direction of General Putnam, a little fleet was built that winter at Sumrill's Ferry, about thirty miles above Pittsburgh. Besides a large boat called the *Mayflower*, there were also a flatboat and three log canoes. "Laden with the emigrants, their baggage, surveying instruments, weapons, and effects," says Walker, "the little flotilla glided down the Youghiogheny into the Monongahela, and finally out upon the broad bosom of the Ohio." Spring was in the air, and doubtless beauty brooded over wood and water. Five days later, the emigrants landed in the vicinity of Fort Harmar, a defense which had been built, two years before, as a protection against the Indians, near the junction of the Ohio and the Muskingum.

It is a matter of pride to the descendants of those who came to Marietta in the first days of the Northwest Territory's development that those ancestors were of the best stock that New England afforded. Among those early settlers were over sixty commissioned officers of the Revolution, one of them the grandfather of the man little Maria Foster was destined to marry. Said Washington: "No colony in America was ever settled under such favorable auspices as that which has just commenced at the Muskingum. . . . I know many of the settlers personally, and there never were men better calculated to promote the welfare of such a community."

The work of surveying and tilling the lands began at once. With great care and much good taste the engineers laid out their city of Marietta, — named for the French queen, Marie Antoinette, — preserving as public grounds the great Mounds left there by a prehistoric race. The first settlers' houses were erected on "The Point," which projected far out into the area where the Ohio and the Muskingum mingled their waters. General Putnam advised building, as protection against the Indians, a strong defense three quarters of a mile from the Point. About forty acres of ground were accordingly enclosed in a stockade. The outer walls of this defense — Campus Martius, as they called it — were made of two-story log houses joined together and opening into an inner court. A heavy picket fence was erected around the log-house wall, and outside that was another high fence of brush. "Suitable plats for gardens," says Hildreth,[1] "were laid out between the garrison and the river. The appearance from without was grand and imposing, at a little distance resembling one of the military palaces or castles of the feudal ages."

A treaty with the Indians was concluded in January 1789. In the spring, settlements were established twelve miles south of Marietta on the Ohio at Belpre, and on the Muskingum at Waterford, at Wolf Creek Mills, and at Big Bottom. Numbers of women soon joined the settlers, though it took high courage to face

[1] *Pioneer History of the Ohio Valley and the Early Settlement of the Northwest Territory*, by S. P. Hildreth.

not only the common dangers, but also the perils of childbirth, unaided, in the wilderness. For a time developments went forward promisingly, and hopes were high, but soon famine, pestilence, and Indian hostility put the courage of the colonists to the test.

For nearly two years the Indians kept the treaty of peace. Then, suddenly, in the early days of 1791, exasperated by attacks of the frontier populations of Virginia and Kentucky, the Indians included in their vengeance the settlement of the Ohio Company at Big Bottom. Five years of horror followed. The Indians were on the warpath continually, and the settlers lived in a stage of siege. All the garrisons were under the strictest military discipline. Every half hour in the night the watchword was demanded. No man tilled his field, or gathered his crop, or milked his cow, except with an armed sentry standing guard. By this watchfulness the settlements were preserved, and yet, in the five years of Indian warfare, what unspeakable horrors were perpetrated without those garrison walls, what fear and sorrow endured within them!

"Oh, that was a terrible time," said Grandmother, shaking her head solemnly. "We often heard old settlers talk about it when we were children."

Two armies were routed by the Indians. But, in 1794, General Anthony Wayne — "Mad Anthony," they called him — defeated the Indians utterly. He burned their villages, destroyed their crops, laid waste their whole country. They sued for peace. At Greenville, on August 3, 1795, the tomahawk was definitely buried. There the Red Man gave up his ancient hunting grounds, surrendered the graves of his forefathers. The white man's rule in the Northwest Territory was never again seriously disputed.

When General Putnam issued, in 1786, his call to veterans of the war and others interested in the purchase of Ohio lands, his neighbors, the Fosters of Oakham, showed no interest in the matter, so far as we know. Lieutenant Foster, head of the family, might be called a war veteran, but he seems to have been well placed in life and, as the father of twelve children, had, doubtless, plenty to keep him tied to the spot where he was. Zadoc, his fifth child, then nineteen years old, was possibly thinking more, just then, of how to ingratiate himself with clever little Sally Porter, daughter of Dr. Samuel Porter of Hubbardstown, who had come to Rutland to teach, than he was of the colonization of the Northwest Territory. He was not old enough himself to have been a veteran of the war. It was not until ten years later that looking for a homestead he migrated to the Northwest.

"Tell me, Grandmother Brown, did n't you ever hear any of your people, when you were a little girl, talk about their life in Massachusetts?" I asked her. "Do you know how your grandparents happened to go West?"

She mused a while, and then she said: "My Grandma Foster — she that was Sally Porter — used to tell me that, when she went to Rutland to teach, there was no schoolhouse, and she was given a room in the Foster house for a schoolroom. This house is now owned and occupied — or was in 1911 when I went to see it — by descendants of my great-grandfather, who had built it. It has always remained in the family. I said to the lady then living there, 'I want to see the room where my grandmother taught school.' 'It must have been the room where Lieutenant Foster held court,' she said, and showed it to me. The house is a good old-fashioned New England structure with one big chimney in the centre. About it are eight large rooms, with a fireplace in each one. 'I want a drink from the same fountain that my grandfather drank from,' said I. 'It is the same water,' said our hostess, as she brought me a glass of it, 'but we've had it piped into the house.'

"A very large old elm stands in front. It measured fifteen feet around the bottom. Our hostess said that she understood it had been there since my great-grandfather's time. He and General Putnam were walking together through the timber, one day, and noticed two little elms. 'Let's take them up and plant them in front of our houses,' they said.

"Grandma told me that Lieutenant Foster said to her, when she came there to teach: 'Sally, we have n't any money in this district. You'll have to take one of my boys as pay for your teaching.' And she said 'I took them both, the money and the boy.' Zadoc was twenty-two years old and she was twenty-one. They were married on January 19, 1789. After that, they moved to Sudbury County, Vermont, and lived there several years. I suppose they were like many enterprising young people — they wanted to strike out and do something for themselves. Then, to leave Vermont and go to Ohio, as they did later, was doing just as many others were doing at the time. And I've no doubt that, having known General Putnam, my grandfather was somewhat interested in going to

Marietta, where the general continued to live until his death."

Not much more about her grandparents' life in Vermont or of their coming to the Northwest Territory did Grandmother Brown know, but in Walker's *History* it is recorded that they came, "like many others of that time, with an ox team as far as Olean Point, on the Allegheny River, and thence proceeded by raft down the Ohio to Marietta, in the autumn of 1796." Remaining that winter in the stockade, Zadoc Foster made a settlement in the spring at Belpre. He is said to have gone ahead of his family, making a little clearing and building a cabin.

Studying the history of the times, I wonder if Zadoc Foster was not one of the multitude who streamed westward from the barren hills of New England as soon as news of General Anthony Wayne's decisive victory over the Indians began to reach them. "During the year 1796," says Walker, "nearly one thousand flat-boats, or 'broadhorns,' as they were then called, passed Marietta laden with emigrants on their way to the more attractive regions of southwestern Ohio." Ohio was reputed to be a land flowing with milk and honey, and to Zadoc Foster, trying to farm the rocky soil of Vermont, tales of its fertility must have sounded alluring. Freed from the fear of savages, inspired by "the siren song of peace and of farming," he joined the living column moving westward.

In making a home for his family in the Belpre settlement, Zadoc Foster had, undoubtedly, full scope for any enterprise and industry of which he was possessed. To make a clearing in the forest and to rear on it a comfortable cabin was real man's work, even though the logs were piled up like children's cob houses and held together by wooden pins instead of nails, even though no tools were necessary in the construction, except an axe, an auger, and perhaps a cross-cut saw. Rude, indeed, were those first log cabins with their puncheon floors, wooden shutters, leather latchstrings, stone chimneys, clay hearthstones. Primitive was the homemade furniture within them. We catch a glimpse of a table split from a large log, a bedstead made of poles interlaced with bearskins, a spinning wheel in the corner, a rifle hung in forked cleats over the door with powder horn beside it, three-legged stools, splint-bottomed chairs, cast-iron spiders, long-handled frying pans, a movable Dutch oven.

In some such home lived the Zadoc Fosters, I've no doubt, when they first came to Belpre. Here were met the needs of the children born to them before they moved to Athens in 1809.

"Pa's brothers and sisters were Sally, Ira, Hull, Issa, Maria, Melissa, and Samuel," said Grandmother. "Most of them I knew during my childhood in Athens. When I remember what kind of woman presided over this household, my dear Grandma Foster, and when I recall all the merry quips of Uncle Hull and Aunt Sally and Aunt Maria and Aunt Melissa, I am sure that that simple cabin must have been a very happy home. But I am sure too that Grandma Foster must have had her hands full. In those pioneer times all sorts of accidents were likely to happen to one's children, besides the kind of thing that may befall any baby to-day. Think what happened to Aunt Sally! She fell into the open fire when she was a child and burned the side of her face so that one nostril was drawn down."

One can easily believe that all of Grandma Foster's daughters, from Aunt Sally down, were early trained to industry. The family had to grow and cook its own food, grow and fashion the material for its own garments. We are told that, at Marietta, silkworms were raised by "the females" in General Putnam's family and the cocoons reeled and spun into strong sewing thread. We know that at Belpre crops of flax, cotton, and hemp were raised.

The Fosters arrived in Belpre at a time of great activity in the settlement. Released by the treaty of peace with the Indians in 1795 from their five years' imprisonment in garrisons, the white settlers began to move energetically over the face of the land, chopping down timber, erecting houses, building roads and bridges, breeding stock, and setting out orchards. Fruit trees in the virgin soil of the Ohio bottoms grew with astonishing rapidity. It was not long before Belpre was noted as the fairest spot between Pittsburgh and Cincinnati. Situated on beautiful meadows set high in a lovely curve over the Ohio River, it had a commanding position.

Just opposite Belpre, an island in the river had been purchased, in 1798, by a rich and eccentric Irish nobleman named Harman Blennerhassett, who became famous in our history. In that romantic situation he had laid out a great estate — a spacious mansion surrounded by lawns and gardens, by stables, dairies, and hothouses. The tragic story of the Blennerhassets is known to all the world — how, fresh from his duel with Alexander Hamilton, Aaron Burr tarried at their island home on his way down the valleys of the Ohio and the Mississippi, and how he interested them in his scheme to establish a colony of wealthy individuals in Louisiana, a scheme that was later declared to be treasonable as making a project to separate the people of the West from those of the Atlantic States. When Burr was arrested, the Blennerhassetts became involved in his fall. Their lovely home was ruthlessly destroyed by the Ohio militia. But during the eight years that the Blennerhassetts — husband, wife, and two children — dwelt there they endeared themselves to all their neighbors, high and low. Mr. Blennerhassett was a man of varied intellectual interests and artistic gifts, Mrs. Blennerhassett a woman of engaging qualities of person, mind, and heart. Socially inclined, hospitable and kind, they made welcome at their home all who shared their tastes. They themselves went often to visit friends in Marietta and Belpre. Mrs. Blennerhassett is described by Hildreth as dashing along forest paths in a riding dress of scarlet broadcloth, accompanied by a favorite black servant.

"Oh, Uncle Hull remembered seeing her in that red habit!" exclaimed Grandmother Brown. "I recall now hearing him tell about it. He was only a little boy when he lived in Belpre, but he had a vivid recollection of seeing Madame Blennerhassett riding through the woods in a red dress on a fine horse."

Whether the Fosters ever partook of the hospitality of the Blennerhassetts is not now known, but it is probable that the families met at the white house of Aaron Waldo Putnam, the Fosters having been friendly with the Putnams, according to Grandmother Brown's traditions. Aaron Waldo was a grandson of General Israel Putnam, whom our school histories used to extol for having left his oxen standing in the field in his haste to enlist in the Revolution. He built himself a fine new house at Belpre. Painted white and surrounded by orchards, it was a conspicuous object to travelers on the Ohio. The upper story was fitted up for a ballroom, and Madame Blennerhassett was said to have led in some of the dances there.

From the earliest days of the Northwest Territory, dancing had been a favorite pastime of the young people. Even in the dark days of the Indian War, it is related that parties of youths and maidens used to come down the river in barges or large rowboats from Fort Harmar and from Campus Martius to dance with their young friends at Belpre. I have no doubt that the Fosters did their share of the dancing. "I remember," said Grandmother Brown, "that Grandma Foster told me she was fond of dancing in her youth, but once, when there were balls three times hand running in one week, she thought it time to stop."

Zadoc erected a gristmill—very essential to the life of the community—on the Little Hocking River, from which he supplied, in 1805, the Southern expedition of Burr and Blennerhassett with corn meal. A number of young men from Belpre enlisted in the expedition. Contracts were made for the building of fifteen large bateaux on the Muskingum River and for purchase of bacon, pork, flour, whiskey, and so forth. The tragedy of that expedition has nothing to do with the fortunes of the Foster family, but doubtless they were stirred by it. The young men from Belpre returned in the course of the spring, and they had adventurous tales to relate that were passed glibly from tongue to tongue.

Like most of the first settlers of the Northwest Territory, the Fosters were staunch Federalists, followers of George Washington and Alexander Hamilton. As time passed, and people from Virginia and Kentucky crossed the Ohio and joined in the settlement of the Northwest Territory, the political faith of Thomas Jefferson gained adherents. Lively discussions between Federalists and Democrats were heard at social gatherings in the river settlements.

The shadow of coming conflicts fell, even in those early days, upon the people of Belpre. Few among them believed in the institution of slavery, but to their shores came often the slaveholders of the states across the river. It is said that one reason Mr. Blennerhassett preferred an island in the river for his countryseat to land along shore was that "its location gave him the privilege of holding colored servants as his own property, which he could not do in the Northwest Territory." At the constitutional convention held in Chillicothe in 1802 there was, despite the clause against slavery which Dr. Manasseh Cutler considered the crown of his Ordinance of 1787, a determined effort on the part of the slavery interests to set that aside. But for the efforts of Dr. Cutler's son, Judge Ephraim Cutler, they would have been successful. In the meantime, at Belpre, runaway slaves were often seen.

"I fancy that it was the sight in his boyhood of those poor fugitives that fixed in the mind of my father the intense sympathy for them which he displayed in later years," said Grandmother Brown.

Another moot question on which the Foster mind seemed made up at that early period was the liquor question. Strong drink flowed freely through the early settlements of Ohio. The luscious peaches grown in the orchards of Belpre made a fine alcoholic beverage.

It was deservedly popular; even clergymen had it for "refreshment" at their conventions. But little Grandma Foster probably entertained prejudices against it, for her sons were known to be teetotalers. Said Grandmother Brown, "My mother told me that when my father used to deal out whiskey to his hired men, as was the custom of those days, he never touched a drop himself. Uncle Hull was the same way. So those boys must have had proper training when they were young."

In 1809, when Grandmother Brown's father, Eben, was eleven years old, Zadoc Foster brought his family to Athens. There he conducted a tavern until he died, five years later, of the "cold plague." "That was probably the disease which we now know as 'grippe,'" explained Grandmother Brown. "It raged with terrible violence, and many died."

Left a widow with a large family of children, Mrs. Sally Foster continued to keep the tavern a few years after her husband's death. Then she went back to the vocation of her youth and became a school-teacher once more, "in which occupation," says Walker, "she was eminently useful and beloved during the remainder of her life."

"With his own hands," Grandmother told me, "my father built a house for his mother to live in. There it was she opened the first 'select school' for young children that was known in Athens."

Why Zadoc Foster and his wife decided, after a dozen years at Belpre, to move to Athens is not now known. Possibly because other enterprising people were doing it. Athens was coming to be a trading point for furs and wild meats.

One of the "principles" dearest to the heart of Dr. Cutler was that of educational opportunity. In dealing with Congress, he had insisted that, in the Ohio Company's purchase of land, there should be an appropriation of land for the endowment of a university. In 1804, Ohio University was, accordingly, established by act of legislature. Two years later, a two-story brick building, twenty-four feet by thirty, was erected as the first home of that institution.

"I remember that old academy at Athens," said Grandmother Brown. "'T was n't torn down till after I was born."

But, perhaps, in moving to Athens, the Zadoc Fosters were drawn chiefly by ties of kinship rather than by desire for gain or learning. Sally's sister, Mary Porter, had arrived in the Northwest Territory in 1802, with her husband, Dr. Leonard Jewett, a capable physician. After a brief period in Belpre, they had settled in Athens.

"I suppose Grandma Foster may have been homesick sometimes," remarked Grandmother Brown. "I never heard her say anything about it. I don't believe she ever went back to Massachusetts. Perhaps she moved to Athens to be near her sister. She had a brother — Uncle Porter — who lived on a farm near there too. I remember his visiting her sometimes."

When the Foster family first came from Belpre to Athens, travel through the woods was by horse path. The population of Athens was about 150. People with good English and Irish names were living there in rude log cabins. Just previous to the coming of the Foster family to Athens, five brick buildings had been erected. There were, besides two residences, a brick schoolhouse, a brick tavern, and the brick academy mentioned above, which was, for ten years, the only building that Ohio University had. Perhaps that was why Zadoc's enterprising son, Eben, began to make brick as soon as he was old enough to seek for ways of getting on in the world.

But, though this so-called "town" showed, as yet, little evidence of architectural eminence, it had certain natural advantages that made it attractive from the first. It was on elevated ground. Round it the Hocking River formed a graceful bend. The prospect over fields and hills and river which the settlers had from their modest dooryards was delightful beyond description. By 1827, when Maria Foster first beheld it, Athens was, indeed, a pretty village worthy of the lovely valley in which it nestled. But to it still clung some flavor of the wilderness.

"I remember," said Grandmother Brown, "that when I was a little girl deer meat was so plentiful that we thought nothing of having venison. That was all wrong. There was plenty of food for us, and the deer too."

Athens's material growth had, undoubtedly, been encouraged by the brickmaking of her father and his brother-in-law, "Uncle Dean." Foster's bricks may be seen yet in some of the Athens pavements, and Dean's have a place in the old college walls. In 1816, a new college building had been erected. In 1822, a complete faculty had been assembled. About the time Maria was twelve years old, Ohio University came under the efficient administration of that Reverend William H. McGuffey whose admirable *Fifth Reader* is among our pedagogical classics. By the time she was of an age to notice college students, the University had entered on one of its most flourishing periods and had nearly 250 students. It has now 2500.

If Eben Foster and his brothers had dreamed, perhaps, that in coming to Athens they were getting nearer to a university education than they had been at Belpre, their dreams were probably disturbed by the death of their father. The question of bread and butter was the one that undoubtedly pressed them for solution in their early manhood. Just as their father had done at Belpre, they, at Athens, turned instinctively to supplying the essential needs of the community, Hull to making shoes, Eben to manufacturing bricks, while their patient, precise, dainty little mother attended in the background to the intellectual needs and social conduct of Athens's youngest set. All were useful and successful citizens, much beloved and respected by the community.

By the time his daughter Maria was born, Eben Foster, twenty-nine years old, had reason to feel proud of the domain he had created for himself. His home was one of the most comfortable and pretentious in the thriving village. And the town records for that year and the previous one showed his name among the town officers: Eben Foster, supervisor.

"My father made steady progress all his life," said Grandmother Brown proudly. "Indeed, he prospered amazingly. When he died at the age of 33, he was counted among the wealthy men of Athens. No other little girls had a home a whole block square. Everyone thought well of him.

"A friend thought that Eben ought to have a wife, so he came to Grandma Foster's home one night and said to my father, 'Why don't you get married, Eben?' 'I can't find time to ask my girl,' was the answer. The friend said, 'Here, Eben, you go right off and speak to her about it now.' Eben was shelling corn at the time, shelling it into a big basket hung over the end of a spout. Suddenly he exclaimed, 'All right, Nick, I'll do it!' Up he jumped, seized his cap, and started off. 'Are n't you going to change your clothes?' called Nick. 'No, if she does n't like me this way, she would n't like me at all,' answered Eben. So he struck out toward his girl's home, which was about a mile from there. 'I looked out and watched him in the moonlight,' his friend told me. 'He went round the point of the hill on the run.' And so Eben Foster told Achsah Culver, that moonlight night, how he happened to come in his working clothes and what he wanted of her. They fixed it up; and that's how I happen to be here now, you see."[1]

II

MARIA FOSTER

"Won't you describe the home you lived in as a girl, dear Grandmother Brown?" I begged. "We want to know just how everything in it looked."

"The land on which it stood sloped toward the east," she answered. "From our front porch we could see Miles Mill on the Hocking River and the hills beyond, but not the river itself. Around our place ran a 'post and rail' fence — that is, a fence that had slots cut in the posts with flat smooth rails fitted into the slots. Within our enclosure was everything to make a happy world for children. We had no need to go abroad for pleasure, although we often did run across the street and down the road to play at the homes of our numerous cousins.

"Our house was of weatherboard inlaid with brick

so that the walls were very thick and the window sills very deep. It was a two-story structure above the cellar kitchen. In the middle of the house, opening on to the porch that faced the street, was the main entrance. This porch had a railing around it and a seat against the railing, all the way around. It was a resort for old and young. There Ma sat with her sewing. There we all gathered on a summer afternoon. The front door opened directly into the big living room with its huge fireplace. Back of this were kitchen and summer kitchen, across the way the best room, — we never called it parlor, — upstairs the sleeping rooms. My mother used to say, after we had lived about in different places, that never was there any place where she could accomplish so much as in that house.

"What kind of furniture did we have? Well, in the best room the chairs were of the kind called Windsor — the bottoms solid, the backs round. In that room too was one large rocking-chair with the most beautiful cushion on it. I think the chairs must have been of cherry — perhaps mahogany; they were red. And in one corner stood a large bureau — the most work on it! — big claw feet, glass knobs. The walls of this room were painted white. The floor had a rag carpet. At that time, all window shades were made of paper, green paper. We had thin white curtains over the shades. No pictures.

"In our living room we had no carpet. The floor was of ash wood, very white, and kept white. Every morning, after sweeping it, we wiped it over with a clean, damp mop. It took but a few minutes and kept the floor sweet and clean. That mop was rinsed then and hung in its place. We were always up at five o'clock in the morning, so that we had plenty of time for everything.

"At the back of the house lay orchard and garden, the well and drying kiln, the milk house and smokehouse, with the stables at the farther end of the lot where my father drove his oxen in. I used to run, when I heard the oxen coming at night, to see them put their handsome heads into the stanchion. My father's oxen were famous for their beauty. Once, a little while after Dan'l and I were married and living in Amesville, we drove back to Athens. Stopping at a wayside place, Dan'l introduced me to the innkeeper, saying, 'This is Eben Foster's daughter.' And the man exclaimed, 'Oh, those fine oxen that he had!' He was more interested in them than in the bride.

"My father was always thoughtful of his oxen. Once he dismissed a hired man who swore at them. 'They work hard for me six days a week,' he said, 'and all they get is what they eat. They can't be sworn at or abused.' Every Saturday in warm weather Pa turned the oxen out for a nice long Sabbath rest.

"He used to send them to his farm. That was the first ground outside the corporation. The Baltimore and Ohio Railway station stands on that land to-day. There my father raised hay for his cattle and there our cows were pastured. We never kept less than two, for Pa always would have plenty of milk and butter. We children used to drive the cows back and forth to pasture. Other people kept theirs on the common. All the hills around Athens were covered with lovely grass where cows could walk knee-deep. But we knew where our cows were if we kept them on our own farm.

"The oxen were used by my father for hauling the brick he manufactured. He always kept at least three teams. The brick he made was eight-sided, like a honeycomb design. Some of it I saw, a few years ago, in a pavement in Athens. The soil about there is full of iron, and the brick made from it was so hard that it would n't break when unloaded. They used to pull out the linchpin of the cart and just drive on."

"Tell me some more about your home," I urged her.

"Close to the house was the well. It was a natural spring. My father had walled it up. Our place used to be a tanyard. Think how much water is needed for a tannery! I 've heard my mother say that in time of drought as many as fourteen families had been supplied from our well. The water from it flowed into the milk house through troughs of cut stone that came from my father's quarry. Everything was so sloped that whenever the least bit of water was spilt around the well it ran into the stone troughs and through the milk house and down to the street. Outside the fence was a great watering trough where Pa used to water his oxen.

"The old milk house was a beauty, everything in it so spick and span and shiny, everything so conveniently arranged, smelling so fragrant too of sweetbrier. Near by, in the smokehouse, we always had a good store of hams and bacon well smoked in corncob smoke.

"Near the house too was the dry kiln where my mother dried fruit for the winter. The kiln consisted of a big oval flagstone, at least six feet long, which had been brought from my father's quarry. It was as smooth as if polished. It was set up on brick legs so as to be well off the ground, and a fire was built at one end with a flue running under the flag so as to warm the stone. The fire was made of chips and sticks and not allowed to get too hot, or it would bake the fruit. On this flagstone Ma spread out apples, peaches, pears, and quinces, cut in quarters. These she covered with a cloth which absorbed the moisture and kept off the flies and bees. From time to time she would turn the fruit over until it was thoroughly dried.

"Fruit! We were rich in fruit those days, our trees and bushes burdened with it. Boys always know where apples grow. I've heard Judge Welch say, 'We boys used to flock up to the Foster orchard. We never got yelled at or driven away from there.' Well, we had all we needed. I never saw such prolific apple trees as we had, such wealth of early sweet apples and Vandevere pippins, such cherry trees. As for quinces and currants, there are n't such any more. Why, our quinces were great golden things like my two fists put together, yellow, the color of lemon, and no 'furze' on them. Currants so abundant that we could n't possibly use them all! Stems as long as my finger and tapering down just like it! My mother used to put them up with raspberries — how good they were!

"My mother was a good housekeeper and used to try to save everything, but there was so much fruit that some of it had to go to waste. I remember that, close at the left of our well, an apple tree grew up slanting, completely covering our smokehouse and milk house. The apples were not considered especially good, — had n't much tang, — but they were solid and sweet. Ma would wash and boil them, press the juice out with clamps, boil it down to make apple molasses. We children loved it on our bread and butter. Then

Ma would boil quinces and apples together in this molasses. Usually a ten-gallon jar of this stood in our pantry. My, how good that was!

"I have never seen any place kept so nice, inside and out, as ours was. In those days bedsteads had no springs, so we used to have straw beds under our feather beds to make them springy. Every spring the ticks were emptied and washed and filled with new straw. I remember hearing it said that my father would n't let the straw be carried through the grounds because some of it would be dropped on the grass and give the place an untidy look. No, everything about our place was neat and in order while my father lived. And there were roses, tidy rows of lovely roses to make things beautiful. I remember a row that ran the whole length of the house, a row of red roses big and round, as big as door knobs. We did n't have so many kinds of roses as nowadays, but we had them in abundance. When Ma would be sitting outdoors sewing, we'd stick roses in her hair. I can see her now with a big one flopping from her comb.

"It was a happy home for ten years; but when I was four years old my father died. And after that things were different.

"I have been told many times about my father by those who knew him and admired him. Once I said to Grandma Foster: 'Tell me, did my father have no faults? Everybody praises him,' and she answered thoughtfully: 'Well, if he had a fault at all, it was his levity.'

"I talked to her a good deal about him. Probably some of the things I think I remember about him she told me when I was helping her on Thursday afternoons. There was no school then, and I used to help Grandma give the schoolroom its weekly cleaning. ('My child, why do you walk so fast?' Grandma used to say to me then. Just as if she did n't fly herself!) You see, Grandma had been teaching a long time before I was old enough to go to school. She may have told other grandchildren about our grandfather, so that it did n't occur to her to talk to me about him. But about my father I asked questions and so I drew her out. When I was going to her school, she must have had her hands full, cutting out and basting all the work for us little girls, besides all her housework to do.

"My mother said she lived with Eben Foster ten years and never heard him speak an impatient word. He was evidently a man of peace, for Grandma Foster has told me how depressed he used to be as a child if his brothers, Hull and Ira, would quarrel. Young as I was at the time of his death, I have some precious memories of my father. I have a clear recollection of him in his Sunday clothes, and he seemed to me very grand and handsome then. Our folks are all proud. We like our Sunday clothes. My father did. Uncle Hull was the same way. And my Grandmother Foster too. Once when she was having a bonnet made and Sister Libbie was making it, there was debate about what the style should be. The newest fashion was to have bonnets stick up in front, and Grandma said she wanted hers to stick up a little too. 'I don't want, when I go into church, to have the young people nudge each other and whisper: "Do look at old Mrs. Noah."'

"I suppose I remember my father in his Sunday

clothes not only because I admired his appearance, but because that was the day when we saw most of him. He had time on Sunday to hold me on his lap. It was a day of quiet leisure with us. No cooking was done on that day. Oh, we might make a fire to boil some coffee, but all the other food had been prepared the day before. And so it happens that, sitting on my father's lap, I studied the last Sunday clothes he ever wore. They were made of a dark navy blue cloth in a heavy weave. With them he wore a white vest and a hat with a kind of bell crown, something like the one Uncle Sam wears in all our pictures of him.

"I remember particularly the kind of buttons Pa wore on his white vest, because I played with them once when I lay in his arms, his naughty, adoring child. It happened this way: We older children were in church with Pa and Ma, but Kate, the baby, had been left at home. My mother suddenly felt the milk come. When they were singing the last hymn, she stepped out of church and hurried home to the baby, leaving us to follow with our father. I began to cry for my mother. 'Daughter,' he said, 'you'll stop this crying, or when you get home I'll have to switch your legs.' I kept on crying. And so he led me home and out into the garden, where he cut a little twig from a currant bush, — one with little nubs along the side, but it would n't break anything, — and he gave me a tingly switching across my legs. Then he took me up in his arms and talked to me as we sat on the front porch, and I played with the buttons on his vest. They were glass buttons held in by a ring. If I should be so fortunate as to get to Heaven, I think my father'll meet me. I always felt he'd be the first one.

"I think I must have tried hard after that to please him, because I remember a scene which would seem to indicate it. We always butchered our own beef. Strips of dried beef hung from the raftered ceiling of our kitchen. I remember Pa standing in the middle of the kitchen and reaching up to cut off pieces of beef for us children. John and Libbie were shouting, 'Give me a piece,' but I said primly, 'Pa, I'm not going to tease.' And he said, 'Daughter, you shall have the first piece for that remark.'

"I know that he must have been a kind and tenderhearted man, a loving husband and father. He thought, for instance, that if a woman had a baby her husband ought to give her something. When Kate was born, he brought home to our mother stuff for two dresses. One was a beautiful black satin. Those were the days, too, when they did n't know enough to make satin without making it all satin. The other was an oil calico, fifty cents a yard, a groundwork of red overlaid with a figure in many colors. Beautiful pieces of goods! Well, a woman earned it when she had a baby.

"My father was good to many. My mother had a brother who was drowned in Lake Erie, leaving behind him a wife and several children. When my father heard of it, he harnessed his team and drove up to Sandusky and brought them home to our place. He gave Aunt Betsy our cellar kitchen and the room above that, and the room above *that*, to live in, gave her practically all her living, and provided a loom for her on which she could do weaving and earn a little herself. I remember that once my father went into Aunt Betsy's kitchen when she and her children were at table. 'What's that?' he suddenly said, quite fiercely, pointing at a pan of milk. 'That looks like skimmed milk.' 'It is,' said Aunt Betsy. 'Giving your children skimmed milk to drink?' he asked severely. 'Well, I took the cream to make a little butter,' acknowledged Aunt Betsy. 'You can have the butter too,' said Pa, 'but I don't allow anyone on my place to drink skimmed milk. That's only for pigs. Children must have the top of the milk.' He made her go to the milk house and get more. After my father died, Aunt Betsy would talk by the hour about how good he'd been to her.

"My mother told me once of how a neighbor came with a silver pitcher, asking for cream, and at the same time the little girl of Mrs. Johnson, a poor widow who lived in the next place, came with the same request. After they had gone, my father said to her sternly: 'Did you put as good cream into that earthen jug as went into the silver pitcher?' He always had his men haul wood from his wood lot to Widow Johnson's door, and he had them cut it where she could get every chip that flew. Every baking day he'd say to Ma, 'Now don't forget a loaf for Mrs. Johnson.' He gave freely, and it never made him poor."

"What about his levity?" I inquired.

"Well, I think he was rather a wag, liked a good story as much as my Gus does, and sometimes played a practical joke that he enjoyed greatly. Even when the matter was serious! I remember hearing about his helping three runaway slaves to get away. He hid them in his haymow and then blacked his own face and had two of his hired men black theirs. Then he and his men showed themselves running towards his stone quarry. The slave owner pursued them into the quarry, thinking they were the slaves, while the real negroes used the opportunity to get away. My father enjoyed playing this trick on the slave master, and telling about it, too!

"But I know he could lay aside his levity long enough to have family worship, for I remember that quite clearly. There were always at least four men boarding with us, men who helped my father in his brick kiln or stone quarry, or on his farm. When breakfast was finished, they'd all shove back from the table and Pa would read a chapter from the Bible. I've heard my mother say she used to think if it was a little bit late, Pa'd select a longer chapter than usual. And then they'd all kneel down and he would pray, and then they'd be ready to go to work. We children had a special place where we sat at this time, on a little bench removed from the others. We were always good and quiet.

"I can remember other times in the dining room when my father's levity was more apparent, when he stood by smiling at me in my red morocco shoes while I danced for the men. They sang while I danced and they beat time with their hands.

> "Heigh, Biddy Martin!
> Tiptoe, tiptoe!
> Heigh, Biddy Martin!
> Tiptoe, tiptoe — *fine!*

"Then they'd laugh and shout —

> "Follow my lady
> On tipty-toe.

"And I would strut and toss my head and lift my skirt and twirl my toes until perhaps one of the men would snatch me up and toss me high and not let me down until I'd tell his name. Ezra Goodspeed! Tom Francis! I could not pronounce them well, and they'd laugh to hear me try. No indeed, my father never objected to dancing. You can't find a thing in the Bible against it, either.

"One of those men, Tom Francis, named his baby Eben Foster after my father. He used to say that Pa cured him of drinking. A man was considered very mean in those days if he did n't keep whiskey for his hired help. But Pa persuaded Tom Francis to limit his drinking. He would only give him a little at a time, and gradually he got him out of the habit of drinking. When the temperance wave struck Athens, my father had two barrels of whiskey in the house. He rolled them out, struck the heads in, and let the whiskey run down the gutter, down our pretty gutter which, with its sloping sides, all neatly paved with his own honeycomb brick, ran from our back door to the street. The first temperance society organized in Athens was called 'The Washingtonians,' and my father was a member of it."

It was ninety-five years since Grandmother Brown lost her father, but there was a tragic quality in her voice still when she told of his untimely taking-off. "I was only four years old when my father died. It was in the month of August and very warm. It had been raining hard for days and the river had risen and overflowed its banks. On the farm Pa had been working hard trying to save his hay, to get it in before it was ruined by the water. He took cold — had a sunstroke, perhaps — anyway, came home exhausted, running a high fever. Ma was alarmed and sent for the doctor, who gave him calomel and forbade him water. Probably he would have recovered if there had been no doctor and he had had plenty of rest and cold water. When the doctor found himself unable to check the fever, he told my father that his hour had come and he would have to die. Pa was only thirty-three years old, but he said: 'For the sake of my family, I would like to live longer, but if I lived ever so much longer I could be no better prepared to go.'

"At the time when my father died, I was very sick too. The doctor told my mother that I would probably recover, but that there was no chance for Pa. I remember her taking me in her arms and carrying me into the room where he was laid out. I remember putting my hand on his forehead.

"Oh, that was a great and terrible loss for us children. If my father had lived, I should have received the kind of education I longed to have. My life would have been very different. Young as he was, my father had made his mark on the community. He had begun with nothing, too. Of course he had made a good many advantageous trades, but that simply showed his business ability. He was perhaps younger than anyone he hired. After Dan'l and I moved into this house here in Fort Madison, an old man came to see me — 'Old Man Orm,' they called him — a bricklayer. He said: 'I worked many a day for your father, back in Ohio, and I never knew a better man.' I never heard anything but praise of my father."

In the three years that followed her father's death, little Maria played happily in the spacious grounds of her pleasant home with the numerous young people of her kin, hardly conscious of what she had lost.

But the fortunes of the family declined. "We were cheated by those who should have protected us," said Grandmother Brown, and her eyes flashed even as she told about it. "And then my mother was no financier. The trustee of our father's estate was not a good one, and somehow he managed most of it away. He was a deacon, but he'd use our cattle to haul wood from our wood lot to my mother's door and then charge her for doing it. And Ma'd be fool enough to pay. All the time, too, he was getting his own wood supply off our wood lot. In time he got to be pretty well off.

"But, dear me suz, 'what comes over the devil's back goes under his belly.' Our trustee lost all his property and, at the last, he lost his mind too. His house was robbed and, after his wife died, he just went to nothing. Finally, he got so he did n't know anything.

"After my father had been dead three years, my mother married again. That was a sorry day for all of us. She married Edward Hatch, a clerk in a dry-goods store. He was a pretty man, but without moral character.

"She had plenty of warning, too, but seemed possessed, poor woman. I remember my Uncle Hull and one other member of the church coming to see her and urging her not to marry that man. I remember, too, that Brother John was much offended when Mr. Hatch came courting our mother. Sister Libbie and I helped him put a mop against the door so that when Mr. Hatch came out it would whack him. 'That cottontail,' John called him.

"But Ma married him. None of her sisters and none of her children were at the wedding.

"And so Mr. Hatch came to live in our plentiful home. He never took care of anything. He would even pull boards off the house to burn them. He was wasteful and dissipated and lazy. He was this kind of a man: If he was talking to a Whig, he was a Whig, if talking to a Democrat, he too was a Democrat. Between him and our dishonest trustee, practically all my mother's property was mismanaged away.

"Three children were speedily added to the family circle — Mary, Ann, and Charlotte. Pretty little girls they were. When Mary was born I was only eight years old, but I took entire care of her just the way I'd seen my mother take care of Kate. She said she had nothing to do but take the baby to nurse. I am glad that I could be a comfort to her, for she needed comforting. The night the last child was born I heard Ma calling me in her distress. My stepfather was too drunk to know what was needed and did nothing except curse and swear, but I went for help, as Ma directed, and got everything ready. The next morning, when neighbors came in to see the baby, Mr. Hatch bethought himself to get some oranges and make a fuss over Ma. But his way was very different from my father's way.

"My stepfather took a notion to keep a tavern. There was an old-fashioned hotel in town called the Brice House, and at three different times he rented it. Back and forth between the Brice House and our old home we moved. Once we went to Somerset, once to Logan, to keep hotel. Libbie and I were growing up, and the older we grew, the more usefully could we be employed in running such a place. But it was a hard life for women. There were no railroads in those days, and people traveled in their own conveyances. Travelers would stop at all hours and call for meals, which Ma, aided by us girls, was expected to provide. All our stepfather ever did was to sit straddle of a chair in front of the fire and roast himself, drinking whiskey and bandying words with every passer-by.

"At Logan we rented a tavern that had belonged to a man named Gilbert Cushing. He had prided himself on keeping a temperance house. Hatch signed an agreement with the widow to sell no whiskey, but he kept the stuff under the stairs and dispensed it as he pleased. When Widow Cushing learned that, she turned him out of the tavern. Our own house in Athens was leased for a length of time, and we had no place to go to. So we had to move to a place in the country where we had rooms in a large home. We were there about three years, until I was fourteen years old."

At this point in her story Grandmother Brown became sorely troubled. "Oh, perhaps I ought not to say anything about my mother's second marriage. She was such a good mother. I would not seem ungrateful. I was a puny little child and no doubt caused her many sleepless nights. I remember her weeping because she thought I could not live. My children all loved her dearly. But how can I tell my life story and not mention the one mistake of *her* life, when it had such a sad effect on us all? Yet we never held it against her, but loved her warmly and obeyed her in everything."

"I wonder what little Maria Foster looked like," I said to Grandmother Brown. "Can't you describe her as she probably was a year or two after her father died?"

"Oh, I was rather a puny child. Not until I got into my teens was I at all robust. I came to be a tall, healthy girl with curly dark hair and high color, but as a child I was small and pale with blonde hair. Little 'Liza Hatch, my stepfather's niece, hurt my feelings one time by saying spitefully, 'Pa says you 're a pot-gutted little thing.' I s'pose I was. I used to have sick spells in school and faint away sometimes. Once I was sent out in the country to a Mr. Richey's. 'Let the little girl go home with us,' he had said to my mother, when he heard I was not well. There I hunted eggs and romped with his little girls, Caroline and Mehaley. What a happy time it was!

"I know that my hair was light once, because I remember the first time it was ever cut. Mrs. Hoge stood me up on a chair and cut my curls. Mrs. Hoge was a friend of my mother's whose husband was a professor in the college. I remember looking at the yellow rings of hair lying on the floor. We girls wore nets over our hair. Our mother made them. She made them of black silk thread, netting them over a pencil — like a fish net. At the top a long portion was left plain so a ribbon could be run through and tied at the top of the head. It was a very nice way to dress children's hair so as to keep it smooth and tidy."

"And what kind of dresses did you wear?"

"Usually Sister Libbie and I were dressed alike. We were for a long time about the same size, and many people thought we were twins. Then I took a start and began to grow, and became considerably the taller. Libbie always liked pink and I blue. I don't think so much pink looks well — I was too big to wear it.

"I remember some of the pretty clothes we used to have when we were little girls. There was a garnet-colored cashmere which was different on the two sides and there was a merino which was alike on both sides. We used to get such pretty lawns in those days in all kinds of colors. Ma made them up with yoke and belt. I remember that the sleeves were cut with a perfect circle for the armhole, making the part under the arms only about an inch long and a puff on the top. I had long mitts of fine brown linen which my mother had embroidered. They reached above the elbow. Our mother used to take great pains with our clothes. We were supposed to wear sunbonnets and mitts to protect us against the sun. It was thought dreadful to get tanned as we did whenever we went out to Uncle John's farm. I can hear my mother saying, 'Oh, my child! I hate to take you to church. How you look!'

"I remember the prettiest little bonnet that I once had. It looked much like a sweet pea. The crown went up this way — oh, you know how a sweet pea looks! It was made of a pretty shade of green silk and lined with pink. This bonnet was made by Miss Crippen, the milliner, and promised for Saturday night. But it was not finished until late and was brought home to us as a special favor on Sunday morning, which impressed me very much.

"I had green shoes to match that bonnet — shoes made of green prunella and trimmed with ribbon pleating and buckles. I had another pair of shoes of which the front part was blue prunella and the back blue kid to match. With these pretty shoes we wore white stockings which were knitted from fine cotton. Our common shoes were made of black morocco or calfskin.

"Though Libbie and I were dressed alike, we were not much alike in nature. I am sure that I was less obedient and harder to control than she was. I was a saucy little girl, I am told. When my mother was pregnant with Kate, she was trying, one morning, to prepare herself for church, but kept complaining that she felt ill. 'If I felt as bad as you pretend to,' I piped up, 'I'd go to bed and have a hot brick to my feet.' She should have spanked me, perhaps, but instead she laughed and thought it funny.

"In all our play Sister Libbie and I were partners. We always did things together. It had to be an awfully hot night when we did n't sleep with our arms around each other. We slept so until we were married, and we were married on the same day. When one of us had a beau and the other one did n't, one would always wait until the other's company had gone before she went to bed.

"We loved and admired each other devotedly. And indeed, Sister Libbie was a pretty, dear little thing. I remember once when we were staying all night at Aunt Maria Foster's, how I looked up and saw her standing there in her little shimmy, looking for fleas and shaking herself over the rose blanket. That's a kind of blanket that has a rose woven in one corner and was made with a very long fibre. Rose blankets were fine things to catch fleas," said Grandmother Brown.

"What?" I asked in astonishment.
"Did n't you ever see a flea?"
"I don't believe I ever did."
"Well, they used to be terribly common. The dust and air seemed to be full of them. The flea is n't bigger than a big pinhead, but he can bite and raise great ugly welts on tender flesh. But he has a beard on his legs, and so, if shaken off into a rose blanket, he is caught by his beard in the long fibre. We used to spread a rose blanket on the floor at night and then shake ourselves over it. As Libbie stood there in her little shift, that night, she looked so sweet that I could n't resist calling out, 'Oh, come, Aunt Maria! Come quick! I've got something pretty to show you!' And I caught hold of Libbie's shimmy and drew it tight around her, calling Aunt Maria to come. But Libbie called out: 'No, *don't* come, Aunt Maria,' and there we struggled, laughing and shouting, 'Come, come quick, Aunt Maria!' 'No, no, Aunt Maria, don't come!' and Aunt Maria came running, wondering what it was all about, and nodded and laughed at us and said, 'Yes, yes, she *has* a pretty shape.'

"Our sister Kate was not with us much in those early days, because, when Pa died, Aunt Eliza, Ma's sister, carried her off and was never willing to give her up again. Not until Aunt Eliza died, when Kate was about ten years old, did she return to her own family circle. She had been spoiled, and at first we found her unbearable; but finally she discovered that she could n't run things at home and settled down to be a very nice child. She was always enterprising and high-spirited, full of life and vitality, ready to try anything. Often I've seen her run and jump and spat her foot against the top of the door. One of her sons — Nelson — inherited her athletic activities and began to jump and wrestle almost as soon as he could walk. I remember one day when she was a little girl we were playing about a friend's stable. Kate and Melissa Dean climbed up on the shaving horse and said they were going to have a ride. Just then, Kate noticed a real horse lying in its stall, ran to it, jumped on its back, and began to shout, 'I've got a live horse, a live one, a live one!' Before the astonished horse could express his indignation, the owner came running in and pulled her off.

"But there was no suppressing Kate for long. As she grew up, she became extremely pretty. She had a lovely fresh color and a very shapely figure. And no one ever got the best of her."

Prominent in Maria's family background stood out her two grandmothers. Each of them made a deep impression on her youthful mind. "Were the two good friends?" I asked. "Oh, yes," she laughed, "both were good Presbyterians.

"Grandma Foster was a tiny little body, always immaculately dressed. She taught school for many years in the house which my father built for her in 1822. Many important persons in Ohio history sat before her in their infancy. Boys and girls were in her classes, her own grandchildren and great-grandchildren among the number.

"I remember well the first time I went to school. I was about two years old. One of Aunt Betsy's children took me as a visitor. There was a new long clock in the corner of the schoolroom which I hadn't seen before. Its little feet were black. I pointed to it and cried, 'Oh, what pretty little feet!' 'You must n't talk out loud, Maria,' Grandma Foster told me firmly, and I was awed.

"At Grandma Foster's school, little girls learned not only to read and write, but to sew and knit also. When the boys got so they could read well in the Testament, they were graduated.

"When I was six years old, I had pieced a patchwork quilt. Sister Libbie had made two. There were nine pieces in each patch. We sewed the pieces together with tiny over and over stitches after Grandma had cut them out and basted them for us. If we took our stitches too deep, we had to pick them out. We were taught to turn a hem and to do it nicely. Sometimes Ma would send a kerchief to be hemmed or an apron to be made. There never was a more useful school.

"We learned knitting, too. First we knit our garters, afterwards our stockings. I knit eight pairs of socks for soldiers in the World War, but I did n't follow the instructions of the Red Cross; I shaped the feet the way Grandma Foster had taught me nearly ninety years before.

"When we were little girls and went some place, we always took our knitting along. We had to knit so many times around before we could play. Children must learn to be useful, they thought in those days. My cousin, Lucinda Gillmore, came to play one day. 'My children have done their task,' said Ma. 'Just give me your knitting and I'll do yours.' We went running down to the orchard to the swing while our mother did Cindy's knitting. It made a great impression on me — Ma's doing Cindy's stint for her.

"After sewing and knitting came spelling and reading. We used Webster's *Elementary Spelling Book*, beginning with the *a—b; e—b;* and so on. Then came short sentences of just one line. Like this: 'Brass is made of zinc and copper.' Then another line telling something else that would be useful to know. Every line different, all important. We had the *New England Primer*, too. Then Grandma taught us the Roman numerals, so that we could open the Bible and know what chapter it was.

"We were taught good manners, too, at Grandma Foster's school. At recess, the little girls used to play under the apple tree, while the boys would romp in the street. I remember that one day, when I had been laughing boisterously, Grandma called me to her and said mildly, — she always corrected us very quietly, — 'My child, if something amuses you, laugh, but not so loud.' When school was dismissed, it was n't just open the door and go out, but first the girls filed past Grandma making a deep obeisance, and then the little boys marched by, cap in hand.

"I never remember Grandma Foster having a rod, never in my time. I do remember the dunce block. It used to stand over in the corner by the fireplace. I can just see the smooth piece of black walnut. Oh, that kind of punishment did n't hurt us, but it *was* humiliating.

"Grandma Foster taught until four days before she died at the age of eighty-one. Every night she used to pray the Lord: 'I beg that I may not outlive my usefulness.' One day she dismissed her school, saying that she did not feel very well. Four days later, she calmly breathed her last. When they went to pay for her coffin they found that she had paid for it herself, several years before.

"She had eight children, and taught school at least thirty-five years after her husband died," said Grandmother Brown. "That's what I call a full life."

Important in little Maria's early life was also her mother's mother, Grandma Culver, or Grandma Perkins, as she was usually called. Maria went to school to Grandma Foster, who thus, as grandparent and schoolmistress, exercised double authority over her, as it were; but Grandma Perkins lived in the same house with her for a number of years and thus brought the weight of her pleasant personality to bear on the impressionable child.

"I remember her well," she told me. "She came to live at our house, with my mother, after her second husband, Dr. Eliphaz Perkins, died. I never remember her speaking my name. It was always 'Here, dear!'—'Wait, my child!' The loving old lady! She had fourteen children of her own, seven sons and seven daughters, and she mothered some of Dr. Perkins's many children too, after she married him. They all loved her. I remember their coming often to see her.

"She came to Athens with her first husband, my grandfather, Bezaliel Culver, from Kinsborough, Washington County, York State, when my mother, who was her youngest daughter, was fourteen years old. They came down the Ohio River on a raft and settled on a farm about a mile from Athens. It was beautiful land, as I happen to know, because it is now the Children's Home of Athens and I have visited it often. I like to think that my grandfather's farm has gone to making a happy place for children.

"My Grandfather Culver was of Irish blood, a warm-hearted man. My mother used to say that he petted his children a great deal. 'I sat on my father's lap until I was married,' I've heard her say. They told that he was a fine-looking man, that he resembled President Washington.

"After my Grandfather Culver died, Grandma used to come often to stay with her oldest daughter, Ann, who lived in town in a large brick house opposite Dr. Perkins, one of the first settlers of Athens and one of the great figures in the early history of the Northwest Territory. I remember that he was one of the first trustees of the University, a man of popularity and influence. He was a very Christian man too. Every time he prepared a potion for one of his patients, he'd pray over it before he gave it. He was a widower at this time, waited on by a colored woman named Violet. When he and my grandmother were about sixty years old, they were married. They lived together very happily — Violet with them, I believe — for about ten years, when Dr. Perkins died.

"Grandma Culver-Perkins was a larger, fleshier woman than Grandma Foster. I remember noticing her figure as she stood wiping dishes for my mother. But during the last years of her life she was crippled by rheumatism and unable to walk. Leaning over a chair, she would stand a while just to rest herself by change of posture, but she could not move without help. She could n't even move her arms freely; she was so drawn down that her backbone was dislocated and her arms rested on the arms of her chair. Every day we placed the open Bible up in front of her so that she could see to read it. From time to time I'd turn the pages for her.

"Grandma was very pretty. No wonder Dr. Perkins fell in love with her. She had the loveliest brown eyes and the prettiest little hands and feet. Her hair was auburn, old as she was. I know, because I combed it for her every day until she died. I was then ten years old. It was quite wavy, in heavy regular waves. I used to put a black ribbon around it, stick a shell comb in the back, and then set on, over all, a white cap made with a full border pleated in.

"I loved her dearly and waited on her more than the other children did. When I'd been a naughty girl and Ma would be about to spank me, I'd run to Grandma and she'd put her arms around me. And so I'd escape the punishment. She was all drawn down with pain, and yet, when I think of her, I can't remember that she was ever anything but cheerful and sweet. Oh, dear, I ought to be a much better woman. I came from better stock than I am myself.

"Grandma wanted to reward me, and so she left me her gold beads. She always wore them — had them on when she died. She called me to her bed one day, and said: 'When I'm gone, dear, I want you to have these. You've been so good about waiting on me.' And so Grandma Perkins's gold beads came to me as a legacy, but I did n't have sense enough to keep them. A peddler came along one day and wanted to buy up gold. Ma thought it would be a good idea to trade off my beads for silver spoons. I should have stood up and said I would n't allow it. Later, the spoons were all lost but one.

"From Grandma Perkins I heard many things about my mother's family. Grandma Perkins, like Grandma Foster, had been a small girl when the Revolutionary War broke out. Her name was Ann Caldwell. She had helped to mould all the pewter platters of the Caldwell family into bullets, and liked to tell about it. When the pewter platters were melted down, her people used turned wooden ones. I remember that Aunt 'Liza had one of those wooden plates and she used to let Sister Kate eat off of it.

"My grandmother was named Ann for her mother. I remember some of the things she used to tell about her parents. It seems that Great-grandfather Caldwell was short of stature, but well built, a very healthy man. When he was past seventy he had n't a decayed tooth in his head, and would mount a horse from the ground with perfect ease. He became a Christian early in life, an Irish Presbyterian. He was a good musician, had a fine voice, and Grandma said that her children always loved to hear him sing. In his old age, when he could not sleep well, he would sing at night, not in a loud offensive way that would disturb the family, but in a sweet low tone that they would love to listen to. In the morning he would say, 'Well, the angels came again last night.'

"Grandma's brother, James Caldwell, was in the Revolutionary War and was taken prisoner. One of the stories I liked best to hear Grandma Perkins tell was about that Great-uncle James. You know that the British had bribed the Indians to help them fight the colonists, and so it happened that when James was taken prisoner he was turned over to a company of Indians to be conducted to a Canadian prison. The

Indians were drunk. They threatened to tomahawk him, and they tantalized him in various ways. In crossing a river, he managed to wet their powder so that they could not shoot. Instead of being enraged at that, they shouted and laughed and called him brave and patted him on the back, and said: 'No hurt Brave!' Soon after, they met another posse of Indians who had stolen a white baby and had it lashed under a horse's belly. One of the child's arms was dangling. Although he knew that he was on his way to prison, my Great-uncle James begged or bought this baby — I do not know how he got possession of it, but he got it — and took it with him to prison. There he enlisted the help of attendants so that he got milk enough to keep it alive and rags enough to cover it. He washed it and fed it and took care of it in every way as tenderly as a mother could have done. Finally, he and another prisoner who was in the same cell with him dug their way out. The prison was built of logs and was situated near the bank of some river. They swam the river and escaped into their own country, taking the child with them. Many people wanted to adopt the baby, but my great-uncle was determined to find its mother. And he did, after two years' patient inquiry. I consider that a better triumph than all the battles Napoleon ever won!"

With a mother who was one of fourteen children and a father who was one of eight, little Maria Foster did not lack for uncles and aunts and cousins while she was growing up. How rich in human sympathy and interest seems the family life of those red-blooded days!

"Naturally," she said, "I saw a good deal of my mother's sisters, who all lived near. I don't remember her brothers so well. Uncle James and Uncle John lived on farms.

"At Uncle John's, we sometimes went fishing in the creek. I remember Aunt Melissa frying the minnows for us that we caught there. And I remember how exciting it was at their house when they renewed the backlog in the fireplace. Queen, the family horse, would be hitched to a log big as a tree trunk and driven right into the house. Then, when the log was deposited on the hearth and Queen was unhitched, the men would take crowbars and roll the log into its place at the back of the chimney.

"All of my mother's sisters were pretty women with good voices. My mother used to sing Irish songs she had learned from her mother. There was one that I liked: —

> "Erin, my country, thou sad and forsaken,
> In dreams I revisit thy sea-beaten shore."

"I remember her singing it once when our singing teacher, Mr. Runyon, was calling, and he thought it fine. All of the Culvers could sing. The daughter of one of Grandma's grandsons — Helen Culver — has been on the operatic stage in this country and Europe," Grandma Brown reminded me.

"Well, my mother had a fine voice too," she continued. "It lasted as long as she lived. We could all sing. Houses in Athens were without musical instruments in my youth, — except the fiddle, — but all the more reason for singing.

"Among my male relatives Uncle Hull, my father's brother, held first place. He was, indeed, 'Uncle Hull' to the whole town. We children loved him dearly and used to stay at his home weeks at a time. 'I don't see why I could n't have had a daughter,' he'd say, as he trotted me on his knee. 'Eb had three. I adopted one, one time, but after a while she took a notion to get married, and off she tilted.'

"Uncle Hull was a maker of shoes, a calling that many people of mechanical skill were tempted to follow in those days when factory-made footwear was unknown and everybody had to be shod.

"Someone asked Uncle Hull one day how he learned the shoemaker's trade," laughed Grandmother Brown. "'Just as a cow learns kicking,' he answered. 'Out of my own head.'"

He was about seventeen years old when that idea came into his head. For four years he traveled through the West and the Southwest, his kit on his back, making shoes as he went, and seeing something of the country that was afterward made into the states of Indiana, Kentucky, Tennessee, and so forth. On his return to Athens, he continued to make shoes for his fellow citizens and kept it up until far advanced in years. Although, judged by the standards of this artificial machine age, he seems to have been merely a humble craftsman, it is evident, not only from Grandmother Brown's testimony, but from various public records, that "Uncle Hull" was an influential person in the community which knew him. As he lived to be ninety-four years old, his was long a familiar figure in the town of Athens. "A man of strong sense, strict integrity, and marked force of character, his life and virtues are known and read of all his neighbors," says Walker.

"Every word of that is true," cried Grandmother Brown with enthusiasm. "To have known Uncle Hull was a joy. Just to hear him coming made people look pleasant. I was at Grandpa Brown's one day, when we heard sleigh bells. 'That's Uncle Hull,' cried someone. Everybody perked up. We knew him by his chimes, the sweetest ones in town. He was a great cut-up. Even in church. His pew was in the front row, and we girls had to be careful when we were singing in the choir, for, if we'd catch his eye, he'd twist an eyebrow or raise a shoulder in such a way as to make us laugh. I remember, that very day, when he came stamping in through the snow and warmed himself at Grandpa Brown's fire, sitting in a light chair that was rather a tight fit for his big body, how we laughed when he got up and walked off with *such* an innocent expression, just as if he did n't know that the chair was hanging to his settee! He could n't help *his* levity.

"After periods at the Brice House or in Logan or Somerset, we were always glad to get back to our own father's dear old home. Nowhere else did we have the same conveniences. We did most of our work there in the summer kitchen. That was where we had the big brick oven. We used to fire it twice a week and do a sight o' baking all at once. We'd make a hot fire in the oven, and then, when the bricks were thoroughly heated, we'd scrape out all the coals with a big iron scraper, dump the coals into the fireplace, and shove in the roasts and fowls, the pies and bread. At other times we'd use the open fireplace. It was n't nearly so difficult to work by as people think. When we went to keeping house in 1845, Dan'l and I, he bought me a little iron stove, a new thing in those days. It was no good, and would only bake things on one side. I soon went back to cooking at an open fireplace.

"You know the look of andirons, crane, spit, reflectors. Our heavy iron vessels were swung from chains. When we wanted to lift the iron lids off, we'd have to reach in with a hook and swing them off. They had a flange around the edge. Many of our dishes were baked in Dutch ovens on the hearth. We used to bake Indian pone — that is, bread made of rye and corn meal — that way. We would set it off in a corner of the hearth covered with coals and ashes, and there it would bake slowly all night long. In the morning the crust would be thick but soft — oh, *so* good.

"For roasting meat we had reflectors. Some joints we roasted in our big iron kettles with a bit of water. And others we put on three-legged gridirons which could be turned. These had a little fluted place for the gravy to run down. Chickens we could split down the back and lay on the gridiron with a plate and flatirons on top to hold them down. Oh, how different, how different, is everything now, encumbered with conveniences!

"The difference between those who were naturally clean and orderly and those who were not was perhaps more marked in those days than it is now. It was so easy, for instance, since we had no screens, to let the flies spoil everything. My mother just wouldn't have it so. We weren't allowed to bring apples into the house in summer, because apples attract flies. If any of us dropped a speck of butter or cream on the floor, she had to run at once for a cloth to wipe it up. Our kitchen floor was of ash, and Ma was very proud of keeping it white. In the summer kitchen the floor was of brick, and it was expected to be spotless also. At mealtime someone stood and fanned to keep the flies away while the others ate. When Sister Libbie went to housekeeping, she had little round-topped screens for every dish on her table. That was considered quite stylish. Ma used to set some tall thing in the centre of her table, spread a cloth over it, and slip food under until we were ready to sit down. As soon as the meal was finished, all curtains had to be pulled down and the flies driven from the darkened room.

"Our dishes for common use were white with blue edges. The finer ones were a figured blue. I remember, also, a large blue soup tureen with a cover and a blue, long-handled ladle, all very handsome.

"Our forks were two-tined. They weren't much good for holding some things. But if we used our knives for conveying food to our mouths it had to be done with the back of the knife towards the face. We had no napkins. We used our handkerchiefs. Tablecloths were made of cotton diaper especially woven for the purpose. The first white bedspread I ever had was made of two widths of that same cotton whitened on the grass.

"In warm weather we washed outdoors under the quince bushes. We used our well water. It was so soft, it was just beautiful. We'd draw a barrel of water, put one shovel of ashes into it, and it would just suds up like soft water, so white and clean. We used soft soap, of course. Our starch was of two kinds — either made from a dough of flour worked round and round until it was smooth and fine or made from grated potato cooked to the right consistency.

"Ma put us girls to work early. It was taken as a matter of course that we should learn all kinds of housework. I know that before I was seven years old I used to wash the dishes. But our mother had village girls to help her also. I remember one Ann Fierce who was with us for years, but it seems to me that Sister Libbie and I usually did the washing. There was need of many hands to get all the work done. It required more knowledge to do the things for everyday living than is the case nowadays. If one wants light now, all one has to do is pull a string or push a button. Then, we had to pick up a coal with tongs, hold it against a candle, and blow. And one had to make the candles, perhaps.

"I remember the first matches that I ever saw. Someone handed me a little bunch of them, fastened together at the bottom in a solid block of wood about a half inch square. 'Lucifer matches' they called them. I tore one off and set the whole thing afire.

"Some people had tinder boxes. Some kept a kind of punk which would give off a spark when struck with steel or knife. Generally speaking, people kept the fire on their hearthstones going year in and year out.

"We did not make our candles at home, but got them usually from Uncle Dean, who made candles for the town. I used to love to watch him and Aunt Maria at work dipping candles — she with the hot tallow in a big kettle on the hearth, he with stillyards beside him, weighing carefully. Occasionally we had some sperm candles made of fine whale tallow. Besides candles, people sometimes burned sperm or whale oil in little lamps that looked like square-topped candlesticks. In the square top was a place for a bowl that would hold perhaps a half pint of oil.

"Even without candle making, there was certainly a plenty to do to keep life going in those days. Baking, washing, ironing, sewing, kept us busy. Not to mention the spinning and weaving that had to be done before cloth was available for the seamstress.

"My mother used to spin. She made beautiful fine thread. She taught Sister Libbie how to spin, but decided, before my turn came, that spinning was doomed to become a lost art, and that I might be better employed in some other way. I used to love to watch her at the spinning wheel. She had two wheels, lovely big ones. She used a wheel boy to turn her wheel. I can just close my eyes and see Ma standing over there spinning a thread as far as from here to the bed — say, twelve feet long.

"My mother and her sister had some beautiful woolen cloth of their own spinning and weaving. Part of the thread was made with the open, part with the crossed, band. They colored it with butternut bark, but the two kinds would never color alike, so that part of it was a light and part a dark brown. They wove it into a plaid and had it pressed, and then they made fine dresses out of it to wear to church. I remember, too, that my mother raised flax, spun it into linen, wove it into cloth, — colored blue in the yarn, — made it up into a dress for me which she embroidered in white above the hem. I wish I had kept that dress to show my children the beautiful work of their grandmother.

"Ma used to use Aunt Betsy's loom sometimes.

When I was eight years old, she wove me a plaid dress of which I was very proud. I remember the pattern: eight threads of brown, then one of red, one of blue, one of red, then brown again, both in the warp and in the woof. It made the prettiest flannel, and that dress lasted me for years.

"Women made their own designs for cloth as well as for dresses in those days. If a woman had taste, she had a chance to show it in her weaving. But, oh, it was hard work. You never saw warping bars, did you? Clumsy things, long as a bed. On them work was prepared for the loom. You had to draw each thread through a reed. I used to love to watch my mother weaving, her shuttle holding the spool with yarn shooting through the warp, then back the other way. When she had woven as far as she could reach, she would bend below the loom and wind the woven cloth into a roll beneath. Blankets made at home used to last a long, long time. Homespun things were good.

"We had all the things that were really necessary for our comfort in those days, and we had quite as much leisure as people have now. Always, too, we had time to attend church and Sunday school.

"You see I had rather a severe course in Domestic Science, but the rest of my education did n't amount to much. I must have been about ten years old when I quit going to Grandma Foster's school."

"Then what?" I asked.

Laughter on Grandmother Brown's part. "Well, my education was about completed. I 've had to get along without anything more than the fundamentals. It was always uncertain, even in our school days, whether we could be spared from work. Some days we could go to school, some days not.

"I used to be able to knit and read at the same time. Not so fast, of course, as knitting with my eyes on the work. But once my mother spoke sharply to me when I was knitting with my eyes on a newspaper. She spoke twice, and I could hardly bring myself to hear her. At the third call, Mr. Hatch snatched the paper from my lap and threw it into the fire. No wonder I never learned anything!" There was bitterness in Grandmother Brown's voice.

"When we lived at Logan, I went for a while to Mr. Parsons's school. I was thirteen years old then. I used to like the spelling matches we had there. I remember getting a ticket for perfect spelling. But I also remember having there the most unhappy experience of my school life.

"Nowadays, when children show a talent for anything good, it is cultivated. I always liked to draw. One day I drew a cow upon my slate. Mr. Hatch — who, with all his faults, was generally kind enough to me — said: 'Now make a picture of *our* cow.' I did. 'Let me show it to your mother!' he said. 'Why it's *our* cow!' she exclaimed, and they were much surprised that I could make a picture of our particular bossy. Once, in later years on the farm, I amused myself one rainy Sunday drawing pictures of Andy Brown and James Mitchell as they sat talking together. 'Why, Mother, you're an artist!' Dan'l said, when I showed him what I had done.

"I think I could have made pictures. I was always wanting to try. I could draw animals and I wanted to make landscapes, too. I remember once, when walking in the country with my mother, the scenery was so beautiful that I just longed to make a picture of what I saw. I wanted to sit and look and look. I sat so long upon a fence looking at the scene that Ma came running back to find me and chided me for lingering. In recent years, at a meeting of my D. A. R. chapter, I won the prize for drawing from memory the best picture of George Washington. I was the oldest woman present, too.

"Well, one day at Mr. Parsons's school I drew on my slate a picture of a lace veil. I drew the string that went around the bonnet and showed the veil all puckered around the face with a heavy border at the bottom. I made it *so* pretty. But Mr. Parsons came up behind me and saw what I was doing. He took my slate, showed my picture to the school, and scolded me for wasting time on things like that. I never did again. I just wept. I thought I had committed a terrible sin. Mr. Parsons was a slender, tall man, but I can't remember how he looked. I had a dread of him. He cured me of trying to make pictures. Well, no matter! I've got along this far without drawing pictures; I guess I can make it the rest of the way.

"But, though I was not encouraged to be an artist, I've always tried to make anything I had to make as beautiful as I could make it. My pats of butter I made in pretty shapes. I've always liked to sew and embroider. I've made some pretty things, if I do say it as should n't. I learned once to make wax flowers and enjoyed doing that. I made them well, too. I know that once when Dr. Rix and his wife were calling on us here in Fort Madison he suddenly noticed a bunch of flowers that I had made and put into a basket, and he called to his wife to come and see. 'Why, I thought they were real!' he said. But wax flowers are perishable, and I'd rather do embroidery. That lasts longer."

"What did you have to read when you were a girl, Grandmother?"

"Well, I remember *Pilgrim's Progress*. And there was *Paradise Lost* and *Paradise Regained*. I always enjoyed poetry. I liked to read Cowper's poems. He was so fond of his mother. He looked at her picture and said:—

> "'My mother! when I learn'd that thou wast dead,
> Say, wast thou conscious of the tears I shed?
> Hover'd thy spirit o'er thy sorrowing son,
> Wretch even then, life's journey just begun?
> Perhaps thou gav'st me, though unfelt, a kiss;
> Perhaps a tear, if souls can weep in bliss —
> Ah, that maternal smile! it answers — Yes.
> I heard the bell toll'd on thy burial day;
> I saw the hearse that bore thee slow away;
> And, turning from my nurs'ry window, drew
> A long, long sigh, and wept a last adieu!
> But was it such? It was. Where thou art gone
> Adieus and farewells are a sound unknown.
> May I but meet thee on that peaceful shore,
> The parting word shall pass my lips no more!'"

That Grandmother Brown loved poetry no one could doubt, hearing the fine appreciation with which she recited these noble lines.

"Every week we had Sunday-school books to read," she went on. "They always had Christian teaching woven around the story of some boy or girl. I remember the first time I read the story of the Crucifixion.

I read it through my tears. It was dreadful to my young mind. It is yet. In the first place, God created the first man out of the dust of the earth. The first one He created without any earthly parent. Then He created one out of the Virgin Mary. How terrible for her to see her son crucified!

"A story that I read as a child that interested me was a tale called *Prairie Flower*. It was the story of a pretty young girl who was stolen by the Indians. There was going to be an eclipse of the sun, a fact she knew. She told them that if they did so and so the sun would be darkened. Sure enough, it was. From that time on, they feared her and did as she directed."

"Did you have newspapers?"

"Yes, the first one I remember was one called the *Western Spectator*, printed by a Mr. Maxon. Then came the *Hocking Valley Gazette*, which Nelson Van Vorhes, who married Sister Libbie, later made into the *Athens Messenger*.

"Two books were presented to me when I was fourteen and sixteen years old that I set great store by. Nelson Van Vorhes, when he was courting Libbie, gave me twelve copies of *Godey's Lady's Book* bound into one volume. When I was about sixteen, a Mr. Cook, who boarded with us, gave me a bound book of the *Family Magazine*. A careless person at the farm left those books out in the rain in later years and they were ruined. No money could have repaid me for those books. Would n't you like to see the fashion plates in colors of the styles when I was sixteen years old? But, oh dear, after a while we 'll be in a place where books won't matter. So why worry?"

"As you grew to womanhood, Grandmother Brown, I'm sure you had some friends among the young men," said I.

"Of course. We had a good deal of attention, Libbie and I. When I married, at age eighteen, I accepted the third offer," answered Grandmother Brown with pretty dignity. "We had plenty of opportunity to have a gay time with young men, because at that time Mr. Hatch was running the Brice House again, and many of the young men studying at the college boarded with us. Some of them were from the South, sons of rich planters, fine dressers and free with their money. But, although we waited on them at table, we never spoke to them. In the dining room was a great coffee urn kept hot by a heated iron rod that ran down the middle. We used to draw the coffee from this urn and pass it to the boarders. Among them was a young man called 'Cap' Reed. 'Why don't you take those Foster girls out somewhere?' he was asked one time. 'I'd just as soon think of asking Queen Victoria for her company,' he answered. Later he married my lovely cousin, Lucinda Dean. But his remark showed how we held ourselves aloof. I remember that years afterward, when my mother visited me on the farm, she said: 'Maria, you never gave me an anxious moment in my life and I never put you to a task that wasn't well done.' Well, I am glad I never hurt her. She had hurt enough."

"But surely you went out with some of the young men, Grandmother," I said.

"Yes," she laughed, "of course; we went around with the Athens boys. We went to picnics and dances, to singing school and campaign rallies. I remember once driving with Dan'l out to Uncle Dickey's, of going through an avenue of poplar trees and craning our necks to look up and up. We just had to stop the carriage and look. You might have to take two or three looks before you'd get to the top!

"I remember going with other young people to see torchlight processions at time of political excitement. We were in the Logan campaign of 'Tippecanoe and Tyler Too.' Our Republican young men called themselves 'The Log Cabin Boys' and they sang: —

"'Oh, Van (meaning President Van Buren), don't you know that
    you're a used-up man?
For the Log Cabin Boys go for Harry of the West
And you'll soon see that you can't shine.'

"They had a float with a live tame bear on it, also a log cabin in which was a cider barrel. This float moved slowly through the streets with young men marching before and after it, carrying lanterns and torchlights, and singing their log-cabin songs. 'We'll beat little Van' was the constant refrain. President Van Buren was very unpopular in that part of the country. It was the time of shinplasters and financial distress of the sharpest kind.

"In Athens our set would go out hunting wild flowers. There are so many pretty hills around there, and in the spring they were covered with dogwood blossoms and other lovely flowers. The grass was so soft and deep you'd think you were walking on top of a feather bed. We'd take along things to eat, things like pickled string beans and pickled peaches — the clings were our choice. After you'd eat one of those, my, but you could sing!

"Our favorite amusement, I think, was singing.

Everybody went to singing school in those days and learned to sing with the help of a tuning fork. I don't like to hear accompaniments. Better the voice alone. Dan'l's cousin, Perley Ward, had a song bird in her throat — I never heard such a voice. I've no doubt it was equal to Jenny Lind's. Dan'l himself taught singing school, and up to the last I loved to hear him throw out his chest in church and let out the Doxology. That was something worth hearing."

"Tell me some of the songs you used to sing, Grandmother."

"All right. This was one of our favorites: —

> "The bright, rosy morning peeps over the hill
> With the blushes adorning the meadows and fields,
> While the merry, merry horn calls 'Come, come away!'
> Awake from your slumbers and hail the new day.
> The stag roams before us, away seems to fly
> While he pants to the chorus of the hounds in full cry.

"I don't like the sentiment of that very much. It sounds cruel, but that is what we used to sing.

> "Then follow, follow music and the chase,
> While pleasure and vigor and health we'll embrace.

"Here's a sad one — though the tune is nice — about a dying girl saying as she draws near her home: —

> "'Are we almost there?
> Are we almost there?' she'd ask.
> 'Are these our poplar trees
> That rear their forms so high
> Against heaven's blue dome?'

"Then comes something I don't remember. Afterwards, —

> "Her quick pulse ceased,
> She was almost there."

"That was something to hold us down a little, so we should n't get too gay."

"What about dancing?"

"Oh, we liked that, too. I remember one night Libbie and I were getting ready for bed — we'd been washing that day and were tired — when a couple of young gentlemen came and asked us to go with them to Judge Welch's house. Judge Welch was a fine violinist. He played for eight of us to dance that night. Jim Hay was my escort. He married Lucy Brown, a cousin of Dan'l's, but her mother would n't let her dance. Dan'l did n't dance either, and so Jim Hay danced with me that winter. Here in my scrapbook you can see a couple of invitations to dances that I've kept all these years."

I examined them with interest, one of them printed on blue, the other on pink paper, and then I said banteringly: "But, Grandmother Brown, you must have been a precocious belle. One of these invitations is for a Fourth of July party at the Perry Hotel in 1839. You were only a little over twelve then, and the other invitation is for a party at the American House in Logan in 1841, just after you had celebrated your fourteenth birthday. I'm surprised that your mother let you go!"

"But notice, my dear! The Independence Party — look at the flag at the top of the invitation! — was at five o'clock, and the Union Ball in Logan was at four in the afternoon. We kept early hours in those days, so that even the children could safely go to dances."

"I'm sure they must have been lovely parties," I said, studying the language of the pink invitation.

"Yes, I think so. But most of my dancing was done at dancing school. When we lived in Logan, Mr. Saunders came from Lancaster once a week to teach us. In Athens, I had lessons two terms from Mr. Crippen. The dancing school always met in the afternoon, girls and boys practising separately at first. When both had learned the steps, then we came together. We danced to the music of fiddles, and they called off, 'First lady forward! Seven hands round.' There were no round dances. Our teachers taught us to take little steps, to move forward and back genteelly. With some pride and dignity! Why, I could do it now if I were on my feet — one, two, three, four, five, then back again; six, seven, eight, nine, ten. That was the way to do it — so rhythmically and beautifully. Now they grab each other and go seesawing around. The contra-dances took in the whole room. It was lovely to see them do it, the girls so pretty and modest, in those days, their dresses ankle-length. When they honored the partner, they did n't just squat that square way, but they must lean to one side gracefully.

"When we were living on the farm I taught my children to dance. Afterward, when Lizzie first came to Fort Madison, she was complimented on her dancing. 'My mother taught me,' she said. A shout went up. They thought her a wicked mother, I suppose, who would teach her child to dance. But, if it had been wicked to dance, it would say so in the Bible. If it had said, 'Thou shalt not dance,' I would not have done it, for I have kept all the Thou Shalt Nots. But it does say that when the Prodigal Son came home and fell on his father's neck and kissed him, the father put a ring on his finger and ordered *music and dancing*."

"And so you were married, Grandmother, when you were only eighteen years old. How did it happen?"

"Well, perhaps it would n't have happened quite so soon if my father had lived. But since I could n't go to school any more, and living at home meant for Libbie and me simply working for a lazy stepfather whom we loved none too well, it was only natural that marriage should tempt me when nice young men proposed it. As I said before, I had three offers by the time I was eighteen. One of them was from a young man who was studying for the ministry. The second proposal came from one who had considerable money. He was a Catholic, but he wrote my mother that he 'd become a Protestant if I 'd have him. My mother and brother rather encouraged him, but I had no love for him. He like to never give it up. He wrote to my brother and he asked a friend to intercede for him. How foolish! But then that's the way men do when they set about wanting a girl."

"And the third suitor, I suppose, was Grandfather Brown?" I ventured.

"Yes, Dan'l. 'Dan Brown' nearly everybody else called him. But I always called him 'Mister Brown' until we were married, and then I called him 'Dan'l.'"

"How long had you known him?"

"Ever since I was born. In a way. You see, his sister Maria was my Uncle Hull's second wife. When I was a new baby she came, bringing that little boy to see me. He was five years old. She used to tell me that she said to him, 'Now this might be your wife some day!' How true it's come about! I used to see him at Aunt Maria's, but not to get acquainted. When I was a little girl I did n't pay much attention to the company — I was more interested in Uncle Hull, who always made a great fuss over us children when we went to see him. Then Dan'l's sister Emma had married my father's cousin, Leonard Jewett, — a son of the doctor of early days, — and I'd seen him going over there. I remember watching that boy go back and forth, the boy with the palm-leaf hat that had a narrow green ribbon round it. I never forgot that little white hat — it looked so clean and bright.

"His folks lived in the country, a mile from the town of Albany. They had come there from Amesville a couple of years before Dan'l was born. Dan'l's father, William Brown, was the second son of Captain Benjamin Brown, an officer of the Revolution, whose people had been prominent for several generations in Worcester County, Massachusetts. Captain Benjamin was one of the first pioneers to hack his way from the Ohio into the interior. He died the year before Dan'l was born, but we often heard old settlers around Ames — which he helped to found — speak of him and his doings. He must have been a forceful person even for those days. His older children, including Dan'l's father, settled on farms around Ames, but his two youngest sons, John and Archibald, were living in Athens when I was growing up. Captain Benjamin spent his last days in Athens with John, who was prominent in the militia and known all over southern Ohio as 'General' John Brown. 'Uncle General' was much beloved. He was very genial and witty. We loved to go to parties at the Brown House. He was honored, too, for his good judgment and integrity. He was treasurer of Ohio University for half a century. His brother Archibald, Dan'l's youngest uncle, was a trustee of the university and an important Ohio judge. Seems to me I've heard he was a member of the convention that framed the present constitution of Ohio. The young Browns were a bookish lot, — those who grew up in Ohio, — but Dan'l's father was nearly grown when they migrated, and never had an opportunity to get far from a farm.

"The farm at Albany was small, and four sons rather overmanned it, I suppose; so when Dan'l was about thirteen he was apprenticed to Ezra Stewart and came to live in Athens. Dan'l was the youngest of eight.

"Dan'l's mother was a Brown, too, daughter of Esquire Samuel Brown, a nephew of Captain Benjamin's. Her name was Polly. You ask about Dan'l's mother," continued Grandmother Brown reflectively. "I could never get acquainted with her. There was a chilly atmosphere about her which I could not penetrate. It seems to me that I never saw her smile. But, though Dan'l's mother seemed cold to me, I realize that she was a very smart, capable woman. She taught Dan'l to spin when he was a little boy. He had to do his stint each day. She made the linen diaper called bird's-eye, and she made very beautiful linen sheets for the beds. She was a woman of strongly marked character. Her face showed that. She had what you might call advanced ideas. She was a great reader. Every afternoon she'd take her paper and lie down on the bed to read. She knew more about politics than any woman I ever met. She was an abolitionist in politics and a Universalist in religion. Not exactly popular causes. She rather courted argument on those subjects, and they used to say that she was hard to beat in discussion, for she read so much that she always had an answer that was pat. She was above the average woman all round.

"I was at the Brown home only once before I married Dan'l," continued Grandmother Brown. "He drove me out once to spend the night. The house was large and comfortable, built of hewed logs and finished inside with walnut paneling. That was handsome, but made the interior seem rather dark. In the best room and the bedroom off of it, where I slept that night with Lyddy Ann, were light curtains that relieved the gloominess.

"From the time he was apprenticed at age thirteen until he was twenty-one, Dan'l lived in Athens. Ezra Stewart had a general store and also conducted an extensive cattle business. He supplied the community with every kind of merchandise it needed. Codfish and molasses, iron and nails, pins and ploughs. He took his payment often in cattle and horses, hogs and sheep, selling them to the Eastern and Southern markets. At first, Dan'l was just a long-legged little boy helping around the store and going back and forth to the homes of his sisters, Maria and Emma. When he grew older he used to go east with the men driving herds of cattle across the Alleghenies all the way, sometimes to Philadelphia. They always used to have one horse and two or three men going along with a drove of cattle, because often one of the steers would take a start in the wrong direction and it would be necessary then for the rider of the horse to head it off and get it going in the right direction. When Dan'l was twenty-one he went into business for himself at Amesville with Austin Dickey, who was his mother's nephew. Dan'l had saved five hundred dollars in his seven years' apprenticeship, and 'Aut' Dickey's father, a well-to-do farmer, gave Aut a like sum. They set up a general store and merchandising business under the firm name of Brown and Dickey."

"Tell me what Grandfather Brown looked like in his youth."

"Well, Dan'l was tall and splendidly developed. At that time, he weighed about 180 pounds. Later, he came to weigh 200 pounds, finally 210, but he was never the least bit fat. He was a good-looking, quick-speaking young man with brown hair, light blue eyes, a friendly smile, and rather a sallow skin. Dan'l used to say that his parents both being Browns was the reason he was so brown!

"After Dan'l began to pay attention to me I would never go to Stewart's store, for fear folks would say I was going in there to hang over the counter with Dan Brown. But about that time he came to the Brice House to board. The first time I remember his ever noticing me was one day when everybody else was at dinner and I sat in the front room by the window. He came by and stopped to speak to me. We looked at each other. That was nothing, but I remember it. And I remember also getting a real love letter from him once when he had gone east with a drove of cattle for Stewart — a love letter with a leaf of wintergreen in it.

"After we left the Brice House and went back to our old home, Dan'l would come up there in the evening to see me when the store was closed. His friend Nelson Van Vorhes was courting Libbie, and sometimes he'd come along. I would usually be knitting. I'd say to Mary and Ann, my little half-sisters, 'I'll knit for one of you to-night, the one that gets her work to me the first.' How they'd scramble! 'Here, Maria, here! Take mine!' One time, I remember, while I sat knitting with Dan'l near by watching and talking, Mr. Hatch popped in on us with a plate of doughnuts. Sometimes Dan'l would take me to dances, but he could n't dance himself.

"One night some of us were invited to a party at Uncle General's. Uncle Dean drove us there — his girls and Libbie and me — in his fine carriage. He told us, as he set us down, that he'd come for us at a certain time and not to keep him waiting. At the party we got to playing 'Pon Honor. You know what that is? You make a pile of hands, then pull them out according to number, and the one that's left has to answer all questions asked him, truthfully, upon his honor. We all put our ring hands on the pile. There was no ring on my hand. Dan'l said, 'I'll lend you mine.' Afterward, when Dan'l had gone into the hall, Uncle Dean came for us, hurrying us along in his quick way. 'Oh, Mr. Brown, here's your ring,' I called. 'Give it to me some other time,' he answered. I did n't want to keep it, and when I got home I woke Ma up to tell her I had Dan'l Brown's ring. 'Child, go to bed and don't worry about it,' she said. A few nights after that I went to singing school. Dan'l was there and I offered him his ring. 'Just keep it a while,' he said, backing off when I held it out. 'I'll tell you. When you get tired of me, just hand me the ring!'

"I never gave it back. Behold the result! Here

I sit with one of his boys taking care of me — some eighty years after."

"How did he make sure you would be his girl?" I asked.

"Oh, I don't know. Lizzie says he told her once, 'Your mother was the prettiest girl I ever saw.' Perhaps he told me that at the time.

"He asked my mother's permission to marry me right before my face. She came in to where we were sitting and he suddenly said, 'Mrs. Hatch, I have a boon to ask of you.' 'What's that?' 'I want you to give me your daughter.' I did n't know he was going to say it then. When the day of our wedding came, the double wedding, — of Libbie and Nelson, and Dan'l and me, — Ma was n't there to see us married. They had to work to keep her from fainting. It touched her very much.

"We were married on the twenty-third day of October, 1845, at eleven o'clock in the morning in the best room of our old house, by the Reverend S. M. Aston, who was a friend. There were no bridesmaids, no presents. Those things had not come in fashion then. We did n't set out to have a big wedding, but when we had assembled all the Fosters and the Van Vorheses and the Browns it made a big company. I know it took two turkeys for the wedding dinner.

"What else was on the menu? Pound cake at that time took the lead. We had fruit and pickles, mince pie, a good fat dinner.

"What did the brides wear? Oh, our dresses were alike, of course. Except in the sleeves. Libbie's sleeves were short, mine were long. I never did like to show my arms. Why not? Oh, I just did n't.

There's nothing wrong with them, either. Once a woman who worked for me, seeing my sleeves rolled up as I worked, said if she had arms like mine she'd never wear sleeves at all! Well, the dresses were white. They were made with tucks and lace. That fine, soft, switchy stuff. I forget what they called it. Oh, yes — India mull! The skirts were plenty full. Girls look so much better with their skirts full enough across the back so they don't draw. Persons should make their clothes according to their figures. At least, that's my taste! We wore white kid shoes and we had orange blossoms in our hair. At the time we were married it was the fashion to part the hair on each side, pulling it straight back in the middle and gathering it behind each ear into a bunch of curls, which we held in place with side combs.

"After the ceremony we young people had a round of parties. First we drove out to the country to Grandpa Brown's. There were fourteen carriages of us. Much joking and laughter, of course. Some of it at the expense of Dan'l and me! The slope in front of our house was awfully steep, and the buggy stood on a side hill. I got in first. Then Dan'l went around on the other side to get in. When he put his foot on the step, the buggy tipped over with him. In a minute we should both have been in the dust, had I not sprung out and back to the step. I was pretty fleet of foot always.

"Finally we were off, Libbie and Nelson at the head of the procession. But after a while there was a halt and a cry down the line. 'The bride's lost her slipper!' Swinging her foot over the side of the light buggy, Libbie had swung off her slipper.

"We had laid off our white wedding gowns and put on dresses of balzarine, an open-meshed, figured cotton goods with a pattern of fern leaves on a blue ground. Very pretty. Our dresses were made with pointed waists and full skirts. We wore bonnets of fine white braid lined with pink sarcenet and trimmed with white ribbon on which were pink flowers. Our stockings were white, our slippers black. We looked very nice. When we passed the college, driving out to Albany, all the students came out and gave us three rousing cheers. Just to think! I am the only one now living of all that company.

"You ask how could so many of us be stowed away for the night at Grandpa Brown's? Well, Uncle John Culver and his wife, Aunt Melissa, lived on a farm not far from Dan'l's father. And Uncle Hull and Aunt Maria — Dan'l's sister — were living, at that time, on a farm near by. And Dan'l's two married brothers, Austin and Leonard, had their farms, too. There was no trouble providing for everybody. Oh, what a time that was!

"The next day we drove back to Athens and had a party at the Van Vorhes home, and the next day to Amesville, where Dan'l and I were to live. There was a party for us at the Ferris House, where Dan'l had been boarding — a big dance. There had been no dancing at our wedding. It seems to me out of place to have dancing at a wedding, but, when with Romans, do as Romans do. Dan'l was always so proud of my dancing. He did n't dance, but he had his partner, Aut Dickey, lead off with me in the contradance. They asked what music I'd like best and I chose 'Money Musk!' Afterward, Mr. Ferris's little daughter came and leaned against my knee, whispering: 'You were the prettiest dancer of all!' The next day we drove to Uncle Dickey's and had another party. That ended it. Our married life began. My happy childhood was over."

III

THE BROWNS

AMESVILLE, or "Stringtown," as it was sometimes derisively called in honor of its one street, was a straggling village on the banks of Federal Creek, when Daniel Truesdell Brown brought home his bride, Maria Foster, in the fall of 1845. When it rained hard, that one street was a sea of mire. "I remember parties at the little hotel in rainy weather," said Grandmother Brown, "when the girls had to be put on a horse and taken across the muddy street that way."

But, rude as was the landscape, the Township of Ames was one of the most progressive of the early Ohio settlements. Nearly a half century had now elapsed since the first white settlers had cut their way thither from the banks of the Muskingum through twenty miles of virgin forest. Three hardy men they were who had thus adventured. One of them was Daniel's grandsire, Captain Benjamin Brown of Massachusetts, an officer of the Revolution who had been attracted by the Ohio Company's advertisements of lands for old soldiers. Coming to Waterford in the spring of 1797, he had made there the acquaintance of Ephraim Cutler of Connecticut — the oldest son of our old friend, Dr. Manasseh Cutler — and of Lieutenant George Ewing of New Jersey, who, like himself, was an impecunious officer of the Revolution. Together these three fared into the wilderness. All were men of sterling quality.[1]

"Yes, the Browns were identified with Ames from the first," affirmed Grandmother Brown, "though Dan'l's branch of the family had moved away from there to Albany before he was born and he himself had passed most of his youth in Athens. But his cousins were as thick as peas around Ames. In setting up a store there, he and Aut Dickey were going back to the neighborhood from which they sprang. You see, Dan'l's grandfather, old Captain Benjamin Brown, who had led the family in from the East, was the father of nine children when he brought them over the Pennsylvania mountains and down the Ohio River. Naturally, his descendants are numerous. Here, you can tell a good deal about them if you'll reach down Dan'l's Family Bible and look over the births and marriages and deaths that are recorded there."

I pored over the records in the old leather-bound book.

[1] It may be interesting to note that great-grandsons of these three men have been associated, in recent years, in the executive work of the Federal Government; Charles G. Dawes, formerly Vice President of the United States, is the great-grandson of Judge Cutler; Thomas Ewing, formerly Commissioner of Patents, is the great-grandson of Lieutenant Ewing; and Herbert D. Brown, Chief of the United States Bureau of Efficiency, is the great-grandson of Captain Brown.

"I know a lot about Benjamin, Grandmother, because his neighbors, Judge Ephraim Cutler and Senator Thomas Ewing, son of Lieutenant Ewing, have both left accounts of those early days which I have been reading. Then I've dug around among War Department records and been able to follow him through practically every day of his four years in the Continental Army. The different witnesses all testify to the same thing: that he was a man of exceptional vigor, physically, mentally, and morally.[1] But I can't find out a thing about Jean Thomas, the girl he married."

Grandmother pointed to the Bible record open before us. "Is n't that enough? A baby every other spring — except when her Benjamin was absent in the war. Shows she had good vitality."

"That's so," I pondered, beginning to figure a little and put my wits to work on what the historians call constructive criticism. "By the time she was thirty-eight, Jean Thomas was the mother of nine children. When the family set out for the Northwest Territory in 1796, she must have been forty-two years old, but, in 1798, to signalize her complete adaptation to the new world in which she found herself, she brought forth at Waterford, on the banks of the Muskingum, a tenth child, her son Archibald, who himself lived more than ninety years."

Grandmother Brown's testimony as to the vigor of her husband's forebears is supported by what the his-

---

[1] Relating the story of Captain Brown's capture, almost single-handed, of Major Butler, the famous Tory leader, and his party, Hildreth speaks of Brown as "a man of great strength and activity." Praising him and his brother John, he says: "These two old pioneers may well be compared to the oaks of our forest, which nothing but the terrible tornado that levels all before it, can overthrow."

torians tell us about them. Captain Benjamin Brown's father, John, for twenty successive years represented the town of Leicester in the Massachusetts legislature. Earlier he, too, had won the title of "Captain" for service in the French wars. One is not surprised to learn that he had four sons in the Continental Army.

Of the four, Captain Benjamin alone came through unscathed. Perley was killed at the Battle of White Plains; William died in a hospital in New York; John's foot was completely shattered at the Battle of Bunker Hill. "Embattled farmers" in the fighting on Lexington Green, the brothers tarried on and enlisted in Colonel William Prescott's regiment. They were all engaged at Bunker Hill. And after John was disabled and Perley and William were dead, Benjamin fought on, not off duty a single day in the campaigns of '76 around Boston and New York and the campaign of '77 along the Hudson. He helped to raise the siege of Fort Schuyler; he captured Major Walter Butler, most notorious of Tory leaders; he was in all the battles around Saratoga, and it was he who there "drove the enemy from the works, and closed this important day in triumph."[1] Invited to become an aide to Baron von Steuben, he refused because "he thought his military knowledge inadequate."

After four years, Captain Benjamin Brown asked to be discharged from the army. The year 1779 was one of acute financial distress, and he was forced to return home to provide for his "aged Father, Seventy-five years Old and entirely Helpless," and his "Large Family," and his "Considerable Farm" that would be "almost useless" if he was longer absent, as he wrote

[1] Hildreth.

his General. We find him joining the westward movement in 1787. In Washington County, New York, he tarried for nine years. Then, in 1796, exhilarated, like so many others, by news of General Anthony Wayne's victory over the Indians, he harnessed up his ox team once more, and set out for Ohio. In February 1797, twenty-three persons of various ages — according to Walker — descended the river to Marietta under his direction.

"It was on that trip that Dan'l's father and mother began to make up to each other," reflected Grandmother Brown. "His father must have been quite a young man by that time."

"Seventeen," I told her, consulting the Bible record. "And Polly was fourteen."

"Big for her age, probably," continued Grandmother. "Tall and angular, dark-complexioned and strong-featured. My Lizzie is a good deal like her. Rather serious-minded always, they said; she certainly was when I knew her. Much given to argument, even when young. Some of my children take after her."

Thereupon I read to Grandmother extracts from Judge Cutler's memoirs [1] with the idea of stirring to life what hearsay of early Amesville days might be buried in her consciousness. Together we retraced the steps of Captain Benjamin Brown as he went from Marietta to Waterford, making the acquaintance of Judge Cutler and Lieutenant Ewing and joining with them in a trip of exploration to the banks of Federal Creek.

The lively account interested her. Judge Cutler tells how the furniture of the two families had to be taken

[1] *Life and Times of Ephraim Cutler*, by Julia Perkins Cutler.

by waterway in pirogues. "What are they, Grandmother?" I asked.

"Canoes made of hollowed tree trunks," she told me.

"Well, it was Captain Brown's task — with the help of some men hired for the occasion — to steer those canoes down the Muskingum and Ohio to the mouth of the Hocking, then up the Hocking to where it joins Federal Creek, then up Federal Creek to within a couple of miles of the clearing, where Judge Cutler and two men, assisted by Samuel Brown, the Captain's third son, had been busy that spring cutting down an acre of trees and making ready the logs for cabin building. From the creek to the clearing they had to cut a road through the woods and brush and haul their furniture over it."

"Why, that's a long journey!" exclaimed Grandmother. "All that roundabout way to go such a little distance!"

"Yes, the water trip was about eighty miles. In the meantime, Cutler undertook to get the horses, women, and children across country through twenty miles of pathless woods. Since their arrival in Waterford, two babies had been born to the Cutlers and one to the Browns, so that the cavalcade of children must have ranged from tenderest infancy on up to adolescence. It was anything but a picnic excursion. But, as the Judge said, 'a gracious Providence' preserved them."

And so we followed the Brown family to the shores of Federal Creek. There, in 1802, Ames Township was incorporated. "See, Grandmother, here in the *History of Hocking Valley*," I told her, "you can read that of the thirty-two men listed at that time six were

Browns — Captain Benjamin and his two married sons, his brother the crippled John, and John's two sons, one of them Polly's father."

"That second married son of Captain Benjamin's must have been William, Dan'l's father," remarked Grandmother. "I know he married young."

"Yes, it was," I said, studying the marriage dates in the Family Bible. "William was twenty-one and Polly seventeen. It was now three years since they had made that memorable trip down the Ohio. They were married by Judge Cutler."

"And then the young couple set up a home in the wilderness near the old Captain's," remarked Grandmother. "They lived there about twenty years. Their nearest neighbors were the Cutlers and Ewings and the family of Judge Silvanus Ames."

"Did you ever hear Grandfather's people tell of their privations in the early days on Federal Creek?" I asked.

"Oh, yes. I know they had it pretty hard at first — harder than the people in settlements along the big rivers. They had a good deal more to fear from the Indians, for one thing.[1]

"Then it was a lonely life," Grandmother went on. "Neighbors few and far between. I've heard Dan'l tell how his father and mother rode over to Marietta once, two on a horse, to go to a dance. And then they

---

[1] Judge Cutler tells how his wife was frightened once by Indians who suddenly appeared at her doorway while he was away in Marietta attending court. The two hired men caught up their guns and ran over to Captain Brown's, leaving her unprotected. One of the Indians threatened Mrs. Cutler with his tomahawk, pointing to a decanter of brandy upon the cupboard. She was afraid that if they once had liquor she would be in danger, so she seized the fire shovel and ordered them to set down the bottle. To her surprise, the Indians called her "Brave squaw" and left just a few minutes before Captain Brown came running in to help.

had hardly any comforts. Even their food must have been monotonous. As for clothes — well, I know the boys wore moccasins and pants made of sheepskin. With thorns for fastenings!"

"But, despite all their deprivations," I reminded her, "the people of Ames Township do seem to have had schools, a library, and public worship almost immediately. The people of Ames evidently had high ideals."

The first school established on Federal Creek was described by Judge Cutler as one of "an elevated character." It was taught by capable Harvard graduates. Five of the twenty pupils were children of Captain Brown. At an exhibition at the close of the term when the children recited pieces for the occasion, Tom Ewing and John Brown spoke the dialogue of Brutus and Cassius.

As early as 1802, thanks to the good marksmanship of the young men of Ames Township, a circulating library was established, the so-called "Coonskin Library." As all the settlers were poor, the question was how they could raise money enough to buy books. Esquire Samuel Brown — Polly's father — was going East in a wagon and would undertake to bring the books back, but how were they to be paid for? Finally, Mr. Josiah True of Sunday Creek Settlement had a brilliant idea. Let people make their subscriptions in the form of peltries which Esquire Brown could sell in Boston for cash and convert into books! Tom Ewing contributed ten raccoon skins — "being all my hoarded wealth," he writes, and one of the Brown boys, at considerable risk to himself, contributed a bear skin. Judge Cutler tells how the young man had crawled into the bear cave expecting to dispatch the animal as Bruin lay sunk in his winter sleep. But he wounded the bear without killing him. Bruin made a rush for the outside air, and young Brown had no other recourse except to lie flat on his face and let the animal crowd out over him. Another hunter shot him through the head, and Brown crawled out afterward, covered with blood. "Pretty hard squeeze," he said. Esquire Brown set out, finally, with about a hundred dollars' worth of skins. In Boston, Dr. Manasseh Cutler and the Reverend Thaddeus M. Harris helped him to select the books. He brought back about sixty well-chosen volumes. Senator Ewing tells in his *Autobiography* of the excitement in the settlement the night they were brought from Marietta in sacks on horseback and emptied out on the floor at Captain Benjamin Brown's cabin. "The library of the Vatican a mere trifle in comparison." Eventually several hundred volumes were accumulated. Different members of the Brown family served steadily as managers, directors, librarians, and treasurers of this historic "Western Library Association," as it was called. I like to think that, living in the wilderness, Polly Brown had some chance to gratify her taste for reading, and that riding double to a ball at Marietta was not the only escape she had from her hard round of pioneer duties.

As for church service, that too was early provided. "The Sabbath was observed as a day of rest," writes Judge Cutler, "and meetings for public worship were held."

"Yes, there were always refined and enterprising people in and around Ames," Grandmother commented. "Both among Dan'l's kin and other families. I suppose that even in the earliest days they got together for good times. I've often heard about the logrollings, house raisings, corn huskings, and quilting bees that they used to have. By the time Dan'l and I came to live there nearly a half century had passed since Dan'l's grandfather had chopped his way through the wilderness. The land had been cleared by that time. Farms had been developed, a village established. It was a prosperous countryside, but Dan'l and I were both so busy, those years, that we stuck pretty close to home and did n't do much visiting. Except for occasional drives over to Athens.

"I was held down by my housework and babies, and Dan'l had a full life in the store, with exciting trips South to New Orleans to sell produce and East to Philadelphia to buy goods. Dan'l always liked to keep a store. Many of the young men of that day were interested in hunting and fishing. He never was. He used to say that men who toted a gun never amounted to much. I think that one reason he liked being a merchant was because, in those days, the village store was a meeting place for everybody who came to town. People talked things over there. And Dan'l was always interested in politics. He liked to argue about public questions. He was like his mother in that respect. Always reading the papers. He never took any part in public life, never held an office, but he followed the activities of government with interest and knew what was going on. His mother died about three years after we were married, so I did n't have much chance to hear her arguing with Dan'l."

IV

EARLY MARRIED LIFE

"Tell me something about the home in Ames where you first went to housekeeping, Grandmother Brown," I begged.

"Oh, it was n't much to brag of," she answered. "We began with two rooms and a porch in a house which stood a little distance up the hill from the store. Across the run or creek which we had to cross to reach the store lay an old gunwale of poplar. It had been intended for the side of a flatboat and had floated down there in some spring freshet. When the spring rains were heavy the water rose almost to the gunwale.

"Though I had n't much house, I had heavy housework from the first. Aut Dickey and two men who worked with him and Dan'l in the store boarded with us. Four hearty men to cook and wash for is all the work one young girl needs to keep her occupied. But I was ambitious to help get ahead in the world. And I was conscientious and used to working hard. So I put my shoulder to the wheel without complaint.

"After a while we built a house near the store. But, oh dear, oh dear, it was n't at all what I wanted or what it might so easily have been. There was no upstairs, and no way of getting up into the attic space. Six rooms we had and seven outside doors. And not a bedroom in it that could be swept properly. It wasn't the plan I wanted. In time, Dan'l came to advise people to have me draw their plans. I made over Sister Ann's house once so as to accommodate two families. Yes, at the end Dan'l got so he thought I knew it all. He told Lizzie, once, that her mother was about the best manager he ever saw. But it took a long time for him to realize it, and there was n't much to manage by the time he was convinced. That first house was one of his mistakes.

"When my father's estate was finally settled a few hundred dollars came to me. With part of it I bought a walnut breakfast table with fall leaves and a drawer in which to keep the tablecloth. I also bought a cherry bureau, a cherry bedstead, and a cherry candle stand — pretty pieces, all of them. The candle stand had a bird's-eye maple drawer with cherry knobs. When evening came we used to set a candle on the candle stand and pull the stand into the centre of the room so that four people could sit around it and see to work. When we left Ames that candle stand was sold, but the cherry dresser I brought with me to Iowa, — all the way down the Ohio and up the Mississippi, — and there it is over in the corner right this very minute."

"And now tell me about the coming of your family," I suggested.

"Well, my dear, I was always one to take things hard. Life has always meant so much to me. So you would n't expect me to have an important thing like a baby without some fuss. The pangs of childbirth! I once knew a woman who said it cost her no pain to have a child, but that was not my experience. In the Bible, whenever there is need to illustrate the utmost agony, comparison is made of 'the woman in travail.'

"We were married in October, and the next October Willie was here. I had grown up among babies and cared for them when only a child myself, and yet I was hardly prepared for the ordeal that awaited me. Even my baby clothes did n't seem to be quite right. Ma laughed when I showed them to her. 'Why, my dear, did you measure the cat?' she exclaimed. 'They are so tiny.'

"And Willie was a big, bouncing boy who nearly killed me as he tore his way into life. Ma was not with me then, only an aunt of Dan'l's and his cousin's wife. The doctor who attended me was a bad man and drunken. First, he bled me — think of it! Then, after he had taken a pint of my blood, he gave me a cup of ergot to hasten labor. I was young and strong and he was anxious to be off. When my agony could go no further, I lost consciousness. All I remember is seeing my hands drawing up in front of my eyes. 'Oh, if they 'll just drop me down, down into that black hole, oh, if they only will,' I agonized, 'it will be all right.' When I came to, I heard a baby cry. 'Your beautiful baby!' they told me.

"Twenty months later Charlie came. He was a nice-looking baby, too. My mother was there that time. When he was born, I said: 'Is that all?' 'My dear child, I should think that was enough,' Ma said. It was really a very happy day. Amesville was having a temperance rally and Charlie was born in the midst of the picnic, you might say. 'So I've been a Prohibitionist ever since,' he always says when reminded of the incidents connected with his birth, and it's true that he has never tasted strong drink or tobacco. You see, it was this way: Tables for the picnic were set in the old orchard next to our place. My mother and the girl we had to help had baked things for the picnic. The Amesville people had prepared a fine dinner, and Libbie's husband, Nelson Van Vorhes, was to be the speaker. Ma had been teasing me right along, saying: 'I guess you're waiting for the rally day, Maria. Then you *will* rally, sure enough!' Well, I was sitting by the window looking out on the picnic grounds when I saw the big band wagon from Athens come driving over the bridge. It was a fine large red wagon, and the band boys wore red jackets and white pants with red stripes down their legs. Brother John was leader of the band. I wanted to see him and visit with him that day, but instead I called, 'Ma, you'll have to fix my bed.' All through my labor I could hear the music and I think it helped to dull my pains. Well, my boy Charlie's been wonderful fond of music ever since; he could always sing, could imitate a horn, too, so that you wouldn't know the difference. When the news of his arrival was taken to John, he said to the members of the band: 'At noon we'll go serenade my sister and her new baby.' They played all my favorite tunes, Brother John knowing my choice.

"When Charlie was four years old, Lizzie was born. She was a big, strong baby with lots of hair.

"Two years later came Gus. He was so good-natured and smiling, the loveliest baby! He's a good boy yet. None of my babies was hard to get along with except Lizzie. She wanted me to hold her in my arms all the time. Gus was so fat that when I tied a ribbon around his wrist you could n't see anything but the bow. I had to be so careful of him to keep him from being chafed and chapped all the time! Such creases in his legs! Such dimples in his back! We had no talcum powder in those days. My mother used to scorch flour, holding it on a shovel over the fire, and rub it on the babies, and I would tear old handkerchiefs into strips and lay them in the creases of Gussie's fat little body. We had no safety pins! It was necessary to be *so* careful in the dressing of little children!

"These were my four little Buckeyes, all born in Ohio before I was twenty-eight. Later, in Iowa, I had four little Hawkeyes. The last one, your Herbert, was born two months before my forty-third birthday.

"If I was busy before my babies came, I was rushed as my family increased. I think now that I attempted too much. My sisters helped me out at times. Until she married Reed Golden in 1852, Kate used to be at Amesville a good deal. She was a nice help for me. But full of mischief, too. I remember one time when Dan'l started off, horseback, on an errand up the road, Kate said she'd like to go along. So Dan'l told her to hop on behind. She snatched up her sunbonnet and stuck her knitting in her pocket. Not far from Ames was a little settlement of homes. 'As we passed those houses,' said Dan'l, 'I noticed everybody staring and laughing, so I looked behind me. And there was Mistress Kate sitting with her face to the horse's tail, her skirts spread out all over his rump, and herself calmly knitting as we clattered along.' Another time when Kate was with us there was a party at Colonel Boyles's. The son of the house came along just as Kate, in high spirits, was talking to a lively group of young folks. 'Kate, your arm's as cold as a dog's nose,' he said, touching her bare arm as he passed. 'Let's see,' she answered instantly, reaching up her hand and tweaking the young man's nose.

"Sister Mary spent a good deal of time with us, too. Though eight years younger than I, and hardly more than a little girl, she could be counted on as everyday reliable help whenever she was with me. She always left crying and wanting to stay longer.

"Our babies were likely children, every one of them, as pretty and smart as parents could want. I remember how we laughed at Willie when we were driving with him and the baby over to Ma's in Athens one pleasant day. We had told him to tell his grandmother that he'd be three in October. Rehearsing his speech, he said he'd be 'f'ee in Knocked-Down.' 'How's that, Willie? Three in October — can't you remember that?' we asked. 'Knocked down same as knocked over,' he answered, with an injured air.

"I was hard pressed sometimes, when the babies were little, to get my work done and look after them too, especially if they were fretful with teething. All my children cut their teeth on one of the Mexican dollars Dan'l brought back from New Orleans. But Gussie's gums were tough, and his four upper teeth would n't come through. So I just took my penknife, wound it with thread all but the point (so that, if my hand slipped, I could n't cut him), and then, while he slept one day, took him on my knee and lanced his gums.

"I found that to keep a baby quiet feathers were great playthings; feathers, or a basket of poppies from the garden that would make them drowsy. Willie was afraid at first of a feather from the bed that floated around the room. But afterward a feather that clung to a drop of honey on his finger amused him for hours. Once when Gus had been very quiet for a long time I found, to my dismay, that he had been picking some little white buttons off their card. He had calmly swallowed the whole dozen, — there was the stripped card as evidence, — but we got them again and Gus was none the worse."

Although Ames Township rather boasts of having led Athens County in the matter of establishing libraries and schools, the educational advantages of the community in the early fifties were not such as to have greatly impressed Grandmother Brown's small sons when they reached school age. "When Charlie came home from his first day at school," said she, "I asked him what he thought of it. 'I like it,' he answered, 'but I would n't be a teacher for anything.' 'Why not?' 'My temper'd fly up and I'd kill some of them, and then I'd have to be hung,' he answered."

His sympathy with the teacher did not, however, prevent him from resenting the way he himself was treated.

"Father asked me how many pupils there were," said Charlie. "'I don't know.' 'Well, why don't you count them?' asked Father. "The next day I stood up and was counting noses, when the teacher jerked me up by the arm and paddled me good and strong. Then a girl drew a picture on her slate, and the teacher scolded her for that and made her cry. It was the foolishest thing I ever saw. Some of the girls in the school were grown women, eighteen or twenty years old. All of them wore linsey-woolsey dresses and pantalets to match their dresses. All of them learned the three R's. Some of the older pupils studied also grammar and geography."

"Did Charlie tell you about the little boy at that school whose neck was dirty?" asked Grandmother Brown. "No? Well, when the teacher reproached him the child whimpered that he could n't help it, because Marm would n't let him go in swimming last summer! Oh, dear, dear! how funny things are!" laughed Grandmother.

The Harvard influence, so strong in the Ames schools of early days, — praised by Judge Cutler for their " elevated character," — seems to have waned a bit by this time. Also, the customs of the people would seem to have become somewhat less decorous during their half century of struggle with the wilderness. According to Judge Cutler, the early settlers had " entered into an agreement not to use ardent spirits at elections, or the fourth of July, at social parties, raisings, logging-bees, or any public occasion, and to this engagement they strictly adhered for many years." But by the time Daniel and Maria Brown took up their residence in Amesville, this self-denying ordinance against "ardent spirits" had been forgotten. Whiskey was freely dispensed in every village store. According to

Walker, even the clergy were active in transporting it — indeed, in profiting by it. The lower settlement in Ames Township enjoyed, indeed, the services of a circuit-riding Free-Will Baptist, one Elder Asa Stearns, who preached to the people once a month and received in pay three barrels of whiskey.

In the meantime, Maria Brown was attending to her home and family, and the firm of Brown and Dickey was pursuing industriously the difficult and delicate art of merchandising.

"When Father went into business with Austin Dickey at Ames," said Will, "they dealt in all kinds of food and grain, dry goods and hardware. Their store occupied the lower floor of a corner on Amesville's one street. Gradually they built on additions until finally it covered a whole block. Their most important addition was a big smokehouse. Raising hogs proved profitable. While hogs, unlike horses and cattle, could n't be driven a long distance to market, they could be fattened at home on soaked wheat, and sold as pork and bacon to the Southern plantations. Then Father had lofts and barns where wool and hides could be stored, so he used to buy sheep, shear them, pack the wool into sacks, tan the hides, and hang them up in his barns, feeding the carcasses to the hogs.

"In the fall, Father and his partner used to go into the tall timber, about a mile from the store, cut down logs, and have the carpenters build them in Federal Creek a scow or flatboat. This they stored with grain, bacon, wool, tobacco, dried fruits. They'd have oxen to load the boat, pulling their goods through the mire. Then they waited for the spring freshets to raise the Creek and float them into the Hocking River. Sometimes the waters would come with a rush before Father was ready to go, before the boat was fully outfitted. I can remember the tense excitement of such days."

"Dan'l could never sleep when he was waiting for the spring flood," commented Grandmother Brown. "In the meantime, Kate and I would be making biscuits and doughnuts all night long, expecting any moment to hear the rush of waters."

"Since the timbers have been cut, that old creek does n't rise any more at all," continued Will. "But in those days it was a thrilling thing to see the boat swing off down the creek, knowing it would be carried into the stream of the Hocking, next into the flow of the Ohio, and finally into the channel of the Mississippi. Propelled by oars and poles, swinging and turning, it swept on its way, irresistibly, to far-away New Orleans.

"At points along the way, Father and his partner stopped to trade off their wares. At Cincinnati they got rid of some grain and tobacco. At plantations along the lower Mississippi they exchanged bacon for molasses. The head niggers used to come to their boat to barter with them. At New Orleans they exchanged that plantation molasses for refined sugar."

"That New Orleans sugar," Grandmother interrupted her eldest, "was shipped in hogsheads up to the mouth of the Hocking River. Dan'l then hauled it sixteen miles to the store. It was white and in sugar-loaf form, covered first with white paper and then with purple. We'd save the purple paper for coloring. I remember that I dyed white silk gloves with it."

"At New Orleans," continued Will, "Father always sold the boat, took the cash returns of the enterprise in the form of Mexican silver, put the money into axe-head boxes, packed those into a small, black, horse-hair trunk, — one does n't see such trunks any more, — and brought the trunk into the stateroom of the steamboat on which he took passage for home. They always tried to act as though the trunk was light; and one person always lay around the stateroom guarding the trunk when the other wandered about the boat.

"The profits of this venture were usually about $2000. With this money in their possession, they would go to Pittsburgh to invest in hardware or push on to Philadelphia to buy general merchandise, — dry goods and household furniture and farming implements, — all of which was later brought over the mountains to them by freighters. This was the long and laborious process by which the products of the Northern soil were collected and bartered through the South for money which was spent in the East for merchandise needed by the farmers of the Northwest Territory. The merchandising of goods was a complicated thing in those days. Most of it done directly without the help of the banker.

"I remember how exciting it used to be when the freighters drove in with their big wagons of goods," Grandmother Brown continued. "'Pennsylvania schooners' we called them — immense wagons, each with six horses, each with a canvas top hooped and drawn in with ropes. The driver used to ride on the horse at the right, next to the wagon. He carried a long whip, and with a whirl of it could hit the front horse. They did n't undertake to move fast, but it was an exciting business just the same — seeing things opened at the store when the boxes of muslins and delaines were brought in. At the end of the first year we had lost a good deal of money, but Dan'l borrowed some more and went ahead, and after that 'the gilt began to stick to our fingers,' as he used to say.

"We lived in Amesville eleven years," said Grandmother Brown. "Then we sold out and joined the Western migration. We bought a farm in Iowa and moved there in the summer of 1856.

"Dan'l had got the Western fever, and I was willing to go to any place where I thought we might better our fortunes. A cousin of Dan'l's who had been in California, going out by land and returning around the Horn, visited us in '55 and told interesting tales of his experience. Dan'l himself had made two trips to the West, looking for land. He thought of settling in Geneseo, Illinois, where cousins had located. But he went on into Iowa, where another cousin named Oliver Brown was living, and came back saying he had bought a farm across the road from Oliver's.

"Brown and Dickey sold their business for $10,000, each getting $5000 in cash. The price of our Iowa farm was $3500 in gold. The rest of our money went to buy a fine team of mares, a new wagon, and a new carriage, which had taken prizes at the county fair. We sold the bulk of our household goods, but I managed to have the cherry dresser packed for transportation and also a big roll of Brussels carpet.

"It was a considerable undertaking, in those days, to move one's family from Ohio to Iowa. There were no railroads to carry us across country and we had to go by steamboat down the Hocking River to the Ohio, down the Ohio to St. Louis, and then up the Mississippi River to Keokuk, and overland the rest of the way by carriage. We were twenty days on the journey. But compared with what our grandparents had had to overcome in moving from Massachusetts to New York and Vermont, and from those places on to Ohio, it was nothing. And then I never thought about its being hard. I was used to things being hard.

"I was very busy, those last days in Amesville, getting myself and children ready for the journey. You may be sure that I fixed my children up so they looked nice. Will and Charlie were nine and seven years old by this time, Lizzie past four, and Gus two. Gus was old enough to be weaned, but knowing that we were likely to move I had kept on nursing him, anxious not to change his food before we got to our journey's end. So they were all rosy and in fine condition. Will and Charlie had such pretty little suits — long trousers with little roundabout coats and hats with visors. I made them ruffled linen collars that were very becoming with their suits, and I did those collars up on the boat, so that the boys looked fresh and clean all the way.

"Whenever I stopped to think, my heart was heavy at the thought of leaving Ohio and going to such a far, strange country. But I didn't have much time for thinking. And one thing made it easier. My mother was going along. Mr. Hatch had died not long after he came home from the Mexican War, and my mother was going West to visit Brother John, who had settled in Minnesota, where his father-in-law was a land agent for the Government. Dan'l's father, Grandpa Brown, also joined us, and a cousin, Will Foster, so that we were a company of nine people when gathered at the mouth of the Hocking, looking for a steamboat to carry us towards our new home in the West.

"Our journey West began with three days of tedious waiting at the mouth of the Hocking River," said Grandmother Brown, continuing her tale of the family migration. "One boat after another refused to carry us, because we were too many in numbers or our freight too bulky for accommodation. But the Lord was watching over us, because one of those steamers that refused us was wrecked soon after it left us, and all lives on board were lost.

"We spent those three days at the Hoyt Williams House. What interested our children most at that place was two parrots. One of them could only say, 'Oh, Hoyt!' but the other was quite conversational. This parrot ate at the second table with the children, pecking away at a plate of things very politely. One morning after breakfast, coming out on the porch with Gus in my arms and the other children following along, I found that this smart parrot was very sick. He was vomiting at the railing, and kept screaming, 'Polly drank too much! Polly drank too much!' Willie regarded him with considerable awe. 'Seems to me, Mother,' he said, 'a bird that can talk like that just *ought* to have a soul.'

"Finally we were off. The boats of those days were interesting places, carrying all kinds of human beings, black and white. The rough work was done by colored roustabouts. Some of the passengers were quite fashionable. There was dancing every night to music furnished by a band made up of colored waiters. There was card playing, too. Indeed, the boat was infested with blackleg gamblers. Every evening after dinner the card tables were set out. There was a bar, too, where you could get anything you'd a mind to pay for.

"Our boat was a side-wheeler," continued Grandmother Brown, "and was loaded to the guards with freight. It moved very slowly. I got *so* tired before the journey was ended. I had my children's clothes to wash and iron every day, but I did n't have much anxiety about the children themselves. All of them kept well. I felt so sorry for a lady who had a baby about the age of Gus. She had weaned him, and said it was *such* a mistake. The baby cried and she walked the deck with him night after night. Will and Charlie were obedient little boys and never wandered far from my sight. Naturally, they were all eyes."

"I never saw a railroad train until we came near Cairo, Illinois," said Charlie. "To most of the passengers it was a curiosity. The people rushed to that side of the boat to watch it go by. Look at the difference now, seventy years after. I've heard Father tell about some of those first railroads in the East that they were just stone abutments with timbers laid on top and spiked down. Travel over them had a tendency to loosen the timbers, and sometimes the ends actually ran up into the car and endangered the people there. What an advance has been made in railroad travel! Just look now at the smooth performances of the Santa Fe!"

"Why, yes," interposed Grandmother Brown, "when first I heard people talking about railroads I thought they meant roads made of fence rails laid across the mud to keep the wheels from sinking into the soft ground! Well, to continue: When we got to St. Louis there was a half mile of boats headed in at the wharf, and we had to wait a long time before we could land. We stopped in St. Louis long enough to buy some dishes and a cookstove. It was a good stove — there never was a better. Made by Bridge, Beech and Company, and called the 'Golden Era.' Those were the years of the California gold excitement, and every door of the stove had the picture of a gold piece on it.

"Finally we reached Keokuk, 'the head of navigation' in those days. We could n't go above the rapids in the river, there being no canal as yet. So we landed at Keokuk, and Ma and I with baby and Lizzie were put into our fine new carriage with Grandpa Brown and Cousin Will Foster to drive us to our farm. That was eight miles from Fort Madison and twelve miles from Burlington, which were towns of considerable size. Dan'l stayed behind in Keokuk with the little boys to look after the landing of our goods.

"After several hours' driving we arrived at Oliver Brown's house. We were welcomed with great excitement, for Oliver had begun to be awfully uneasy, fearing that Dan'l had been robbed and murdered for his money. The care of that money had been our main concern all through the trip. Dan'l had the paper money in a belt around his waist — see, I have that old belt yet, that and Dan'l's tuning fork (it's a *C*), here in this box. The gold for the farm was left with me. The gold pieces were wrapped separately in paper and put in a sack of linen bird's-eye which had been woven by Dan'l's mother. (I gave that little sack to Lizzie not long ago, thinking that she might like to have a piece of her Grandmother Brown's weaving.) This sack of gold I kept in a carpet bag where I had the children's soiled clothes. We did not, of course, want to give the impression that we had any quantity of money with us. I felt deeply the responsibility of looking after it.

"As we were leaving Keokuk, Dan'l brought the carpet bag and, depositing it at my feet, said cheerfully: 'There, Mother! There's your farm!' Then off we drove.

"There were so many of us that we could not all be accommodated, that first night, at Oliver Brown's. Ma and I went up the road with the little ones to sleep at the home of a cousin named Tom Stephenson. 'Where shall I leave the carpet bag?' I asked Oliver Brown's wife. 'Why, put it in the room where Oliver and Will will sleep. Put it behind the door,' she said. And so I went peacefully to bed.

"But the next morning, when I looked for my gold in the carpet bag, it was *gone*. Oh, I shall *never* forget the horror of the next few hours. I thought I should lose my mind. The gold simply was n't there. Oliver and Cousin Will had risen early and started with a wagon and team back to Keokuk to help Dan'l move our things. Of course we thought that they might have moved the gold, which was, in fact, what they had done, having taken it out of the carpet bag and locked it in Oliver's desk before they set out that morning. But they neglected to tell anyone that they had moved it. I kept remembering how Dan'l had called out at Keokuk, when he put the gold at my feet: 'There, Mother! There's your farm.' And I imagined that some thief hanging about had overheard, followed us, and robbed us in the night. Tom Stephenson got out his horse and rode off in haste to meet the party coming from Keokuk to announce to them the misfortune that had befallen us. In the meantime I walked the floor. The fruits of ten years' work and saving entrusted to my care and lost in a single night! Oh, why had I, at the very last, let that carpet bag from my sight? My hair turned gray early; I think it must have started to turn that day when I thought that our farm had been lost, and lost through me."

"In the meantime," said her son Will, taking up the story, "we folks coming up the road from Keokuk were having a little excitement of our own. Oliver Brown and Cousin Will Foster had joined us with a team of farm horses, but one of the horses took a notion to balk. We could n't move him. There we stuck. And then, just in the nick of time, came Tom Stephenson pounding down the road, his horse all lathered, waving his arms and shouting, 'The gold's gone.' But Oliver Brown and Will Foster knew where the gold was, and naturally could n't be excited about it. 'Oh, the gold's safe,' was all they said. 'It's in Oliver's desk. Get off your horse, Tom.' And they took Tom's horse, all covered with foam as it was, put him in harness in place of the balky one, and we all moved forward again. It seemed very exciting and dramatic to us small boys, but we should have called it a drama of 'The Balky Horse,' I suppose, whereas to Mother it was a tragedy of 'The Lost Gold.'"

MIDDLE AGE

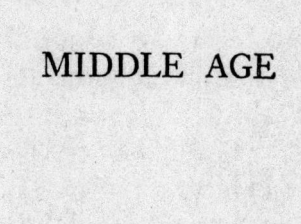

V

AN IOWA FARM

AND so it was that the Brown family came to Iowa.

"How did it seem to you when you got over your excitement about the gold and looked around you?" I asked Grandmother Brown.

"Oh, my heart sank. 'Don't let's unpack our goods,' I said to Dan'l. 'It looks so wild here. Let's go home.' But we had bought the farm and there we were.

"We lived there fourteen years, and I was never reconciled to it. I had never lived in the country before. The drudgery was unending. The isolation was worse. In time, we knew a few families with whom we had friendly relations, but they were very few. At first we had the Oliver Browns across the way. They were always great readers, were educated and sent their children away to school. But they were frontiersmen by nature, always moving West, and a couple of years after we came to Iowa they sold their farm and moved on.

"We had a good farm of rich black soil. But it is people that really make a country, not soil. Those who had settled in that neighborhood were of American stock, but it was poor in quality. I like to be with people who know something, who want something. One of our neighbors let three years go by before she came to see us. 'I woulda come before,' she said, 'but I heard you had Brussels carpet on the floor!' Why, she should have come to see what it was like. She was mistaken about the carpet, anyway.

"Soon after we came to our farm there was a Fourth of July celebration not far from us in a grove on Lost Creek. I packed a picnic luncheon and took my children over. Long tables were set for dinner. There was plenty to eat of a kind — but the people had no more manners than so many pigs. They stared not only at us, but particularly at the jelly cake I had set on the table. Without apology, they grabbed at my cake and gobbled it down.

"The nearest town to us was Augusta," continued Grandmother Brown. "It was about two miles away on Skunk River, a narrow winding little stream not entirely without beauty. Augusta once showed some signs of life, though not a very cultivated life. It had two mills and two blacksmith shops, and several stores. But now it's a strip of desolation, all grown up with weeds. You can't find it on the map."

"It's not quite so bad as that, Mother," interrupted Gus, "but I drove past our old farm the other day, and I must say things did n't look as prosperous out that way as they did fifty years ago. The road past our farm, which was once a main highway, is now a bypath only. Where a double row of shade trees ran along the road, a half century ago, one sees now only rows of stumps. We had three bearing orchards when we left and a fourth coming on. Where are they now? To be sure, we knew nothing then of the pests that prey on fruit trees. But nowadays one sees few flowers and gardens about the houses. And the fields seem deserted. To be sure, with all the new machines not so many men are needed to work the fields. But it does seem as if all people care for out here now is to get the crop. There is less pride in the way things look. Perhaps the bad Iowa roads have something to do with it. But the road that runs past Denmark — which the railroads have missed all these years — is part of the system of permanent State roads, and perhaps in time this part of the world may look like something again."

"Denmark was a pretty village, a really charming town in some respects," said Grandmother Brown. "It had an air of refinement. It had been settled by educated people from the East. They had a fine academy and a good church there. But it was five miles from us, and five miles in days of bad roads was a real barrier. We could not often spare the time or use the horses to drive so far to church. The first Sunday we were at the farm we drove to the poor little church on Lost Creek."

"It used to have two front doors," quoth Gus. "Men went in one and women in the other. When a man and wife from town came in and sat beside each other, the children giggled."

"And what a woodsy congregation it was!" sighed Grandmother Brown. "Lizzie kept whispering that first Sunday: 'Oh, Mother, I'd rather be in Ohio. I'd rather hear Aunt Ann sing!' It brought tears to my eyes and a homesick lump to my throat to hear her carry on so. It was just the way I felt. The next Sunday we drove over to the Congregational Church at Denmark. The singing was better there, and Lizzie whispered: 'Oh, Mother, there's an Ann here!' A later Sunday when we were there they were doing something in the church, and held services in the schoolhouse. I set Gus up on a desk in front of me. Over in the corner sat a square-faced old lady, lovely old Mrs. Houston. She tossed me a cooky for my baby. Right in meeting! It kept him quiet. That sweet old lady — to think of her tossing that cooky to my baby!" mused Grandmother Brown. "She and her daughter Rowena and her two sons used to drive over to see us sometimes. And so did Pastor Turner, the good Congregational minister. But it was only once in a great while that we could go to church. If the horses were used all week, they needed rest on Sunday. And we were tired ourselves and glad to be quiet at home. It was a lonely life. Practically no close neighbors or associates for fourteen years!

"Oh, there was one bright spot I must not fail to mention. Good old Dr. Perkins of Athens who had married my Grandmother Culver had a grandson, Mr. Chauncey Perkins Taylor, who was a Presbyterian minister and preached in Fort Madison while we were living on the farm. The first time Dan'l and I went into the Presbyterian Church in Fort Madison, the service had not begun. Mr. Taylor came down from the pulpit and shook hands with us and seemed to be so glad to see us. After that we exchanged visits often, and had the best time ever talking about our grandparents being married in their old age.

"There never was a nicer family than that of the Reverend Taylor's, but visiting with them or anyone else in Fort Madison was restricted while we lived on the farm. When Ma took leave of me after seeing us settled on the farm she said to me, rather solemnly, 'Now, Maria, you'll be tempted to grow careless, living off here away from everybody. People who live in the country seldom change their dress in the afternoon, the way you've been brought up to do. Now keep on doing the way you've done all your life. After dinner, take a bath and clean up and keep yourself nice, even if there's no one to see you.' And so I always did. Coming in, Oliver Brown would say, 'Going some place?' 'No.' 'Company coming?' 'No.' They learned after a while that it was my way. I could sew and I could wash and iron, and so I was independent always in the matter of wardrobe. I always had plenty of clean white wrappers and fresh cuffs and collars. I can't help but think that children have more respect for a tidy mother than for a clatty one. Webster says a 'slut' is a careless, dirty woman, or a female dog.

"And it took the same sort of watchfulness to keep from sliding backward in other ways. The work of the farm interfered with regular family worship, but Dan'l always asked the blessing. I had been brought up to keep the Sabbath Day holy, and it seemed to me that my children should be taught to do so also. On our farm were many acres of hazel nuts. The boys gathered them and laid them out on top of the woodhouse to dry. Charlie wanted to climb up there and shell them out on Sunday. 'Can't I shell them out on Sunday, Mother, if I sing a hymn all the while?' he teased. 'Seems to me I'd have let him do it,' Sister Libbie said. But I wouldn't. I'll not compromise when I think a thing is wrong."

"Was your land virgin soil?" I asked Grandmother Brown.

"Much of it had never been broken," she answered, "but the farm was twenty years old when we bought it. It had been entered with the Government by old Uncle William, Oliver Brown's father. He sold it to a man named Thompson, and we bought it from him."

"Father paid $17.50 an acre for that farm," volunteered Charlie. "There were 202 acres, which was about the average size of the farms in the neighborhood. The two acres were thrown in extra. Eighty of the 202 acres were timber land, a grove of walnut trees on Skunk River. The timber had been used most wastefully. The best logs had been cut. There was an old log house on the place that had a siding of walnut boards and a roofing an inch thick made out of walnut logs. The granary and barn were also made of wide walnut boards. Such wastefulness!"

"Just think," said Grandmother Brown solemnly, "if Dan'l had only been a financier, those eighty acres of walnut trees would have enabled him to die a rich man. But then, what's the use of fretting about it now? We lived and worked and had our being, and burned that nice walnut wood in our stoves, and kept our house warm and comfortable. Otherwise there was no wastefulness in that house of ours," she went on grimly. "Four rooms with cellar and attic was all we got. It was a well-built, good house painted white, but without a single extra thing. No shutters, no porch, no closets. Not even a nail to hang a dish rag on! Just house!

"The biggest room was used as joint kitchen and dining room. In it we installed our good St. Louis cookstove. I missed the open fires of Ohio. I remember that I thought it pathetic when Gus asked me one time in his childhood what a 'mantelpiece' was. Across the tiny hallway was a sitting room from which a door opened outdoors. The two other rooms were bedrooms, and sometimes we had a bed in the sitting room, too. In the attic there was a window at either end. On either side of each window we put up beds — those at one end for our boys, those at the other for hired hands, when we had them.

"All about the house, at first, was a tangle of hazel brush. It grew so close about us that the cows could n't get between it and the house."

"Oh, well do I remember that hazel brush," exclaimed Lizzie, "and the thorn-apple trees which grew in a circle near the back door. They had the sweetest-smelling blossoms. Father made me a playhouse out there, not twenty feet away from the kitchen door, but so dense was the brush that I could n't see the house. Mother tied a clothesline to me, spread my playhouse with an old red-brindled sheepskin, and put Gus down on it beside me inside a horse collar turned upside down. Baby pens had n't been invented then; the inverted horse collar served just as well. I had some of Mother's fine dishes to play with, ones I had broken for her. But once or twice, before she tied me, I'd follow some other path and get lost in the hazel brush. Oh, there must have been forty acres of it. And beyond was a grove of wild crab apples. Father cultivated them and Mother mixed them with pumpkin and cinnamon, and they really made pretty good apple butter. Father's cousin wanted to know where she got her apples for the butter."

"Yes, it was wild enough when we first came there," assented Grandmother Brown, "but when we left, after fourteen years, it was pretty much all under cultivation. All our stock was under shelter. At first we had only a log barn, but later we built two new barns, one with a fine stone basement with room for our carriage and with five stalls for horses. Once we had reached the farm we had very little use for our carriage and for our silver-mounted harness — a rarity in Iowa. One of the first things that Dan'l did was to get me some muslin in Fort Madison, and I made a cover for that beautiful carriage. We set it away on the threshing floor and kept it clean and bright until we had a chance to sell it in later years.

"Another useless luxury in the first years was our Brussels carpet. Until we had walks and fences and an orderly domain, it was folly to spread out carpets. I was thankful if I could keep my bare floors clean. I can remember how Charlie would say in the harvest time: 'Come on, boys, turn down your pants and shake out the chaff; don't carry it upstairs.' But, oh, how Grandpa Brown would stamp in with chunks of mud hanging to his boots! And so it was several years before our Brussels carpet was unrolled. Not until we had a nice board fence all around the house and garden.

"In time the place came to look rather nice. No amount of cultivation could make it beautiful in the sense that the hills around Athens are beautiful. It was doomed to be flat and uninteresting by comparison. On the farm one could see a mile in every direction. The first morning there Lizzie looked about her and exclaimed, 'Oh, Mother, is n't this a wide town!'

"Our road drove in past an orchard which was half grown when we came there. Later we planted others, and had a nice selection of fruit. At the left of the barn grew a clump of jack oaks — they have one smooth leaf, you know, not the leaf with scalloped edges like the big oak. There we had a box for the martins. And there was a rather pretty tree near the house, a silver poplar with white leaves that were always shaking. In the hazel brush the wild violets were as thick as could be. How Gus loved to gather them! He would come with his fat little hands full of the blossoms, and Ma would put them in water for him. He was so fond of her, and Lizzie would be jealous, because she was fond of Grandma, too, and wanted her attentions.

"We had so many more birds then than we have now. One time I shall never forget. I was washing outdoors on the shady side of the house and I heard a bird with an unfamiliar note. I left my washing and followed it into the orchard, where I saw it quite plainly. I rushed into the house and consulted the bird book I had bought for my children. A Baltimore oriole! They build their nests of thread. Is n't it wonderful how a bird can do that — take thread and weave a nest for its babies and line it soft and nice with feathers from its own breast?

"At night it used to make me so lonesome, sitting at the front door in the dusk, — we had supper at five o'clock, — to hear the prairie chickens calling over the meadow, 'Boo-hoo! Boo-hoo! Boo-hoo!' Charlie could make a noise exactly like their three calls.

"'T was sufficiently settled up in Iowa by the time we got there so that there were no prairie wolves about. It was n't like Chicago when my cousin Mary Harper went to live there. I have heard her tell how one time, when Mr. Harper lay very sick, the wolves howled about the house all night. But I did see three wolves go past our house once — just once — on the lope. They went the length of our farm as far as I could see. I don't know where they were going, and I guess they did n't know either.

"We were too late for the Indians, also. They too had gone before we came. But once, driving home from Fort Madison, Dan'l did overtake two braves. He asked them to ride. When he reached home they sat down under a tree in the yard. I fixed up a big trayful of good things to eat and sent it out to them. There they squatted in paint and feathers, showing their nakedness as they ate. They were the first Indians I ever saw.

"One thing we did have in Iowa that was terrifying. That was thunder and lightning. I don't remember that the Iowa storms ever hurt our crops, but the lightning tore a splinter out of a walnut tree and tied it around a little tree in the yard. I never shall forget the crash that shook the house when that happened.

"But Iowa was ahead of Ohio in one respect. It had no poisonous snakes. In Ohio, when we were in the country, we were always afraid of the snakes."

"That first year must have been very hard for you, dear Grandmother Brown," I said.

"It was, especially after Ma left to visit Brother John. I don't know how I could have gotten through it if it had n't been for Lyddy Ann, Dan'l's good old-maid sister. She joined us in the fall. She was a lovely, sweet-natured woman and a great comfort to me. She was quite good-looking, but had suffered terribly with neuralgia, so they drew out her teeth to ease her pain, — such pretty teeth! — and it made her face fall in.

"Like Grandma Hatch, Aunt Lyddy Ann humored Gus to death. She would give him biscuit dough to play with and he'd wallow it around and have a fine time on baking days. In the morning she'd usually say to me: 'Now you get the children washed and dressed and combed, and I'll get the breakfast.' We tried to pay her when she left in the spring, — she was far better help than we could get around there for two dollars a week, — but she said, 'Oh, I can't take it! The idea!' But I insisted on her taking twenty dollars.

"Oh, those were busy days! Besides the everyday routine of cooking, cleaning, washing, ironing, and baby tending, there were many things to be done that nowadays women might consider extras. I never did any gardening — that was thought to be men's work in our house — and I never milked any cows or made the cheese. But I looked after the chickens and eggs and butter. We stocked up with big Shanghais, but we could n't afford to live on chickens that first year. I would never sell all our cream, but always saved enough to make good butter. I never made soft, runny butter; you could always cut a slice off *my* butter. Only the other day, Lizzie said to me: 'I can just see how you used to work your butter, Mother. I can see you shaping the roll, tossing it over and over and rolling it, and tapping it at the ends, making it so pretty!'

"I often did the washing with and without help. There was no running water in the house in those days. Still, we women had it pretty convenient with a well on the porch and a good cistern. In summer we washed under the cherry trees.

"There was always enough cooking to be done, and at threshing time we had to lay in unusual quantities of food to feed the extra hands. The men of the countryside helped each other in their harvesting, and the neighbor women took turns helping each other feed the men. Often, at those times, Dan'l would let Charlie come in the house to help me. Until Lizzie was twelve years old, Charlie was my chief assistant in ironing and making pies. He would take the moulding board down cellar where it was cool and where flies did n't bother him, and would roll out as fine a batch of pies as threshers ever ate.

"One of my best helpers in time of stress was my neighbor, Mrs. McChord. She was the loveliest woman. There never was such a neighbor. She used to help me pick hog guts all day long. The men would bring in the whole entrails of a hog they had butchered and lay them on the table before us. There is a leaf of solid lard above the kidneys, you know, which is considered the best. All along the entrails is fat which we would pick off. This gut fat is just as clean as any of the animal, but I had a notion that it did n't go in with the other lard and always put it by itself.

"And the sewing we had to do! We could get

almost nothing ready-made, and sewing machines had not been invented. Men's shirts and underwear, as well as women's clothes, had to be made at home by hand. I think I had more faculty for that sort of thing than most women have, but, goodness knows, it was hard enough for the most skillful of us. Probably it was I who made the first knit underwear for babies. At least I used to feel very proud of the beautiful gauze-like shirts I'd make for my babies out of the tops of my old white cotton stockings, and I never knew any other woman who thought of doing it.

"I even made the men's clothes at times. Dan'l came home from Fort Madison, one day, bringing cloth for a suit. 'Why, Dan'l, I never cut out a man's coat,' I told him. 'Well, if you can cut a coat for the boys, why not for me?' he asked. Emma Farnsworth was to come and help me; her mother had been a tailoress. She was amazed. 'You don't mean to tell me you cut out this coat!' she exclaimed. 'Are all these chalk marks yours? Why, *he'd* have sold a cow before he would have done that himself.' I suppose I *was* a big simpleton to do such work. Oh, no. I guess it was right. It didn't hurt me, and it saved money. We got ahead.

"But I really had to draw the line at making clothes for the neighbors. Once when I was making a suit of clothes for Gus he wanted me to make a suit for his friend Henry, a little German boy, whose mother was dead. 'But, Gus, I can't buy clothes for outside children,' I remonstrated. 'Why, sometimes you can find old clothes around the house to make new ones out of,' he told me. 'You'd have to make the suit,' he went on, ''cause Henry's sister Julia couldn't do it.' But I didn't see how I could undertake to make clothes for Henry, and had to say so. When I washed and dressed Gus for Sunday school, putting on the new gray suit, he heaved a big sigh and said: 'Oh, dear, I'm going to talk to Henry more than ever to-day, because I'm afraid he'll think I care 'cause my clothes are better than his.'

"When everything else was disposed of, we women always had knitting to do. Everybody's stockings had to be knitted by hand, and so a ball of wool with the knitting needles stuck through it was carried around in one's apron pocket or set up on the kitchen window sill ready to be taken up when one had a moment free from more pressing duties. Mrs. Glazier in Amesville told me that in Ireland it was the men who did the knitting, the women the sewing. That seems to me like a fair division of labor. Of course the men were pretty tired in the evening after a day in the field, but the women were just as tired after a day of cooking and ironing.

"Our work had to go on after dark by light that was none too good. We had only candles on the farm at first. I had an iron candlestick with a hook on it that hung on the back of my chair, so I could get light on my work. The wicks of those candles were as thick as your little finger.

"Making the candles was part of our work too, winter's work, for candles must be made in cold weather. I remember that once we dipped four hundred candles in four hours. We brought our candle rods with us from Ohio. First, we laid down paper to keep the drips off the floor. Then we brought in the scantling and set it up in rows. Next the wash boiler, with hot water in the bottom and hot tallow on top. We took up a candle rod with wick hanging from it, dipped it once, straightened the wick, dipped again, and laid on the scantling. After a while the tallow grew thin. Then we poured in beeswax and moulded the candles in candle moulds. A dozen at a time. We laid them away in the coldest part of the cellar.

"The first lamp I ever saw Will brought home from Denmark when he was a young man. It was made of glass, and it exploded. Dan'l and I had gone to bed when Lizzie came downstairs into the sitting room carrying the lamp in her hand. I heard a pop and an exclamation. I rushed to the door and saw her still holding the lamp in her hand. The wick had blown out over the top and half the oil was gone, but scattered in so fine a spray that we could n't see any shadow of oil in the room.

"Just think what I have seen in my lifetime in the way of development in illumination! When I was a child, the only kind of lantern known was the tin can with holes punched in it to allow the checkered candle-light to shine through. Lanterns, candles, oil lamps, electric incandescents — I have seen them all.

"I suppose that the most unusual piece of work I ever did while we were living on the farm," continued Grandmother Brown, "was to make a casket for a little dead baby. It was my brother's child, and had been born dead. My brother himself was ill at the time and had little money. 'You can't afford to buy a casket,' I said to him. 'I'll make you one.' 'You! How can you?' he exclaimed. 'What's that dog lying on?' I asked him. 'A pair of old pants!' He shooed the dog away. The pants were of fine broad-cloth and were lined. 'Rip out the lining!' I said. The inside was like fine black velvet. I looked about and saw some thin boards that had been laid down to step on, to keep the mud out of the house. Brother John cut them out the proper shape for a little casket and tacked them together, and I covered them with the black broadcloth. I lined the box with cotton batting, tacking it neatly in the corners. I had an old white dress of thin stuff. I folded it in pleats and tacked it over the batting. I covered a board for the top in the same way. Brother had some pretty little white tacks that looked like silver. I tacked them in around the edge like a finish. And then I made a pillow of the white stuff and laid the baby on it. Brother John wept, and said: 'My! Sister! What *can't* you do?' 'Better that,' I told him, 'than buying a casket when you have so little money.' We buried the little baby on our farm.

"Whatever the work to be carried through to completion, whether for the dead or the living, one's children must not be neglected. Gus used to follow me around sometimes, those first years on the farm, saying doggedly: 'Mother! Mother! I've got me some tiredness, I want to be took.' Poor little fellow! It was only a little while after we went there that Will and Charlie had him out in the barn one day sitting on a box, and he fell off, striking his head. A great lump raised up on the soft place in his skull. I sat up all night long, night after night, and dripped water on to his head. Grandpa Brown said he hoped he'd never get well, as he would n't have any sense if he did. But Grandpa was wrong.

"It seemed as if the only time when I felt justified in taking up a book or paper was when I sat down to nurse my babies. I always nursed them till they were pretty big. I could n't bear to wean them — they kept so fat and pretty as long as I fed them at the breast. And so it happened that Frank would sometimes pull at my skirt and hand me a newspaper, as a hint that he would like to be taken up and nursed. Herbert declares he can *remember* the last time I nursed him, and perhaps he can, for it was the only way I could quiet and comfort him. It was one day long after he had been weaned and was running around independently in house and garden, when a bee stung him. (I was stung by a bald hornet once, and I never had anything hurt me so much in all my life as that did.) Anyway, for many years all my household tasks were performed with an ear cocked for the cry of a waking baby. How often I used to think: 'What happiness it would be if I had nothing to do *except* take care of my babies!' There was one terrible period when, for two years, I carried my little sick Carrie around with me on a pillow as I went from stove to table or from room to room, doing my work.

"Such a way of living is hard, *hard*, HARD. The only thing that can make it endurable for a woman is love and plenty of it. I remember one day on the farm when Dan'l was going up to Burlington. I remember that before he left he kissed me — kissed me and my little sick baby lying so white on her pillow. I had many things to do that day. But, my! how the work flew under my hands! What a difference a kiss can make!

"Outside in the fields the men folks had their full share of trials before our farm was well under cultivation," went on Grandmother Brown. "To begin with, soon after we arrived Dan'l began shaking with fever and ague, having got infected on the river as we came here. I myself never had a chill in my life, but Dan'l suffered one season terribly. He always claimed that he cured himself eating wild plums.

"Then the weather was very trying during our first years on the farm. The summer of '57 was terribly wet. Soon after came a summer that was just as terribly dry. The grass actually crackled when we walked over it, and the corn shriveled and dried up in the stalk. Then the winters of '58 and '59 were unheard of in their severity. For months the snow was knee-deep between the house and the outhouses. To cultivate and develop a farm in a new country when the weather is unfavorable is no easy task. Charlie can tell you some of the difficulties the men encountered."

"The first piece of ground Father undertook to break," said Charlie, "was a twenty-acre piece that proved to be full of bumblebees. One boy always had to follow along behind the team with a shovel, smothering the bees with earth wherever the plough turned them up. The horses used to get panicky. Old Sal wanted to run off, and our sober Bob was so scared by the bees that he jumped and cut his foot on the plough. Grandpa advised us to buy a yoke of oxen. We did so, but they'd twist their tails when the bumblebees flew out about them and run just about as fast as the horses did. People used to say that clover wouldn't grow unless there were bumblebees about to carry the pollen, and Father always kept half a dozen swarms of bees; but I don't believe it. The bees stung me on the face once so that I had to stoop over close to the earth and cut for the house. Mother was frightened. But finally we got that field ploughed."

"I wonder if Charlie remembers that time our threshers disturbed a skunk?" said Grandmother Brown. "He came rushing toward the house, smelling to heaven. I called out frantically, 'Don't come in the house!' But he did. Spoiled the butter and everything with the scent he carried on him. Isn't that a strange weapon of defense for an animal to have?"

"We kept those oxen four or five years," continued Charlie. "Good, honest old beasts they were. I've hauled many a load of logs with them. Most of the neighbors used horses in their work — with the exception of old Miss Moon at Augusta, who ran a saloon. Oh, yes, she had a husband, but he was a kind of cipher — so we always called her 'Old *Miss* Moon.' She used to drive her oxen past our place on her way to the Fort Madison distillery for whiskey. They'd take all day for the trip. Slow, but sure."

"I wonder if Charlie remembers how he and I made one of our good oxen cry one day," remarked Grandmother. "All the men were gone when he came driving in the oxen. I went out to the barn to help him unyoke them. We didn't know that the right way to do was to take the bowpins out of both sides of the yoke before releasing either ox. Instead, we took the bowpin out of the right side of the yoke and let that ox walk away. The yoke fell clattering down about the shoulders of the left-hand ox. Charlie couldn't lift the heavy yoke high enough so that I could loosen the bowpin on that side and release the poor beast. There that ox stood crying great mournful tears all the time. Finally Charlie gave the yoke a mighty boost, and I got the bowpin out. I've often seen cows cry when their calves were taken from them, but this was the first time I ever saw an ox weep.

"Our poor old bossy! When she wanted her calf and would cry for it, the tears would run down her hairy face. Many times I'd go to the barn and try to comfort her!"

"Father was looking out for any kind of help he could get, to do the farming," Charlie went on. "He bought the first mowing machine I ever saw, one of the first lot ever shipped west of the Mississippi. It was made by Walter A. Wood and Company and cost about $65. The first hay put up in Iowa was cut with a scythe. We did n't have much meadowland on our farm — not more than about three acres — because of the difficulty of cutting it with a scythe. A traveling man who had met the agent for the mowing machine told Father about it. 'If there's a machine like that, I'm going to have one,' said Father. It cut four feet wide. The mowers nowadays cut six or seven feet.

"In Ohio, where the soil is very stumpy, we had used cast-iron ploughs. In Iowa, steel ploughs made in Moline were considered the best. But they were not polished — were made of raw black steel. We had to polish them ourselves — go into the road and drag them up and down. It used to take a week to get them so they'd work.

"The first farmers of our Middle West ploughed the land too much. They loosened the ground so thoroughly that it would n't hold the moisture. When the rains came the good deep soil ran off and left the clay banks. And then, they had no idea at that time of rotation of crops.

"We did n't have any reapers until a year or two before I was married. The first was a Buckeye reaper and mower combined. McCormick put out a harvester about the same time, but it was no good for mowing.

"The Atkinson self-raker we had when we came to Iowa. That raked, but did not bind. We had to bind by hand.

"In Ohio, folks used a threshing machine that was a 'chaff piler' — that is, it ran the grain through the machine all together, scattering the wheat and oats about. After the machine was gone it was necessary to take a fanning mill and run the grain through it to get it clean. For threshing buckwheat they used a hickory flail. In Iowa, we tried to thresh with a treadmill. It did n't work very well, because Jule and Sal, the horses, got rebellious."

"I don't blame 'em!" ejaculated Grandmother Brown.

"We finally attached the horses to poles and drove them round and round. That was threshing by so-called 'horse power,'" explained Charlie. "Of course no motors were dreamed of in those days."

"We had a good deal of stock at times," remarked Grandmother Brown. "We kept sheep for a while. Always we had hogs, which we butchered ourselves and sold. We always saved enough hogs for our own use. Fine hams and shoulders came out of our smokehouses — not hams like the soft white things these present-day ones are. Father used to drive a wagonload of his hams and shoulders up to Burlington. Or perhaps he would drive the hogs up there on foot. In the fifties there were no railroads in Iowa. It was some years after we came to Iowa before there was a bridge across the

Mississippi or even a railway between Fort Madison and Burlington. In disposing of farm products we were not much beyond the period of barter and exchange that we had known at Amesville. Dan'l was more of a trader than he was a farmer. When our boys had raised things, he could drive a bargain with them."

"What did the children do for schooling in this Iowa wilderness?" I next asked Grandmother Brown.

"Schooling!" she echoed, with a sad shake of her lovely white head. "That was the great mistake in our moving West. There were no educational facilities on Skunk River that could compare with those in Athens or Amesville, and even such as there were my children could not take full advantage of.

"There was a little white schoolhouse a mile up the road from us where children could receive instruction three months of the year. I remember only once when there was a four-months term. Our children went to school there, when their father did n't have something on the farm for them to do. If there was any work going on in the fields or orchards at which the children could help, Dan'l seemed to have no scruples about keeping them out of school to do it. It is a very poor way to educate children. The work of the farm always seemed to Dan'l more important than that of the schools. Nothing I said would change him. I never could understand why he was so blind on this one subject. Generally speaking, too, the Browns were a bookish lot and set great store by education. That was one thing I liked about Oliver Brown. He sent his children away to school."

"Well, Father believed in education," commented

Will, "but he had the idea that if a person had it in him to profit by any particular kind of training he'd reach for it himself. Just as Tom Ewing did, who lived on the next farm to Grandfather Brown in Ohio. He knew from earliest childhood that he wanted to be a lawyer and go to Congress. He never gave up the idea, but kept studying by himself until he actually made himself ready for college and realized his ambitions, becoming a United States Senator and member of two Presidential cabinets. Father thought it was not necessary to force on a child anything beyond the ability to read and write and cipher. The rest he could get for himself, if he wanted it badly enough, and if he did n't want it why waste education on him anyway? The pioneering, self-made man was the hero of Father's day, the typical American of that time. Father himself had a logical, active mind and a natural faculty for reasoning out a problem. He used to say that he could solve any mathematical problem he ever heard of by the Rule of Three. Fact was, he could think straight, straighter than most of the young men around Athens or Ames whom he had to cope with, including those who had been to college, and I think he knew it, modest as he was. He could write a better letter than any of them and he was an easy talker, too, and could beat them in an argument if he set about it. He was interested in public questions, and that was one reason he liked to keep a store. He was a good mixer, Father was, and enjoyed drawing people together under his roof in a group for sociability's sake. He felt equipped to meet the life of his time. He honestly thought he did his children a service by forcing them to stand on their own feet at an early age. He did n't realize that times were changing and his children would have to meet competition in a very different world from the pioneer society he had helped to make, a new world where technical information would be at a premium."

"Indeed he did n't realize it, and I could n't make him," said Grandmother Brown broodingly. It is probably the subject on which she felt most deeply. Other disappointments and sorrows were softened by the years, but nothing ever reconciled her to the fact that her children were denied "advantages" they might have had.

"But I must say this for Dan'l," went on Grandmother Brown. "He felt differently late in life — after his own children were grown up and gone. He was eager to do for Lizzie's children what he never thought necessary for his own. He saw, too, that his own boys were resentful of the way he had let them scramble for an education or go without, and it hurt him. He grieved over it a good bit at the last, especially over Herbert, who was having a hard struggle about the time Dan'l died.

"I know, too, that Dan'l did n't feel things just the way some of the children did and so he could n't understand, because when he was a boy he had n't wanted the *kind* of things some of them wanted. But *I* knew that Willie wanted to make music the way I had wanted to make pictures when I was a little girl. And I knew that he loved birds and bugs, too, the way I did, and would have liked to study about them. And Herbie was crazy over machinery of all kinds and should have had an engineer's education. All my sons are better mechanics than Dan'l was. They get that faculty from me. I always liked to invent ways of simplifying my work. For instance, long before I ever saw an egg beater for sale in a store I had made one for myself. I took heavy wire and bent it into the shape of a spoon, and bound it together with lighter wire. If there was any tinkering to be done about the house, 't was I who did it. Dan'l was n't so much interested in finding out ways to make things run slick and smooth. But my boys were. Charlie always contrived to have everything conveniently arranged where *he* was working. While selling sewing machines, Will invented a ruffler that another man patented and made a fortune out of. In the paper mill Gus invented a machine for putting up paper in rolls instead of packages. He got a patent on it and made a good many thousand dollars out of it, until someone invented a better machine. At another time he invented a machine for working over leather scraps. Frank has experimented with numerous devices to facilitate the work around the ice plant, and Herbie began when he was just a child to work out mechanical short cuts of one kind and another. Why, I remember, when he was n't more than ten years old, how he rigged up a piece of old board with some burlap and wire and hitched it to the back of the lawn mower to save himself the trouble of raking the lawn. A few years later he built himself a snowplough. To this he hitched his pony and so he saved himself the work of shoveling off the walks. And when he began to use a typewriter he worked out a touch system of his own — a new thing then — that made him very proficient. Oh, my children all had special talents that nowadays parents would delight to develop.

"Well, back in Amesville, Willie had teased hard for a little fiddle which his father had brought from

Philadelphia and had for sale in the store. Dan'l said, 'I can't afford to give you that, Will.' Sister Kate was there at the time, and how she laughed when Willie answered, mimicking a Quaker friend of ours: 'Did n't thee know, Pa, when thee got me, that I 'd need fiddles and things?' Sure enough! He should have known. But later, on the farm, Dan'l did get Will a fiddle, and taught him to play it. He was soon playing better than his father."

"Well I remember the day when Will got his fiddle," said Charlie. "I remember Father bringing it home one night from town, and scraping away at it, letting Will try it. And the next morning I remember Will going into Father's room where he lay in bed — it was hardly light — and getting him to tune it. Why, within a week Will was playing all sorts of things. He could make up as he went along, too."

"Yes, yes," cried Grandmother Brown. "Often I 'd hear Will playing after I went to bed. Just making it up as he went along! Oh, it would be beautiful. He should have had violin lessons.

"Then, Willie shared my love of living things. On the kitchen at the farm was a lean-to, in the corner of which an old spider built her web. I used to want to sweep it away. But Will would always stop me. 'Don't, Mother, I want to watch her!' And at noontime he 'd sit and watch the spider. Once Dan'l called to me to see what an undutiful son I had. 'See that boy Will,' he scolded angrily, 'squatted down in the road there. I sent him up to the barn an hour ago. What's he doing?' 'I s'pose he 's watching a tumblebug,' I answered. Tumblebugs are very interesting. They lay an egg in a little manure, roll it around in the dust until it gets to be a good-sized ball. 'Never mind about Will,' I told Dan'l. 'Morning after morning, he's out cutting hay before you and Charlie are out of bed. I never have to call *him* in the morning.' He did his share of work on the farm as all my children did — but I think he might have been a naturalist if he had had encouragement.

"I think Charlie perhaps was kept out of school the most. He was such a good little helper on the farm, such an honest, conscientious little boy about everything he did. Fact is, I think he was about the most honest child I ever knew. We used to sugar cure and dry our hams at home. They were mighty good. Often Charlie would take his knife and cut out pieces around the bone. I heard him in the pantry once and called out: 'Charlie, what are you doing?' 'Oh, I had to work at this ham again,' he told me truthfully, though he knew I'd scold. We used to keep two kegs of sugar in the pantry, one of granulated and one of Orleans sugar. I heard the tramp of feet there one day, and called, 'Charlie, what are you doing?' 'Oh, I'm going to get some lumps of sugar for these boys,' he told me. Mrs. Akins was sewing with me, and she said, 'Are you going to let him do it?' 'Why, of course,' I told her. 'I wouldn't spoil all that good time for a few lumps of sugar, especially when he's so honest about it.' And Charlie has certainly made his life an example before men as good as a man could make it. He has never tasted liquor, never smoked. And his father said that he never told a lie. I remember that Charlie was once summoned to court here in Fort Madison as a witness. When Dan'l heard of it, he said, 'Well, whatever Charlie tells them will be the truth.' But the truth is, I guess, that Charlie was most too conscientious for his own good when he was a little boy. He did his work at home so well that it was hard to spare him when school time came. He kept a record of his school attendance one season and found that he 'd been to school only thirty days that year. That was n't right. And then, when he was older, Dan'l sent him over to Denmark to be apprenticed to a blacksmith. The idea! One of our neighbors said to me that it would have been more to our credit if we 'd sent him over there to attend the Academy, and so it would."

"And what did that blacksmith business amount to?" commented Charlie scornfully. "I received my board and $4 a month. I was there a little over a year, earned $52. My clothes cost me $72. Finally, one Saturday night, I went home, telling the blacksmith that if he could n't raise my wages I would n't be back. I quit anyway; I was afraid he *would* raise them. I learned some things from him, it is true, that I found handy to know on a farm. No, I never did any horseshoeing, I never drove a nail. I was allowed to take the shoes off the horses and pare their feet, but I never got to putting them on. We used to make our own horseshoes then. Now we buy shoes for horses just as we buy shoes for folks."

"My Charlie's done remarkably well in the world!" exclaimed Grandmother Brown proudly. "All my sons have done well. 'All 's well that ends well,' I suppose."

"Yes, Mother," was Charlie's comment, "but I 've always felt kind o' cheated. I did n't realize myself, when I was a young fellow, how much I needed an education. I 've prospered in a worldly way, but I 'm shy with people. I notice when there's a big meeting people don't want for chairman or chief speaker someone who is n't trained in school ways. I see now how I might have got more education by my own efforts, but I did n't see it then. At the time I was sent to Denmark I could have earned my living as a farm hand and gone to school part of the time. Men offered me a dollar and a half a day to cut corn for them."

"What could a little boy do on a farm?" I asked.

"The first work I ever did," answered Charlie, "was to cut cornstalks with a nigger hoe. We cut the stalks close to the ground, raked up the stalks into rows, and burned them."

"It was too hard work for him to carry that heavy hoe," declared Grandmother solemnly. "He used to get so tired. Once he said to the hired man, 'Elias, will you kill me? I want you to.' Elias told me about it. Was n't that dreadful? 'I took the back of my knife, Mrs. Brown,' he told me, 'and just sawed around his neck. "It's too hard, Charlie," I told him. "I can't kill you."'

"Sometimes there would n't be more than half a dozen children at school," observed Lizzie. "The rest would be dropping corn. That gave me more of Het Mullen's time. She was the teacher. She took me through long division and compound numbers by the time I was eight years old. We worked through McGuffey's Readers and Spellers and Ray's *Third Part Arithmetic* with her. She taught mental arithmetic, geography, and history as well. Sometimes we stood up and had a spelling contest. But Father and Mother were n't much for having us go around at night. I went only once to a spelling bee. When I was fourteen they sent me over to school at the Denmark Academy and later to Ohio. Will attended school at Denmark one winter, too.

"The Denmark Academy was probably as good as any school in Ohio," continued Grandmother Brown, "but we were not so situated as to be able to take advantage of it. Mr. H. K. Edson, the man who was principal of the Academy, was a remarkable person and some well-known men came from that Academy. At one time they had an enrollment of several hundred, the children of Illinois and Iowa farmers. The people of Denmark were unusual too, known, far and wide, as abolitionists. Denmark was famous as a station on the underground railway in the days before the war. Unfortunately, we didn't live in Denmark, but five miles from it, and the roads of those days were often almost impassable. When children were sent to school in Denmark, they had to board there."

"Those first years of yours in Iowa were the bitter years just before the outbreak of the Civil War, Grandmother. Did any of the bitterness and excitement reach you off there in the country?" I asked.

"Yes indeed. We were abolitionists, of course. It was bred in our bones to hate slavery. Both Dan'l's people and mine were clear on that point. We were accustomed from our earliest youth to seeing runaway slaves along the Ohio River, and advertisements offering rewards to anyone who would return them to their masters. I remember seeing slave owners coming over from Kentucky with chains and whips, looking for their slaves. I remember, too, my horror at the sight. I remember particularly, one time when we were living at the Brice House, seeing a man there who had caught his slave and was taking him back handcuffed. The black man had to eat so, weighted with irons. Think of a nice little girl standing in the dining-room door seeing that pitiful sight! Someone said the other day that the negroes were better off in slave days than they are now. How could that be, when now their children are taught and they are treated like human beings? See what good ministers some of them are! One of them preached a fine sermon here in our Presbyterian Church not so long ago.

"Oh, I never could have been anything but an abolitionist, a Whig, a Republican. Once, Mr. Richey, a very pleasant man who boarded with us, a Democrat, said to me: 'You don't know the difference between the Whigs and Democrats. You're just a little girl!' 'Yes, I do.' 'What is it?' 'Democrats believe in buying and selling people, and Whigs don't.' 'You're just about right,' he acknowledged.

"Dan'l felt the same way. Once, coming home from New Orleans, he saw a slave sale in St. Louis; saw men and women exposed for sale on a block in front of the courthouse, saw the auctioneer trying their agility and running his finger around their mouths exactly as if they were horses. We all *hated* slavery. My father helped many a slave get away on the underground railway, and Dan'l's folks did, too."

"Don't I remember what Uncle Jack Brown did in that line?" exclaimed Will. "You know, Albany, where Uncle Jack lived, was quite a station on the underground railway. Uncle Jack was a big fat man. He used to drive about in an open phaeton with Aunt Susan sitting up beside him in a poke bonnet that had a green veil hanging over it. Aunt Susan always made a great fuss over me when I was a little shaver. One day they drove up to Father's store in Amesville. Uncle Jack called Father to one side and they talked together very earnestly. But Aunt Susan never answered a word when I threw myself upon her. Rebuffed, I hurried home to Mother and told her about it. 'Sh!' she said. Later, I learned that it was n't Aunt Susan behind the green veil that day, but a runaway slave, whom Uncle Jack was helping to get away."

"Naturally our children imbibed our feelings in regard to slavery," said Grandmother Brown. "That meant trouble for them almost from the first in the country schools of southeastern Iowa. Denmark was an exception with its abolitionists and fugitive slaves. We had a colored cook from Denmark once, Old Tishy, who had been a slave and a runaway. But in Augusta and most of the other places near the Missouri border Southern sympathizers were numerous. It was soon discovered in school that the Brown children were abolitionists."

"I remember how mad I was," said Lizzie, "when some children at school called me 'a black abolitionist' and sang: —

"'Douglas rode a white horse,
Lincoln rode a mule;
Douglas is a wise man,
Lincoln is a fool.'

But when I wept about it at home, Father said: 'Why, of course you're an abolitionist, a black abolitionist. *You* don't want slaves.' He explained it all to me, and I went back to school and said to the children, 'I am what you say I am, and proud of it.' And when they'd abuse Lincoln I'd fairly yell and dance with rage. Lincoln did n't know I was such a booster. During the war there were continual rallies in Fort Madison and Denmark. Often a Copperhead would make a slighting remark about Uncle Sam or about Lincoln, a soldier would resent it, and then there would be a fight and much excitement."

"There were about as many rebels along the Missouri border as there were Union men," said Charlie. "Our countryside was very unsafe in those days. They would drive off each other's cattle, steal anything they could lay hands on. When the Lincoln and Douglas campaign was on, Will and I joined 'The Wide-Awake Boys' in hip-hurrahing for Lincoln. We'd get together down in Augusta and march back and forth, carrying lamps filled with crude oil. It looked rather pretty as we described figures in our marching. There was a tonguey lawyer over in Fort Madison making speeches for Douglas, but nothing he or anyone else could have said about how Kansas should come into the Union changed our allegiance to Lincoln. We were thoroughly grounded in the principles of the abolitionists. Father and Mother had read aloud to us Harriet Beecher Stowe's book, *Uncle Tom's Cabin*, as it came out serially in the paper. We'd just get 'raring' mad over that story. I'm sure that book was most influential, indirectly, in freeing the slaves. And over in Denmark there was a good man named Cable, who had known Grandfather Foster back in Ohio and worked with him helping slaves get away. I remember his driving over to our farm one day and telling us about his experiences. We boys sat on the edge of our chairs taking it all in. He told about staying somewhere one time in Kentucky and being wakened in the morning by the sound of terrible groaning. He looked out of his window and saw a poor black man tied to the ground while a white man was lashing him. 'Oh, massa, hab mercy! Hab mercy,' the slave cried. But the master whipped him until he brought the blood, rubbed salt in his wounds, and then started him off towards the field. Mr. Cable said that back in Ohio he had always kept a horse and carriage ready to come to the aid of any fugitive slave who appealed to him for help."

"It seemed afterward as if we had seen that war coming all our lives," said Grandmother Brown, "but at the time when Fort Sumter was fired upon we were as excited as if the course of events had been wholly unforeseen. Feeling against President Buchanan was very strong with us. He was clearly a Southern sympathizer. He had allowed the Treasury to be robbed. He had let the arsenals be stripped of their guns and be put in the hands of Democrats. Fortunately, a great many Republicans had their own guns. Dan'l had his.

"Lincoln's call for volunteers reached many of our folks in Ohio, but our own particular family in Iowa was hardly subject to call at first. Will was only fourteen years old when the war broke out. But before it was over he and Dan'l both went up to Burlington to enlist. I could n't eat that day. I felt that it was no worse for my men than for thousands of others all over the land, but, oh, how glad I was when they came home again after only a day's absence! Both were rejected. Dan'l had broken his arm and shoulder when he was a young man, and they had been so set that he was never again able to straighten out his arm completely. And a chisel had fallen on Will's bare foot when he was a child and cut off two of his toes. The doctor had sewed them on again, but Willie had worked one toe free from the bandage so that it turned under his foot. He could never have tramped like a soldier.

"Back in Ohio there was great excitement among our relatives. Sister Libbie's husband, Nelson Van Vorhes, and Sister Kate's husband, Reed Golden, — he was a Democrat, but not a Secessionist, — went around with Brother John getting volunteers for the 92nd Ohio Regiment, of which Nelson was to be colonel. Reed was a cripple — one leg shorter than the other — and could n't go to war, but he had an eloquent tongue and was good at drumming up recruits. As for Brother John, his forte was another kind of drumming. He drilled the musicians. On one occasion, after Reed Golden had spoken Brother John was called on, and created a great laugh by saying: 'I'm no speech maker; just a plain musician; but I was born with drumsticks in my hand and my mother was singing "Yankee Doodle"!'

"Brother John organized a drum corps. At the beginning, when soldiers were being mustered from town and country, he and his drummer boys were put on a steamboat that headed a procession of boats down the Ohio to Cincinnati, every boat loaded with soldiers. All the way they kept playing rallying tunes, such as 'The Girl I Left Behind Me,' and: —

> We're coming from the hillside
> We're coming from the shore
> We're coming, Father Abraham,
> And many thousand more.

"When they played 'The Mocking Bird,' they would tap on the side of their drumheads to accentuate the time of the chorus. It was beautiful.

"Brother John was never in much danger from the enemy, because when the battle began the musicians were always sent to a safe place, since they had no arms with which to defend themselves. But he succumbed to camp diarrhœa, developed asthma, and came home after a year. He was never in really good health again, although he lived to be an old man. The war, you might say, left him his life, but ruined it.

"With Brother John was his eleven-year-old son, Eben. After John returned home the boy stayed on, drumming through the war. He saw many hard battles, but was not in them. He marched with Sherman to the sea and was mustered out at Columbus with the rest of the Ohio veterans at the close of the war. In all that time he did not grow an inch. The little drummer boy's jacket he wore when he went in fitted him when he came out; but afterward he made up for lost time and grew to be six feet tall.

"Was n't that a terrible experience for a little boy? I never could see how his mother allowed it. I've heard Brother John tell of how once, when they were fleeing for their lives, crowded together in a wagon, Eben hung on to the feed box of the wagon at the rear. Brother John could hardly see him in the dark, and every time he could make himself heard he would call out: 'Are you there, Eben, are you there?'

"Oh, that was a dreadful war! Soldiers were n't provided with doughnuts in those days. Often they had nothing but wormy hard-tack and black coffee. The worms would float to the top of the coffee, but the best they could do was to skim them off and swallow the coffee thankfully. They used to beg in their letters for onions, for most of the soldiers got the scurvy for lack of fresh vegetables. Like the Irishman, they might have said: 'I prefer onions to strawberries; they're more expressive.' No one sent them things in packages or cans; we did n't have canned goods in those days. No one knit socks for them. We scraped lint for them; now army surgeons use absorbent cotton.

"As the war went on, everybody grew more and more anxious about their loved ones," went on Grandmother Brown. "Those who were n't killed by shot and shell seemed doomed to die by camp diseases. We got a Cincinnati paper every week and followed the movements of our Ohio soldiers as best we could. How anxious we were, looking through every paper for news of our people! I worried over Brother John and his boy Eben. Dan'l was always looking to see if Austin Brown's three boys were among the dead or missing. One of them did die of smallpox contracted in the army.

"When my brother became so ill, Ma went to the hospital in Kentucky where he was and brought him home. He was too sick to walk. He told Ma that Corwin Culver, one of her nephews, was in the next ward shot through the wrist. She hurried to see him. Poor boy! Such a pitiful story! He had thought that he was not severely wounded and he had sent the doctors to wait on others. But they let him go too long. Gangrene set in, and he died. Just think, there were no disinfectants then, no anæsthetics. What those boys must have suffered!

"I had no sons in the ranks. I had one day's experience only. I don't know anything about the real agony of war mothers. In the World War, a neighbor's son came in to tell me good-bye. A tall, straight, fine-looking young man in his brown suit. The work of a good woman. *Isn't it terrible that he was there to be shot at?*" said Grandmother impressively.

"Once in Iowa we thought that the war might touch us. It was reported that Denmark was in the line of Morgan's raid, that he was sweeping on toward us."

"He *did* come over the state line from Missouri," remarked Charlie. "There was a little battle on the Des Moines River. Everybody in our neighborhood got out his gun and promised that Morgan should be sent back on the skedaddle."

"Yes, I remember that Dan'l took *his* gun and went over to Denmark with the rest," narrated Grandmother Brown. "But Morgan probably heard that Denmark was ready for him. He never appeared. After scouting around for hours, Dan'l came home about frozen, got into bed, cuddled up to me, and gave me the awfulest cold I ever had in my life.

"When the reports of Lincoln's assassination reached us, we were about sick. The sad news just flew!"

Charlie took up the story. "It was as blue a day as ever I experienced," said he. "I was about seventeen years old at the time and was working in the shop of the Denmark blacksmith. Our leader was gone. The governor of Iowa issued orders that every cannon should be fired. There were no cannon in Denmark. But *I* shot off anvils every thirty minutes that sad day after Lincoln was assassinated. I turned the anvil bottom side up, filled the hole with gunpowder, put on top another anvil, and shot off the powder. Lincoln was dead, and who knew what to do except make a big noise?"

"Oh, that was a sad, sad time!" mourned Grandmother Brown. "But the Lord was on our side. Lincoln was his instrument. Against all odds, we conquered, and Lee had to surrender. If the Lord is on your side, you're bound to win. It's all summed up in the words: 'Do right and fear not.' The Southerners thought of slaves as property — in so thinking they did evil and not right in the sight of the Lord. He would not uphold them."

"But, Grandmother," I argued, "if the Northern climate had permitted us to raise cotton, we too would have had slaves up here to work our fields. Property of that kind was not economically profitable in the North, and so the Northerners had no interest in slave holding."

"Nonsense!" declared Grandmother Brown with energy. "Every farmer could have used the slaves. The Lord led us to victory because we did right in His sight and turned from evil."

"There was quite a space, wasn't there, Grandmother Brown," I asked, "between your two groups of children, your little Buckeyes and your little Hawkeyes?"

"Yes, six years; it was four years after we came to Iowa when our blessed little Lottie was born. We never meant to give her the name of Lottie. It wasn't pretty enough for her. But while we were trying to choose a name, Gus, who was very much in love with a little girl in school named Lottie, began to call her that. She was born in the afternoon of a lovely April day. That evening, Dan'l took her up and held her to the light. 'Did you ever see anything prettier, Mother, in your life?' he exclaimed. Dan'l was always anxious to see our babies. Lottie was beautiful enough to please the most fastidious father, and she never did anything but what was beautiful in her short little life.

"She must have everything in order. When the boys pulled off their shoes and left them by the stove, she would say: 'Oh, may I put them away?' If the corner of the rug was turned over, she must wriggle down off your lap to turn it back. The boys would often disarrange it just to tease her. When she undressed at night, she would hang her little clothes on the knobs of a chest of drawers. She would run in her nakedness to hang them up. 'Put on your nightie first,' her father used to say, as he watched her. But she could not bear to drop the garment in an untidy heap and must hang it up at once.

"She was a happy little thing. She loved beauty. She noticed that the leaves of the smartweed all have that same little heart in the centre. I had never noticed that, although I was accustomed to use the leaves of the smartweed to color things yellow.

"Down by the garden gate grew a bunch of four-o'clocks. Gus said to her, one day before he went to school: 'Don't pick any of them until I come back, and I'll make a wreath for your head.' Before he came, hundreds of them were out. 'Go pick them, Lottie,' I said. 'I deth could n't do it,' she answered, 'when my Duthie thaid to wait.'

"Another time, when she and Gus and I were walking along the road, Gus found three little blackberries and gave them to her. 'Eat them, Lottie, eat them,' he said. But she held them in her hand. 'No, one for my Papa, one for my Libbie, and I eat one then,' she answered.

"Ah, she was such a loving little soul. The whole family were her slaves. 'My Papa! My Mamma! My Will! My Cha-Chu! My Libbie! My Duthie — all *tho* good to me.' I think we felt at times a premonition that we could not keep her. I used to feel impatient with Het Mullen when she called her 'Little Angel.' And I remember one lovely morning waking early to find her and Gus sitting together in the doorway. They slept together in a trundle-bed that was pulled out from beneath our big bed every night. There they sat in their nighties, on the doorstep flooded in the summer sunshine, Gus with his arm around Lottie. Just then Will rushed through, stepping over Lottie as he went. 'She's my morning-glory,' Gus called out. 'Don't call her a morning-glory,' answered Will. 'They fade too quick. Call her a rose or something that lasts longer.' Oh, before those same morning-glories had faded she was gone.

"That spring of 1862 we went back to Ohio, Dan'l and I and Baby Lottie, two years old. It was our first visit back after an absence of six years. We left in February, driving in a sleigh up to Burlington and across the Mississippi River on the ice. Since we had come West the railroad had crept to the river's edge. There was a box-car station on the Illinois side where we bought our tickets. We took the train for Chicago. We had to sit up all night, Lottie sleeping in my lap. At Chicago, we had to wait until evening to get a train for Cincinnati. It took us four days to go from our farm to Athens, but that was considerably shorter than the twenty days it had taken to go from Ohio to our farm six years before.

"Coming out of the Athens depot, we met Reed Golden on the street: 'Good Lord, Dan!' he exclaimed. 'What are you doing here in war times? Most of the folks are up at our house. Let me take the baby and go on ahead. I'd like to see if they know whose 't is.' He walked off limping, and Lottie went with him, not the least bit afraid. She had on a little crocheted cap that matched her dress, and she was pretty as a picture. 'Mighty nice-looking baby; might be one of your own, Reed,' said Sister Kate when he set Lottie down in the middle of the party. But they did n't know whose child she was. 'Come in, folks!' called Reed then, and that brought them all out in the hall to fall on Dan'l and me. My mother kissed me and kept patting me on the arm. Suddenly a little voice piped up: 'I don't want my mamma 'panked.' And everyone turned then to look at Lottie, all exclaiming: 'Why, she can talk!'

"The following summer, on our return to Iowa, she died. She had diphtheria. With any fair treatment, she would have pulled through. But old Dr. Farnsworth gave her terrible doses of quinine and cayenne pepper. She would say, patiently: 'Is this like the last, Mamma? Oh, I can't take it.' But she would. Or sometimes she would say, 'I want something to look at, when I take it. If I could hold a rosy in my hand!' And we'd bring her a flower from the garden.

"When the last night came, Mrs. Johnson, a good neighbor, was there to help me. 'Let me hold the baby,' she said. But I could not give her up. 'I'm not tired,' I would answer. And then the child herself said: 'Mamma, you let Mrs. Jossie hold me and you rest a while.'

"We never got over the sorrow of losing that sweet child. Dan'l just worshiped her. After she was buried, he said to me it seemed to him as if he just must dig her up. We buried her not far from the house and put a little white fence around the lot. Every day, as he came from the field, he used to stop there.

"It seemed to me I could never be reconciled. The child was continually with me in my mind for years. I dreamed, one time, that I came into a great light rotunda and Lottie came towards me. 'Come this way, Mamma, I'll show you,' she said. Light was shining down the stairs. Her figure was as plain as could be. She seemed to lead me up and up, a long way, but before I got to where I could see into the Above I woke up. She was gone."

"Isolated as you were, dear Grandmother Brown, you must have had many anxious hours when sickness came," I said.

"Yes," she answered. "The country doctor of those days was n't much help. I learned to rely on myself. When my little Lottie was dying I just did everything the doctor said. But after she was gone, I said to myself: 'Never again! When the next trouble comes, it will be between me and my God. I won't have any doctor.' I recalled the old saying: 'I was sick and wished to get better, took physic and died.'

"I had a pretty hard test. Three of my children, Charlie, Lizzie, and Gus, came down at the same time with scarlet fever. All but Will were ill, and I was expecting another baby. Nevertheless, I nursed them through without the help of doctor or nurse, as I later did my brother's son, after we moved to Fort Madison. I did n't call the doctor until the baby was almost there. 'I can't have that baby now,' I thought desperately, 'while these children are so sick.' I had my bed set up in the sitting room, where I could direct an old woman of the neighborhood in nursing the sick children, while I lay in the next room with the new baby. I gave them no medicine and no food except the juice of grapes and of canned peaches. When they began to get better, I gave them a little egg soup — that is, egg beaten up with salt and hot water. I kept them cool and clean. One good thing about the old house was that you could let the windows down from the top. I had a clothes horse hung up with wet sheets to cool the room. I kept a bottle of slippery-elm water sitting in the well curb all the time and gave them some of it frequently to soothe and heal their parched mucous membranes. I never gave them water that had stood in the house, but took it always fresh from the well. 'You make such hard work of nursing,' Dan'l used to say; but it is care with the little hard details that makes the difference between good and poor nursing. Dan'l was not to be depended on in illness, because he could not keep awake. If anyone was sick, it was Will who helped me through the nursing.

"When Charlie began to dry up, after scarlet fever, he was yellow all over. Old Doc Farnsworth came over for potatoes one night. 'Now you can go in and see the boy, if you want to,' Dan'l said. But Farnsworth would n't look at him. He was mad because I had ignored him throughout the illness.

"I had plenty of opportunity to test the strength of my resolution to get along without doctors if possible. The locality was reeking with malaria. Water stood all through the prairie grass in the pools of Lost Creek and Skunk River. Nobody had screens to keep out the mosquitoes; in fact, nobody knew then that there was any connection between mosquitoes and malaria. Dan'l, Charlie, and Lizzie all shook with fever and ague. Doc Farnsworth, called in to look at Lizzie, left some of his black physic. He called himself an 'eclectic.' He gave no calomel, but was generous with quinine and 'black physic' — which was the root of the May apple. He gave a good deal of aconite, too. I distrusted the medicine he left for Lizzie. I knew he had two other patients down on the bottom lands of Green Bay, which was a terrible place for typhoid and malaria. 'How are the little girls at Green Bay this morning?' I asked. 'One is dead and the other soon will be,' he answered shortly. So, with prayer and trembling, I took his dose and divided it. And yet, even so, it physicked the child so that she was too weak to hold her head up.

"More and more I came to rely on my own judgment in illness. When there was a smallpox scare, we called on Dr. Farnsworth to vaccinate us all. Three more babies came to us for him to usher into the world. But the rest of the time I ministered to the family myself. That is, with the help of good Dr. Gunn. Dr. Gunn was the author of a big book entitled *The House Physician*, which told how to care for the sick and make them remedies from the herbs that grew all around us. Whatever the ailment, from hiccoughs to tapeworms, I consulted Dr. Gunn.

"I think I have an instinct for nursing. When my youngest sister was a new baby, only a day old, she had a spasm. I was just fourteen years old and had never seen anyone have a convulsion. My mother was in bed, of course, and there was no one about just then except Sister Libbie and a servant girl. I called them to bring a pail of water, and I dashed it on the baby's head. Soon she relaxed and was all right. 'Child, whatever put that into your mind?' said Ma. I don't know; I just instinctively seemed to know what to do when people were sick.

"Whenever one of my children was ailing, the first thing I tried to do was to clean him thoroughly, inside and out, to open skin and bowels, and then put him to bed. The warm bath would bring out any latent trouble. Of course we had no stationary bathtubs in those days. But I had a large wooden tub. I put a board across it and made my child sit on it, gave him a washcloth, and took another with which I washed his back and feet. Then he'd climb into bed and usually sleep off his disorder.

"Once Dan'l and a girl named 'Liza, who was working for us, were taken sick the same day. 'Liza wanted the doctor. He came and looked at them both. 'They're in for about three weeks' sick spell,' he said. I did n't give Dan'l the doctor's medicine. Instead, I put him through one of my scrubbings and gave him some grated rhubarb. When the doctor came next day Dan'l was out chopping wood, but 'Liza was in bed. Sick for three weeks and more — sure enough!

"One time I came to Eben Foster's house when he was very sick with bloody flux — very low indeed. I went to the drug store and bought some slippery elm and laudanum, grated the slippery elm and beat it to a fine cream, added fifteen drops of laudanum, got my brother to give his son an injection with a baby syringe, put a hot plate on his abdomen. He rested all night. 'Good morning, doctor!' he called to me when daylight came. I just knew that slippery elm was very cool and healing, that laudanum was soothing. And it worked!

"Surgery has made great strides during my lifetime. It's wonderful. Just see what the surgeons have done for Gus — given him a new opening to his stomach. But they don't know much more about drugs than they ever did. Except that they've learned to use them less. That's good.

"I've done a little surgery myself in a modest way. Once my baby Herbie touched his hand to a hot stove lid that I'd taken off the stove and put on the floor. He burned himself cruelly, and I was afraid that his fingers would be drawn up when they healed. I made a splint out of a thin board and bound the fingers to it."

"That wasn't the only time Mother saved my fingers," commented Herbert. "I cut off three of them one time when I was cutting sheaf oats for my pony in a cutting box. I rushed into the house with the ends of my fingers hanging by shreds. Mother washed them, fitted them together carefully, and bound them up so that they grew into perfectly good fingers again. Another time she saved my foot. I was running barefoot down the street in front of the Court House. They were repairing the roof, and the sidewalk was covered with old shingles. I ran a rusty spike straight through my foot. Mother pulled out the spike and syringed the wound with hot salt water and hot soda water until she washed away every bit of the rust. Saved me probably from lockjaw."

"There was one time," reflected Grandmother Brown, "when I was forced into performing a really important surgical operation. While we were living on the farm a woman came to live temporarily with our neighbors, the McChords, while her husband was in the war. She was about to have a baby. Dr. Farnsworth was away. No midwife could be found. All the help the poor woman had was what three of us neighbor women could give her. She had had children before and said that none had ever been born to her without the help of a knife. She begged us to help her. Oh, it was terrible. I could see that the body of the child was unable to break through into the world. She suffered horribly. None of the other women would do anything. 'It can't be born without a knife. It can't be born without a knife,' the poor thing kept saying. I was afraid to use a knife for fear of sticking it into the baby's head. Finally I just plucked up my courage and tore the membrane with my finger nail. The baby was released and the mother relieved. That night Dr. Farnsworth stopped to see me. He had been to see the mother after being told, on reaching home, that she had sent for him earlier in the day. 'I came to congratulate you,' he said to me, 'for having had the moral courage to *do* something. That woman could n't have lasted much longer. She would have gone into spasms and died.' The baby lived to be an old woman, and died here in Fort Madison only recently."

"Tell me about the baby who arrived in the midst of your scarlet-fever epidemic," I urged.

"Dan'l had hoped that this baby would be a little girl," answered Grandmother Brown. "But it was another boy, and we named him Frank. With Will now eighteen years old, Charlie sixteen, Lizzie twelve, and Gus ten, he was very much a baby in the family. He was a cheerful little fellow, who slid off my lap the day he was ten months old and started to walking. Round and round the room he ran in great glee; but the next day, of course, he was tired out and hardly stirred. He was always light on his feet. A Fort Madison neighbor said to me, later: 'Does that boy ever walk? I never see him except on the run.' One Christmas, I remember, he said he wanted for presents a Bible with flexible binding and a pair of dancing pumps.

"Ma came to visit us soon after Frank began to run around. Every night she would rock him to sleep. She had a nice voice and was a good singer. There was one song that he always demanded, 'The Pony Song,' that took a great deal of action. Much prancing and ha-ha-haing! I wonder if children know it now:—

> "One bright morning early,
> My pony I bestrode,
> And by my Anna's cottage,
> I took the well-known road.
> There stood my gentle Anna,
> For 't was my greatest pride
> That she should see me ride.
> Then prance, prance, prance, Pony,
> Prance, prance, prance waggishly!
>
> "There stood my gentle Anna
> Beside the blooming bower,
> Training the opening roses,

>   Herself the sweetest flower,
>   Then prance, prance, prance, Pony,
>   Prance, prance, prance waggishly!
>
> "To show my skillful riding
>   I spurred him very sly,
> Alas, he reared and threw me
>   Into a ditch hard by.
> Then off he went like wind
>   And left me there behind.
>   Stop, stop, stop, stop,
>   Stop, stop, Pony, amicably!
>
> "On hands and knees I scrambled
>   To reach at length dry land,
> And, oh, in such a pickle
>   Before her face I stand.
> But worse than all by half
>   To hear my Anna laugh,
>   Ha, ha, ha, ha!
>   Ha, ha, ha, ha!

"I can't remember that my son Frank ever made anybody any trouble," said Grandmother Brown. "That is, after he was once weaned. He has always been correct in every way, as baby, boy, and man. But he was very reluctant to take up a new line of diet. Finally, Will took him upstairs and made him sleep with him; but every time Frank came downstairs he did want his mother's dinner. One day, one of our mares had a colt, and then Dan'l told the baby that he'd give him that colt if he'd give up his dinner and eat like a man. He said he should have a ride the very next morning if he did n't cry for me that night! That evening our neighbors, the Stevensons, came to call. Frank circled around them announcing: 'I don't suck any more. I've dot a pony.'

"From that time on he never was a bit of bother, and, necessarily, he was rather a lonely little figure in the household, as the others were so much older. But he liked to be busy, and I'd give him a paper of pins and a tack hammer and he'd be happy for hours pounding the pins into a pine block.

"He seemed to be a very outspoken little boy, because he often repeated the speeches of the older people around him, speeches not intended for repetition. How we laughed one time when he gave Newt Tyndall a piece of the family mind! Newt had once worked for us, but he went away and learned to be a dancing master, and never did any real work afterward. Sister Mary sat in front of the fire one day, with her baby on her knee. 'Oh, dear,' she said, 'this fire's pretty nearly out. If anyone will hold this baby, I'll go get more wood.' And then Newt said: 'I will hold the baby.' And Sister Mary let him, and he let her bring in the wood! Dan'l complained about Newt to me. 'He comes here and never does a stroke of work. The lazy dog lies in bed and lets the boys get up and milk the cows and never offers to help.' That night, Frank, the solemn baby, walked around and around Newt eyeing him severely, as he sprawled in front of the fire. 'What's the matter, Frank?' the man finally asked. 'Newt, you lazy dog, you lie in bed and let the boys get up and milk the cows, and you never do a stroke,' piped the child. Oh, dear," giggled Grandmother Brown, "I always had something to laugh at!

"Frank used to stand up on a chair by the vat to watch the cheese making. One time a new man we had helping us kept coming to me to ask what to do, and every time I'd tell him he'd say, 'That's just what the boy said.' When the cheese would get the size of kernels of wheat or small grain, Frank would come running with a few grains in his grimy little hand for me to taste.

"One time when he was a little older, Frank used to sit in front of the beehive, laying sticks up against the hive for the bees to climb up on. He said the bees had such heavy loads on their legs that they were tired. (Of course they could *fly* in!) 'You'd better look out, Frank, the bees will bite you!' said a visitor one day. 'You'd better get a bee and look it over and you'll find out where its needle is,' answered Master Frank rather contemptuously."

"Frank was too little, I suppose, while you lived on the farm, ever to help with the work," I suggested, drawing Grandmother back to our main theme.

"I think he did his share of corn dropping," she answered.

"Indeed I did," said Frank. "I was less than seven years old when we left the farm, but I remember that plenty of work was found for me to do. I remember starting to school one day with a lunch basket into which I had watched Mother put a little jar of the peach preserves that I liked so much. But I didn't get to school with it, for as I passed along the meadow where Father was at work he spied me and set me to dropping corn. How I hated it! Then I often carried cool water or buttermilk to the men at work in the field. And after we moved to town, and Charlie was running the farm, I used to spend my summers there. I used to drive a team of horses hitched to a stalk cutter — a dangerous business for a boy."

"Did you make any money from your farm, Grandmother Brown?" I asked.

"Yes, as time went on we became quite prosperous," she answered. "The thing that set us on our feet was cheese making. Our neighbor, Mrs. Andrews, had a little vat big enough to make small cheeses in. I borrowed it once and made a few little cheeses. I pressed them under the fence rail with a weight on top. They were very nice. It put Dan'l in the mind of cheese making on a larger scale. He concluded to sell the fine carriage which we had brought with us from Ohio and so seldom used and to buy cows with the money we received from the sale. We kept increasing the herd until it brought us an income of about $300 a month for cheese. At that time, $300 looked bigger than it does now. The 'Dan Brown Cheese' made quite a name for itself in southeastern Iowa. A good deal of it went to the Union Army.

"Cheese making itself was not heavy work. A boy could do it. The hard part was caring for the cows and milking them. The older boys did that. Gus stayed in the cheese house more than any of the others. One thing that I did not like about cheese making was that it kept someone at work every Sunday. We could n't let all that cheese spoil; the cows gave milk on Sunday the same as other days.

"I found it interesting to watch the process of cheese making. We used to strain the milk, put the rennet in, and then go to breakfast. When we had finished breakfast, it was time to cut the cheese lengthwise of the vat, then crosswise, later to drain off the whey, gather the cheese into hoops, and cap it. One has to be awfully clean with cheese, scraping out the corners of the vat thoroughly in washing it, or the cheese will be sour. I never made the cheese; merely fixed things so they'd be clean — the vat, the frames, the cloths — and so the work would be easy.

"Oh, yes, I did make one cheese. It became a family joke — 'Mother's Cheese.' I read in a magazine that one could make good cheese of skimmed milk. I followed the recipe. When I thought the cheese should be ripe I tried to cut it — but, goodness, it would n't cut any more than a piece of wood. So Charlie tried to cut it, first with a knife, then with a hatchet, finally with an axe. Half he gave to Dash, the dog, who was delighted, at first, to have for once all the cheese he wanted. But Dash grew quite melancholy working over that cheese. He had it around for months. He even buried it in a manure pile, hoping to soften it, but his hopes were never realized. The boys used to pass the other half at table to all newcomers. It looked like cheese, it smelled like cheese, — an elegant smell! — but it might as well have been rubber."

"As you became prosperous, were n't you more reconciled to life on your Iowa farm?" I asked Grandmother Brown.

"No," she answered. "I took satisfaction in the improvements we had made, but it seemed to me that our life grew more burdensome each year. The family was larger. It seemed to take more strength to keep things going, and I had lost some of my courage when our little Lottie died. And I could n't see much opportunity in that part of the country for my children.

"When Frank was about a year old, I had a bad sick spell and was very miserable. One day I suddenly lost consciousness. Dan'l was away at the time. Will, who was with me, was much alarmed. After putting a hot iron to my feet, he jumped on a horse and rode off for the doctor and then on over to Denmark to get Charlie. He thought I was dying. In the meantime, Dan'l returned. When Sister Kate came in, he was on his knees beside the bed. 'Get up and do something,' said Kate. 'She's dead,' he answered. But after a while I came slowly back. 'Don't touch my feet. They're glass. They'll come off,' I shrieked. Then they looked and they found that my feet were cooked. The hot iron had burned them. But it was the shock of the burn that probably saved me. 'I've seen some very sick people,' the doctor said, 'but I never saw anyone else go so far around the corner and come back.' I was needed for something, I suppose, as here I am yet, nearly a hundred years old.

"Poor Will was just about broken-hearted when he saw that he had burned me. But, oh, he was so good to me. Sister Kate took hold and ran the house for a long time. Lizzie, a big girl of thirteen by this time, looked after the baby. She would put Frank in his little wagon — a chuggy, solid little wagon with iron wheels — and trundle him all around the fields after her father. That suited her much better than staying in the house helping Aunt Kate.

"Gradually I got better and took up the burden again. But Will came in one day when I was about to scrub the floor and just took and emptied everything, put away the brush and mop. Did n't say a word. Charlie would say, 'You 'd better not do that, Mother.' Will's way would be to walk off with the things so I could n't work, and say nothing.

"But, oh, one could n't baby one's self long. There was so much to do all the time in the house and in the fields. I remember once, at harvest time, I suffered terribly with the toothache. But no one had time to hitch up and take me in to town to the dentist's. Besides, all the horses were needed for the work. In the daytime I did n't mind my aching tooth so much, but at night I could hardly stand it. So, one evening, I went out on the porch with the shears and an old looking-glass and just pried it out. I had cut my wisdom teeth when Willie cut his first ones. We were teething together. I was just beginning to get my senses about that time, I suppose. The tooth came out all good and smooth. I took it in the house and dangled it before Dan'l in the light. 'Why, Mother, how in the world *could* you do that?' he exclaimed. But it was *out!*

"When Frank was four years old little Carrie was born. 'Brown, come here,' Dr. Farnsworth called to Dan'l. 'She's a little Venus. I've brought a good many babies into the world, but never one of prettier shape.' It seemed for a while almost as if our lost Lottie had come back. Yes, she was a little beauty, but she was never well. The nurse bathed her till she was chilled. It was the Fourth o' July, but it was a cold day. And then the baby nursed my hot milk. It seemed to poison her. I weaned her,— tried cow's milk, goat's milk,— but nothing helped. Twice a doctor came all the way from Burlington to see her and advise me. But she never thrived. I tried in every way I could to tempt her appetite. I made her the daintiest food I could devise; made it taste nice, look pretty. Trimmed her tray and dishes with flowers. 'Baby want some more?' I would coax, but she would always shake her head. She understood everything I said to her. She loved me. But she never talked or walked. She was just too weak. I carried her about on a pillow. As I went about my work I used to think my heart would break as I looked at her lying there, so frail and beautiful, and I so powerless to help her. To have lost one lovely little girl so suddenly and then to watch this one die so slowly — oh, it was more agony than I deserved! She breathed her last one morning at daybreak, when everyone else in the quiet house was sleeping except us two. And when she died, I knew that in seven months I should bear another child."

"Surely there are some pleasant spots in your memory of the farm, Grandmother Brown," I said.

"A few," she acknowledged, but without enthusiasm. "I look back to those years on the farm as the hardest years of my life. But there are of course some happy memories of the life there. Always where there are growing things — plants and children — there is beauty. Though I had not much companionship with the people of the neighborhood, we had visitors from time to time from Ohio. Once, dear old Uncle Hull came. Dan'l was always hospitable to my sisters and their families. He loved a houseful. And though their coming made more mouths to fill, it also brought more hands to help with the work.

"Sister Libbie was not there so often. She spent a number of those years in Columbus and Washington, for Nelson went first to the Ohio State Legislature and afterward to Congress. But Sister Kate (her husband, Reed Golden, was the leading Democrat of that time in the Ohio Senate) and Sister Mary visited us frequently, both before and after their husbands died, on the farm and later in town.

"For the children it was great fun to come to the farm. How they'd romp and play! It was Sister Kate's idea, when she first came, that her children should do all their playing in the morning and must be washed up and put into starched things when afternoon came. She held to that idea for a while, but later she let them go more recklessly than I did mine. One afternoon her little daughter Frankie was playing with Lizzie in the creek at the bottom of the garden, each child smearing her legs with black mud to see how high their gaiters should go, when who should drive in at the gate but Frankie's father, Reed Golden. Mischievously, I sent Frankie in to see him just as she was. 'Good Lord, Kate,' he exclaimed, 'how are you living here?' That was mean of me, but I thought Kate had gone to the other extreme.

"And so they never had to think of their clothes, but were allowed to climb and jump and roll around with all the freedom that children love. Once, however, when Lizzie didn't have any too many clothes on, she was caught in the apple tree with her skirt hanging over her head, and had to stay there until rescued. The boys took their time about it, too. The maddest little girl in all Iowa she was that day, scolding and crying and waving her white legs above her soiled feet while the rest of the children roared. Poor Lizzie! She had a standing grievance, too, that they always made her be the candlestick in the 'teeter' and gave preference to Gus and Frankie on the ends of the Flying Dutchman.

"The boys had their own fun, too — sometimes a

little rough and dangerous. They used to have a good deal of sport with a certain billy goat. Once when Nel Golden, Sister Kate's boy, was visiting there, they took an old ram out in a ploughed field, and offered Nel a ride, telling him to hang on tight to its hair. The ram made for the fence, butting against it to the terror of us elders, who heard the commotion and rushed to see what it was all about. But Nel happily tumbled off before his brains were butted out.

"Sometimes the boys slipped off for a swim in Skunk River. There was a shallow place below Augusta that made a good swimming hole. And occasionally they went fishing. The river was dammed in those days at Augusta and the fish could n't go above it except in high water. Our boys would dip nets and catch buffalo, catfish, red horse. The first time Nelson Van Vorhes ever visited us at the farm, Dan'l took him fishing over on Skunk River and Nelson caught a very big and beautiful pike; we had never seen anything like it before. I baked it in the oven and it was the subject of much comment.

"Hunting never interested my family much. As far as I know, the only time Gus ever went hunting he killed a mother squirrel, and that took away his appetite for killing. He and one of Sister Mary's boys started out for a day of sport. When Gus shot into a tree and a mother squirrel came tumbling down at his feet, he felt so grieved that he lugged up the tree and brought down her three little ones. It so happened that our old cat had just lost her kittens. Someone had closed the cellar door one night when she came up for a turn in the fresh air; she could n't get back to her babies and they perished in the cold. She brought them up and put them under the kitchen stove, but they did n't come to. You could just see how the poor thing felt about it. Well, Gus brought the little squirrels home and put them in a basket back of the stove. I was sitting there with little Carrie on my lap. The cat roused up and began purring the way cats do when they are in a good humor. She got into the basket and tucked the squirrels up against her. I called Gus. 'See, kitty has got into the basket with your squirrels.' In the morning we found that she was nursing them, but one poor little squirrel had been shot and the milk ran out of a hole in its stomach. The other two lived and thrived and afforded us much entertainment.

"It was interesting to watch the cat play with them. She'd bring in a mouse; they would n't touch it. But they'd run up on the dresser and eat hazel nuts and hickory nuts they found there. They'd eat cookies, taking them in their hands as little babies do. The old cat would seem to look on in amazement. But they were very playful with the cat, rolling and tumbling with her, and at times it seemed, when she watched them jumping from limb to limb of a tree, as if she wanted to say, 'Have n't I remarkable children? I myself am astonished!'

At first the squirrels would sleep with the cat. I put them in an old tea chest under the stairs. But later they wanted to get away. They nested in a bag of scraps that hung on the sewing machine. (We had sewing machines by this time.) Finally, they made a nest for themselves in the trees, though for a long time they'd go to the woods every day but return to us at night. Gus wanted to make a cage for them, but I would n't let him. I always feel sorry for animals in shows. Of course, we'd never have the privilege of seeing wild animals if it were n't for menageries, but it's punishment for them to be shut up. So the squirrels were allowed to go and come as they pleased, and finally they failed to return at all. Gus had put bands of red morocco around their necks. A neighbor once told us that he had seen a squirrel in the woods who wore a red collar.

"And so our good old cat lost her adopted children too. That was the smartest cat I ever saw. I would praise her when she came with a mouse. She'd make a peculiar noise, as if she were calling me, and I would say to her, 'Kitty, that's a good kitty to catch the mouse.' And she'd seem glad to have pleased me.

"Indeed, all my life I've been amazed at the understanding of animals. On the farm I was continually noting it. Our farm dog Jack, for instance, a big black dog with a white ring around his neck, often showed that he knew what we talked about. We'd usually drive him back if he attempted to follow us — that is, unless we had gone considerable distance before discovering him. And so he adopted strategy to get ahead of us. If he heard us say, for instance, that we were going to Burlington the next day, and we started off early in the morning, lo and behold, when we got to the first rise of ground, there would be Jack waiting for us. If we said we were going over to Mrs. Johnson's, off he'd go, and she would say when we got there, 'Well, I knew some of you were on the way, because Jack appeared.'"

"Most of your family pleasures seem to have been found at home in those days, Grandmother," I commented.

"Yes," she answered, "young people didn't do as much going then as they do now. But there were nice concerts and ice-cream sociables at Denmark sometimes. I remember Lizzie going once to a picnic that Denmark young folks had down in our walnut grove on Skunk River. Afterward she brought them all home to supper, about twenty of them. The boys made ice cream and I stirred up a warm cake, and the evening ended in a big sing. There was always singing at our house, especially after we got our piano. Many came from Denmark then to play on it and join in the singing. Dan'l taught Lizzie to sing by note when she was a little girl of eight or nine, and later she and Charlie went to singing school at Augusta. Lizzie says she knows the words and tunes of at least a thousand songs and hymns, and I expect she does; she's been singing all her life. I feel sure she could recite the whole hymn book. She memorized easily; she had Aesop's *Fables* by heart as soon as she could read. Before we had the piano, she used to sing to Will's violin accompaniment, and he was always so delighted to have her sing with him, going higher and higher. 'Hear, Mother, hear!' he would say. 'Just listen to Lizzie!'

"Then there were nights on the farm, especially in the earlier days, when we danced. Dan'l would play the fiddle, and then Will and Charlie and Lizzie and I would make a French four. I used to think that people passing would think, 'How funny! They're there by their lone and they're dancing!' But I think that's a very nice entertainment. It's one of the happiest things I remember about our life on the farm."

"How did you happen to leave the farm?" I asked Grandmother Brown.

She thought awhile. "I think it was the coming of the piano that made the big change in our lives," she answered, "the change that eventually led us away from the farm. Will and Charlie were young men by this time, reaching out towards a life of their own. Restless. Looking for entertainment, of course. Fine-looking young men, both of them. Both were fond of horses. Each wanted a nice team to drive. They used to go over to Stevensons' a good deal, where there were young people fond of music. One son played the violin, another the bass viol, a daughter the piano. Will would mount his horse and ride over with his fiddle under his arm to join them. And Charlie was off with a horse or team to see his sweetheart, Lyde McCabe. Why, Will even wanted to have a horse to go off riding round on Sunday. Charlie was a more serious nature and would n't have done that, but Will would. It got so that when Dan'l wanted a horse he almost had to ask the boys for it."

"Yes, he threatened to sell the horses," laughed Will. "Don't I remember? And just then there drove into our yard a strange man and woman, agents for the Chickering piano and the Wheeler and Wilson sewing machines. We made a deal with them for a piano worth $700. Father turned over in payment a team of horses worth $150 (fine scheme to keep us more at home) and the rest in cash."

"Which included $300 that had come to me from my father's estate," interjected Grandmother Brown.

"The day that piano was brought in was a great day," said Will. "We sent word to the Stevensons to come over and bring with them Libbie Knapp, who was going to school at Denmark Academy and played the piano.

How we made the welkin ring! The Stevensons could read music. I could n't read a note, but once I got the melody in my head, I could keep up with anybody. We played and sang for hours that day, and the old lady who had sold us the piano, an old lady named Mrs. Cole, leaned back in her chair, listening to us and watching us all. Before she left, she suddenly pointed to Charlie Stevenson and me, saying, 'I want this boy and this one'—Charlie to help her sell pianos and me to sell sewing machines.

"Well, we were ripe for such offers. Gus was big enough by this time to help Father. I wanted to get away from the farm and see what the world was like.

"Charlie Stevenson and I went with Mrs. Cole to her headquarters in Milwaukee. She kept me there until I learned all about sewing machines. Then she gave me a horse and wagonload of machines and sent me through the country to sell them. I spent a couple of years driving thus over the State of Wisconsin. Charlie and I met regularly at the county fairs and then we had a great time, Charlie playing the piano and I the violin. We drew crowds of rubes around us, and when we had attracted the crowd we 'demonstrated' the sewing machine.

"After that I never went back to the farm for any great length of time, although I would have stayed in the country, as Charlie did, if Father could have bought the Andrews farm for me. It was next to our place and Father offered Andrews $40 an acre for it, but Andrews held out for $45, and Father would n't pay that much. I went to firing on the new railroad that ran between Fort Madison and Keokuk, but not for long. About that time I heard that a bookstore in

Fort Madison, which had a branch store in Keokuk, was for sale. I remembered that on a farm just outside of Fort Madison lived Libbie Knapp, whom I had known at Denmark Academy. I persuaded Father to buy the bookstore in the hope that he would let me run it."

"That fall we all moved into town except Charlie," said Grandmother Brown, taking up the story. "We were all glad to go, even Dan'l. Gus had broken away the year before and come to Fort Madison, where he got a job in Schaefer's drug store. Charlie was married the January after we left, Will the next June. Dan'l took Will and Gus into the bookstore with him and he rented the farm to Charlie for five years until Charlie could finance the purchase of a farm of his own in Missouri. Then Dan'l sold the farm — sold it for $10,000.

"I've often thought," said Grandmother Brown, speaking slowly and with conviction, "that a considerable part of that $10,000 surely belonged to me. All our married life I was just saving, saving. We should n't have had anything if I had n't been saving. The secret of the whole thing was just dimes, dimes. I never got anything I did n't need, and, when I had it, I took care of it. A neighbor who saw me patching an old dress said, 'I'd never try to save an old calico dress!' Well, *I* would. I'd save anything that could be used. Our neighbor, Mr. McChord, said to Brother John: 'Some of the rest of us could own a farm and store and move into town if our wives knew how to save the dimes as your sister does.'

"We received $10,000 for a farm that had cost us only $3500. But it had cost us, in addition, fourteen years of our lives and most exhausting labor. It had been little better than a wilderness when we took it; we left it in a good state of cultivation. Those fourteen years seemed a long time to me, a big price to pay. We had buried there two children, and our youth was gone. Eight months before we left the farm our last child was born there, a boy whom we named Herbert Daniel."

"Tell me about the coming of your last baby, dear Grandmother Brown," I begged. "I'm specially interested in him."

"It was while Will was in Milwaukee that Herbert was born," she made reply. "Will came home just after that. I was very sick and I remember how nice it seemed to have him come in and show such an interest in me and my little boy. He was in his twenty-fourth year, as much older than Herbert as Dan'l was older than him.

"The eighth child in a family is, of course, no novelty. This one did not seem to be needed at all. Then, of course, our boys were farmer's sons and knew something about stock breeding. They knew that the little baby I had lost, the year before, had been born to a mother who was too tired to nourish her offspring properly. They naturally did not want to see a repetition of that experience. I felt that they regarded the last baby as an unwelcome addition to the family circle. But Will looked him over very kindly. 'I wonder if these little hands will ever milk a cow,' he said. We had so many to milk just then.

"That last year on the farm had been terribly hard. I had nineteen in the family most of the time. I don't know how I could have got through it all, if it had n't been for Lizzie. She had always been a wonderful help for a little child. She was only four years old when we came to Iowa, but the next year I could put a dishpan on a chair beside the table and she'd wash the dishes for me. She'd wash out the dishpan properly, — we always used soap freely, — rinse and wipe the dishes, and do them well. I could go on with my work. They'd all be nice and shiny. She very early learned to use a needle. She made a man's shirt — with a bosom — at a tender age; I'm quite sure she was n't more than eight. And when Dan'l and I went back to Ohio on that first visit she was only ten, and we left her knitting her own long woolen stockings.

"Before Herbie came, Lizzie said to me, 'Don't worry, Mother. Don't cry. I'll help you.' And she did. I had childbed fever, and, for a good while could n't nurse him. She took all the care of him, washed and dressed him and fixed his food. Before he was born she had said hotly, 'I hope the baby will be a boy — a homely little boy. We don't want any more pretty little girls to love and lose.'

"But, with all Lizzie's help and thoughtfulness, it had been a very hard year. Before we had any thought of moving to town we had commenced to enlarge the house and build it over. The carpenters who did the work boarded with us for months and were just so many more to feed. And there were the harvest hands part of the time, besides all our own family. The young folks seemed to get a good deal of pleasure out of the excitement, but for me it was only drudgery."

"There were often jolly times in the noon hour

and the evening," explained Lizzie. "Pen Sharp, a fiddler who worked for us every harvest, had his fiddle along as well as his scythe. He was a great, strong fellow. Even Father, who prided himself on being able to outdo any harvest hand, could n't keep up with Pen. We had a swing in the new part of the house, a swing that went way up to the upper joist. The harvest hands would swing us girls in the noon hour way to the roof. Father said it looked as hard work as pitching hay. And Pen Sharp said yes, it was, but lots more fun."

"As for me," said Grandmother Brown, "I did n't care about having an ark of a house in the country. I did n't want to live in the country, even though by this time we had things fixed pretty nice, outside and in. The Brussels carpet and piano made a big difference and I had other pretty things. There was the walnut table with harp legs that we bought at Burlington. Dan'l had brought home an ugly table at first, but I grieved over it so that he took it back and bought this one. It always gave me joy to look at it. Still, I did n't want any more house in the country.

"When I felt the first birth pangs at the coming of my last child I was on my knees scrubbing the pantry floor. To give him birth caused me almost as much suffering as my first child had caused me. But he was the last.

"I was nearly forty-three years old, and my hair was gray by this time. My neighbor, Mrs. Johnson, said she 'd be so ashamed she would n't know what to do if she had a baby after her hair was gray."

"She did, did she?" I asked fiercely. "What became of *her*, I 'd like to know?"

"Why, she died after a while," said Grandmother Brown, and then, with a flash of humor, "I don't know what *became* of her. Everybody around here has died except me. She was a very kind neighbor really — after hanging off three years on account of my Brussels carpet. But she was there when my little Lottie died. Only — I'm proud of the baby of my old age that Mrs. Johnson told me I ought to be ashamed of. He's a useful man down there in Washington."

"Yes, he is, Grandmother," I agreed, " he is saving dollars for Uncle Sam just the way you saved dimes for Uncle Dan'l. I think he learned the way of doing it from you."

VI

AN IOWA VILLAGE

"Fort Madison in 1870! What was it like?" I asked Grandmother Brown.

"In 1870," said Grandmother Brown, "it was a town of perhaps five thousand people, with about forty saloons and no plumbing. It was hot in summer down here between the river bluff and the river. Only two or three families had then thought of building up on the hill. But, after the farm, it all looked good to me.

"It was several years before we had a home of our own again. For the first few weeks we lived on Front Street. The life on the river fascinated me. Steamboats carrying passengers and pushing raft boats plied up and down the stream. I was never tired of watching them. I would get up in the night when I heard a boat coming; I used to think it a beautiful sight to see one steaming up the river at night, all aglow with lights. Come to think of it, the very first electric lights I ever saw were on a river steamboat.

"Next, we lived for a couple of years in a house next to Dr. Toof, the dentist, on Third Street. Dr. Toof stuttered. He came across to get some water from our well one day when I was on the back porch cutting Dan'l's hair. 'Th-th-at's the w-way you s-s-ave your d-d-imes, is it?' he ha-ha'd as he went by. Why, of course I always trimmed Dan'l's hair and beard. I cut the boys' hair also as long as we lived on the farm. I did it well, too.

"When Herbert was about five years old we bought this old home, and I have lived here now for over half a century. It had been built in 1841, the year that the Court House was erected. Two stories in front, one at the rear. Back of that were the washhouse, woodhouse, and stable, with a warehouse above. Gus said that the house 'looked like a cow lying down.' It was n't much. We bought it of an old seafaring man who had a wife as rough in her speech as he was. When I made some criticism of the house, she said, 'I'm not selling you the damned old house. I'm just selling you the lots.'

"Those *were* beautiful. The trees — fine old oaks full of squirrels — would have made any corner beautiful. Then Dan'l planted a maple tree at the back which shaded our kitchen so nicely for years and years. I hated to have Gus cut it down when he made over the old house. Herbie — the little baby boy — had held up that maple tree while his father was planting it. But it offended Gus; a limb fell down and broke his bird basin. He tore down the grape arbor, too, that used to flank the house just outside the dining room and he closed up the well. I think the way we had it with the brick pavement and the grape arbor just outside the dining room was nice. It was pleasant and cool to sit there in summer and look out into the depths of the garden in the days before we had given Will two of the lots to build his house on, when the garden really *was* something. 'T was a beautiful place those first ten years.

"The corner of the fence was just full of roses. And to the left of the house there was a row of hollyhocks; they were like great double roses. At one time we had quantities of sunflowers at the back. I remember how Herbie trimmed our Jersey cow from horn to horn with little sunflowers, a wreath around her neck and a girdle of big ones across her back. Then he drove her down to the watering trough in front of the *Democrat* to show her off. Oh dear, oh dear!

"We always kept a cow, of course, and a few chickens and turkeys; at first also some white pigs and a hive of bees. I was amused one time when we had nine little turkeys. Coming home from church Sunday morning, I found the whole nine sitting in a row on the front porch as if waiting for me. We ate some of them, but Herbie did n't like the idea. 'It 's just a shame to pet them and then *eat* them!' he said. He was like Lincoln with his pig. We had one turkey that kept going over into a neighbor's yard where there was a high bunch of weeds, higher than your head. The turkey made her nest there. Dan'l told the neighbor about it and asked him to spare her, but he was a sour old man — cut down the weeds, and spoiled her nest.

She flew up on the fence and never would come down to eat; stayed up there until she fell off dead. I had no idea a feathered fowl could be so sensitive, but she was. We couldn't tempt her with any kind of food. She just sat there until she died. Well, I'm happy to say I never *borned* a child who would harm a bird. We had guinea fowl, too, and a couple of peacocks. The peacocks used to like to strut across the front porch and look at their reflections in the long parlor windows.

"There was a bluebird's box on a pole at the back of this place when we came here. I haven't seen a bluebird for years, but Will tells me they have them in South Dakota. When I was a little girl, I used to think there was nothing so lovely as a bluebird.

"We had a house for martins, too. They're interesting birds to watch. You know they make their nests of mud. One spring it was so dry after they came that there was nothing for them to work on. Gus made them some mud, and you should just have seen their excitement. They could hardly wait to get it.

"I always had a wren box, too. One year a wren arrived just as I was getting ready for church. I saw him flying around the grape arbor. I thought I'd hurry and get a home made for him before I went to meeting. I always had things to do with, my own saw and hammer and nails. I got the box — a little cigar box — all tacked up on the grape arbor before I was off; I had a little short stepladder. The wrens weren't a bit afraid of me. When I came home from church, there they were all started to housekeeping, the two of them. I love to watch them courting and to hear them sing, so clear and sweet.

"Among our Fort Madison livestock I should n't forget to mention our house dog, Benny. His box stood in a corner of the sitting room. We used to think so much of him. He was a little black and tan dog that Will had sent to Frank from St. Louis. He knew just as much as folks. He got mad at Dan'l once about something — we did n't know what — and stayed over at the market house with Al Casey for several weeks. But one day he came running home and whimpered up to me as I was lying on the couch. And, only a few days before, Dan'l had said, 'I met Benny on the street and he would n't speak to me.' Once Herbie harnessed Benny with white and red strings and tried to drive him to a little wagon. But Benny got away. Gus was singing in the Episcopal choir. Benny smelt his tracks and ran clattering into the church in his harness with the wagon at his heels. What a commotion! Later, Benny got into a fight and was so hurt that we had to have him killed.

"Our house was reconstructed according to my directions. Mr. Emerick, the carpenter, seemed amused one day when I called to one of the men who was working on a joist, 'You're pushing your crowbar wrong. It should go to the left.' He said to my neighbor, Mr. Doerr, 'She's the best architect in town. She knows what she wants done and she can tell the workmen how to do it.' Well, why should n't I know something about building homes? My mother's brothers were carpenters. It's always a pleasure to me to make and mend. I want things smooth. If a pane of glass got broken, I 'd put a new one in myself. How silly to call a man! I always had a putty knife by me and a scraper for taking paper off the wall. If a lock wanted fixing, I'd take it off and fix it. I craved to do things.

"I could n't do much in the next dozen years," lamented Grandmother Brown. "During the whole of Herbie's childhood I was a poor, sick thing."

"But you got well, dear Grandmother; and look at you now, with a record that few can equal! I've heard Herbert say that his mother was like a fine watch; she could n't be dropped, but handle her gently, and she'd run forever."

"He did n't see it that way, of course, when he was a little boy. I remember that when he was about five years old he looked at me disapprovingly one day and said, 'When I get me a wife, I'm going to have one with red cheeks — a stout, strong lady like Mrs. Case!' Mrs. Case was the grocer's wife, a nice, pretty woman. But she died years ago, and here I still am.

"Living in town was a very great change from the farm, a welcome change. I was glad to be relieved of the farm drudgery and happy that my children could have the advantage of better associates, of better schools and churches.

"The children met for school in the basement of the Baptist and Methodist churches. But not long after we came a building was erected on Fifth Street, and Nelson Johnson, the superintendent, graded the pupils. Up to that time, mothers would bring their children and say they wanted them put in Miss So-and-So's room. One teacher taught all classes from the First Reader to the Philosophy Class.

"I was glad of all town advantages, but sometimes I felt as lonely as when on the farm. And I had more time to think. The two oldest boys were married and in their own homes. After five years both moved to Missouri, Charlie to a farm near Revere and Will to St. Louis, where he was in the employ of a lumber firm. Gus and Lizzie soon became absorbed in the affairs of the town and entered into all the doings of the young people. Gus was always a great cut-up — when he was n't down in the dumps, for he swung both ways — and was soon in demand at all the dancing parties and sleighrides and amateur theatricals. He had a period of acting, when he was the funny man, singing the comic songs of all the shows given in town.

"Dan'l and Gus were at the store all day and often they were there at night, though I must say that when Gus was at home he'd fuss around me like a girl; sometimes would fix up a tray of food himself to tempt my appetite. 'Now, Mother, I'm going to poach you an egg and have it *just right*,' he'd say. Lizzie was my mainstay at home, but she went to school for a while after we first came to town, and later had her natural interests with the young people. Frank, too, was in school. And so there were a great many days and weeks at that time when I lay in bed all day with only my baby boy to keep me company. For a good while, life seemed to pass me by. I felt old and worn. I thought that I looked prematurely old. My hair was white. Stung by Mrs. Johnson's amazement at my having a baby after my hair had turned, I dyed it, using a recipe that I found in a paper."

"You with dyed hair! You, Grandmother Brown! I can't believe it."

"Yes, I was just silly enough to do it. I continued to keep it dyed for a while after we came to Fort

Madison. And then I suddenly came to my senses and saw that my face did n't match the dyed hair. A servant girl who came to us stared at me and then at Dan'l. She had only one eye, but she should have seen better than that. 'Be you his wife? I thought you was his mother,' she said. I decided to let my hair be any color it would. But I suffered a lot in my pride before I had it all white again. Slowly, so slowly, the clean white streak got wider and wider, while the rest was a dirty green.

"I got rather melancholy, being in poor health, and alone so much. And I was n't happy in my church associations. I wanted to unite with the Presbyterian church, where I belonged, but I had persuaded myself that it was my duty to go with Dan'l to the Baptist church. When we were living on the farm, a minister of the Baptist church came out to the schoolhouse near by and preached. Dan'l and Charlie united with the church. Later, Will and Charlie and Dan'l and I were all immersed in the Fort Madison church. In black alpaca slips with bare feet! Why, the whole front of their rostrum was a bathtub!

"Dan'l was religiously inclined all his life; seemed to like to go to church. All his people were Universalists, but at Amesville we went often to the Presbyterian church. However, as long as he was with those Universalists, he never came right out.

"I thought it did n't make much difference what church we went to, so long as it was a Protestant denomination. But I always thought that the Close Communion of the Baptists was wrong. I used to wonder what I'd do when my mother came to see us some Communion Sunday, and, because she was a

Presbyterian and not a Baptist, would have to be excluded from the communion table where Dan'l and I would be welcome. I worried about it quite a bit. And then, when such a Sunday came and we were on our way with Ma to the Baptist church in Fort Madison, a terrible rain cloud appeared in the sky. We whirled around and drove home again. And that was the way of that. Afterward, in Fort Madison, Sister Ann and her husband, both Presbyterians, were visiting us on Communion Sunday. When they got up to go out, I went with them, stared at by the whole congregation.

"It's just like this: We've no right to say who is worthy of Communion. If Jesus were here on earth now, there would be a multitude following Him all the time, just as there was then! Every request a poor soul made of Him was granted. No place would be big enough for the crowds, unless the park. He would bid them all come to Communion. It's what the heart feels that counts. It reminds me of what Hedel Schultz, a girl that worked for us, said to me. She had been to confession. 'God is the only one that can forgive our sins,' I told her. She answered: 'Mrs. Brown, you don't know how I am inside. I'm praying when I am peeling potatoes.' I've had so many Catholic girls working for me who were exemplary in every way that it does n't become me to say anything against Catholics, even though I am a Presbyterian. There was Mary Voigt! I said to her: 'Why, this is n't Friday! You've eaten no meat. You've hardly touched your breakfast.' And she answered, 'Well, Mrs. Brown, if you must know, I'm fasting while I pray for a friend.' Now that's *real*. Ah, there's lots o' good in Catholicism. Remembering Lent's a mighty good thing. And so I decided that Close Communion would n't do for me. It is n't right to say who shall and shan't commune. Let God be the judge!"

"But how about 'the elect' of the Presbyterians, Grandmother?" I questioned. "Does n't that doctrine bother you? Such ideas disturbed your Herbie. I 've heard him say that when he left home you extracted from him a solemn promise to go to the Presbyterian church every Sunday, and he meant to keep the promise, but one day the minister whose church in Kansas City he was attending chose to expound the doctrine of 'infant damnation.' And then Herbert reached for his hat, got up, and walked out, never to return."

"I don't blame him!" said Grandmother Brown, warmly. "Just think! A little innocent one that has never lived to do either right or wrong condemned to eternal punishment! Oh, no! We know that Jesus loved little children. So does His Father. The little ones are safe in His arms. I think these lines are so pretty:—

"How I wish that His hand had been laid on *my* head . . .
How I wish that I could have been there when He said:
'Let the little ones come unto me!'

You see, it's this way. There's so much I don't understand in all the churches. I pass it over. I just live by what I understand. I understand what love means — that's enough."

"But you were n't happy among the Baptists!"

"No, I was n't; I was very unhappy. But all the time I did my duty. Dan'l was a pillar of the church for many years, and I stood by him, going to meetings when I felt able and feeding generously all the brethren he brought home. All the visiting deacons and itinerant preachers stopped with us when in town. It makes me think of what Georgiana Rochester said when my brother drove her home from a party and the chickens all began to fly as they turned in at the gate: 'Dear me! they think it's a preacher coming!' The fatted calf we killed for preachers in those days was usually fried chicken.

"I remember once when Lizzie expressed herself freely, to the horror of her father and great satisfaction of her brothers. We had a houseful of Baptist preachers. Lizzie went and slept crosswise in bed with Hedel Schultz and someone else, I don't remember whom, so that a preacher could have her room. In the morning he told at table about some home at which he'd been entertained where the mattresses were humpy and there were pin feathers left in the chicken. I could see that Lizzie was getting redder and redder as he talked. Finally she burst out: ''T wouldn't do for you to go away and talk about how you'd slept or what you'd eaten *here*. I slept crosswise, three in a bed, last night, so that you could rest easy in *my* bed. And I was up at five o'clock this morning to dress the chickens you see before you, and, believe me, if you ever speak a word in criticism of our hospitality I hope it's the last time you will enjoy it.'

"For a while the Baptist minister and his wife lived at our house and boarded with us. They did a good deal to wean me from their church. In the first place, Brother Jones — that name will do for him as well as any other — was always preaching Temperance, and he was one of the most intemperate people I ever saw.

He used to get all tea'd up on tea — the strongest anyone could drink, cup after cup. And then how he'd carry on, berating everyone! He had ten weeks of 'protracted meeting' that winter; about wore us out, scolding and scolding. One night he got hold of a nice comfortable text. It was so restful for a change that I rose in meeting and made a speech myself, saying that we were so glad to be praised a little after having been scolded so much. Once while he was having meetings Gus had a carbuncle and I stayed to dress it. I came in late. And then Brother Jones knelt down and scolded away to the Lord about my being so late. That's no way. God is Love. He does n't rave and go on at us like that.

"My dissatisfaction with the Baptist church worried me for years, but finally I made up my mind to go back where I belonged. We were visiting a cousin, Sarah Glazier, who had married a man named John Patterson. John had been brought up a Quaker and had the nice Quaker ways. The Wednesday night prayer meeting was led by John. On the way home, John and Dan'l lingered behind, talking together. Next morning, Sarah said to me: 'Dan'l told John that he expected you would leave the Baptist church and go back to the Presbyterian, and that if you did he meant to follow.' Well, it did n't take me long to change over after that.

"It took years to work out my church relations," said Grandmother Brown. "In the meantime, I had a long struggle with ill health. My little boy, Herbert, was my closest and most constant companion in those difficult years. I was n't equal to any more hard work. When I could sit up, I occupied myself as usefully as possible with my needle. I made dozens of yards of carpeting. At one time I had four rooms and the stairs and hall upstairs all covered with my own carpeting. I was particularly proud of the stair carpet. I made it so that the stripes — made of bright colors — ran up and down the stairs. I bossed the weaving of it, invented a special way of having it done, and got the woman who did it to follow my instructions, so that every step looked just like every other one. I've had more people admire that carpet and wonder how it was made!

"While I sewed, Herbie was always at my side. He was the best-natured child I ever saw. As he grew older he always wanted to be working. I'd say, 'Go pick up some chips.' 'What I do next, Mamma?' 'You may cut out some papers for cleaning the carpet.' (We used to moisten scraps of paper to scatter over the carpet when we swept. They helped to pick up the dust.) 'What next?' he'd ask. 'Cut them smaller.' And so he kept me busy, thinking up jobs he could do.

"One result of Herbert's being by my sick bed so much was that he learned to spell at a tender age. It was one of the games I had to think up to keep him amused. He soon knew all the letters on his blocks. Then I began teaching him to spell the names of things around the room. Before he was five years old he could spell about two hundred words — hard words, too, like 'bureau,' 'cupboard,' 'biscuit,' though they were words that he used all the time. And so it happened that he spelled the town down when he was only five years old.

"You see, they were having a spelling bee in the

Court House. Herbie heard it talked about. I listed the words that I knew he could spell, and I said to Gus: 'Now I want you to take Herbert to the spelling bee. You tell Mr. Johnson, after the school has spelled, to call off these words and hear the baby spell.'

"It was a warm night, and the windows were open. After a while, I could hear a terrible stomping and shouting. I said to myself, 'They like the baby's spelling.' And so they did. But Mr. Johnson had n't done just what I had asked. He had put Herbie in the class with the others, and then he had given the class Herbie's list of words. One after another missed a word and sat down, and finally Herbie stood there alone — or sat, rather, for Judge Van Valkenburg held him on the desk, standing beside him. 'Good for you, Herbie. Don't be frightened!' he kept saying. And Herbie was n't the least bit frightened, but spelled steadily away, not only the words others had missed, but all on his list.

"Then some of the people said he had no right to the prize, as he did n't go to school. But Mr. Johnson said that that made his right all the better. The prize they gave him was a handsome book.

"After that, Herbert used to ask: 'What for does John Van [as everybody used to call Judge Van Valkenburg] say, "Hello, Noah Webster!" when he meets me on the street?' 'I suppose it's because Noah Webster made a dictionary,' I told him. Well, mothers are foolish things. They're so wrapped up in their children.

"I did let Herbie do some things that the rest of the family scolded about. For instance, let him use the sitting room at times for a workshop. He had a fine time making a bird house there for the martins. He made it of old shingles that had come off the house. It had nine rooms. He took great pains making it. Dan'l was away at the beginning. When he came home, he said, 'A pretty-looking place!' 'It's all right, Father,' I told him. 'I know where my boy is.' Later, Herbie made a turning lathe — made it himself. I let him set it up in the dining room. What a good time he and Leon Rizer did have turning things! I had for years rolling pins and potato mashers that they turned. Herbert was always handy with tools of all kinds. This was about the time that he made Jennie Mason a bedstead and bureau for her doll.

"But Lizzie objected to the muss, and said I was 'humoring' Herbie. 'It's all nice clean shavings,' I told her. 'And when he's here I know what he's about.' Later, when she had children of her own, I noticed she 'humored' them quite as much as I ever did Herbie. Herbert and Frank were never away from me an hour when they were boys when I did n't know where they were. Gus laughs and says, 'You could n't keep tab on me that way.' But he forgets that he grew up on a farm and not in a rough river town.

"Sometimes Dan'l felt it necessary to take Herbie to the woodshed and administer justice in the old-fashioned way. 'Spare the rod and spoil the child,' Solomon said, but Solomon was n't always wise. Herbie was likely to holler, 'Help! Help! They're mur-r-r-dering me!' on such occasions, and Dan'l was rather afraid the neighbors might think he *was* doing violence to the child. I never thought it did much good. I tell you how I feel about disciplining children. If I had it to do over again, I'd be mighty slow to spank a child. I'd piece out my patience an inch or two and wait longer before I spanked. When one is overtaxed and a child makes trouble, it is easy to use the rod. I think it is wiser often not to seem to see — to be looking the other way. Children get tricks that don't last. It's one thing this week and another the next.

"Herbert really needed a little extra support at home," continued Grandmother Brown, "for the other boys in the family — not only Gus and Frank, but Sister Mary's boys, too — were all so much older, and they used to tease him unmercifully, and treat him pretty roughly. They'd torment him until he'd say something smart, — his only adequate weapon, of course, was his tongue, — and then they'd roar. 'First they devil me and then they dance,' he'd complain to me.

"It really was funny, one day, when he came home from the store crying over a special outrage. The big boys had pinned a Democratic badge on his coat so that he couldn't get it off, and he'd run home all the way with his hand over it so no one could see it. 'What would any of my folks think, if they'd see me with *that* on?' he raged.

"He got to be pretty sharp at defending himself. Even as a baby he was determined not to be imposed upon. I remember once, when there was a lot of company, and the table was pretty full, Gus bribed him with a nickel to wait until the second table. But when Herbie heard them all pulling up their chairs and smelled the good dinner, he came around the table to where Gus sat and slapped the nickel down beside him, saying: 'Here! Take your nickel and wait yourself!'

Everybody shouted, and then they squeezed up and let the baby's high chair in.

"Once his father laughed at some smart thing he'd said, and remarked, 'I guess you'll make your mark in the world.' Herbie set up a howl. 'I won't do it! I won't do it! I'll learn to write my name to-day.' He had seen men at the store who could n't write and had to sign their name with a mark. He did n't intend to be one of them. Fact is, he soon astonished everybody by learning to write forward and backward and with either hand — all kinds of ways.

"No, Herbert did n't like rough play. He liked to go to school, but he would n't stand for being imposed on there, either. He would never snowball anybody. 'I don't throw snow in anybody's neck,' he used to say to me, 'and I don't want it in mine.' On snowy days, he'd wait until the last bell rang before he left. I can see him standing in the kitchen window with his books in his arm waiting until the bell had rung and the boys had formed in line. He could see the schoolhouse door from the kitchen window.

"He was always looking for peace, but when attacked I noticed that he was ready to defend himself well. I think he had a strong sense of justice that kept him from doing things that many boys do to show off — the cruel, tormenting things. And he'd hold on to his own idea, however much he was tempted or tormented.

"There was a show in town one day, and he was very anxious to go to it. He pulled out his money at the gate. 'How much is it?' he asked. 'That's what it is — what you have there,' the ticket man said, trying to take advantage of him. 'Now you've lost the whole thing — I won't go at all,' said Master

Herbie, and he put his money back in his pocket and came running home with the perspiration just rolling down under his hat. 'There'll be other shows,' he told me, stiffly.

"We used to sell some of our milk. Herbie was always worried about what Mrs. Hesser got. He'd always give her a quart and then some. Our girl Betty would say, 'A quart is a quart and that is enough.' But a quart did n't fill the pan Mrs. Hesser had set out, and away Herbie would go, carrying some more over. That was just like my father — everything must be well supplied and generous. Father was uneasy if he did n't do his part, and that was the way with Herbie.

"I never knew a family with a number of children where there was n't some bickering. Children, like other people, have to have their ups and downs. Charlie used to aggravate Lizzie, and Lizzie used to worry Gus. Lizzie doted on Frank, and was good to Herbert, and adored Will. Frank and Herbert were really devoted to each other, but they had their quarrels, too. Once Gus put a log of cordwood lengthwise in the bed where they slept. 'To keep you apart!' he told them severely, when they complained. The next night he found it laid crosswise, under the sheet, in his own bed.

"Frank used to tease Herbert by calling him 'Mr. Trill.' Herbie loved to whistle and he did it better than anybody I ever heard. It was just like the birds themselves. And his whistling to a song was like a violin accompaniment. Why he should have minded being called 'Mr. Trill' I don't know, but it was a sure way to make him flare up. Dan'l used to scold Frank for getting among his tools. 'Call him Mr. Tinker-Tonker,' advised Hedel Schultz, always Herbie's friend. 'That will cure him!' And sure enough, it did.

"The two boys used to sleep, when they were small, in the little room adjoining ours. Through the open door one night, Dan'l and I saw Frank on his knees saying his prayers and Herbie standing over him, saying severely: 'Frank, while you're praying, I just wish you'd ask the Lord to make you treat *me* a little better!'

"Like Will, Herbert had an ear for music; but he did n't appear at all interested in learning to play by note. As soon as he could reach the piano he was picking out tunes. He had a few music lessons. But when he had heard his teacher play a piece once — while he perhaps stood whittling a stick — he knew it and could play it as well as she could. 'If I ever want to play, I 'll just do it,' he used to say. And so he went through childhood playing everything he heard, but learned nothing about music.

"There was n't much opportunity to hear good music in Fort Madison. But one night, when Herbert was in his teens, beginning to be a big boy, a troupe came to town singing a comic opera — *Pinafore*, perhaps. Herbert came home about midnight with his head full of the melodies, walked into the back parlor, sat down at the piano, and began to play the whole thing through. He was having a beautiful time, just going it, when Dan'l woke up out of a sweet sleep. 'What in thunder? That boy again! Waking us up at this time o' night.' And he went hurrying downstairs to put a stop to it. I felt so sorry for Herbie. But what could I do? Can't you just see them? Dan'l all het up, standing there in his nightshirt and bare legs, — my turkey-red stitching all down the front of his shirt and across the pocket, — and Herbie, blinking at his father without an idea why Dan'l should be so indignant.

"Herbert was always very intense about anything he did, very persistent, especially about any kind of task or problem that was mechanical or mathematical or had to be puzzled out. It seemed as if he just never would give up trying until he'd got a thing to running smoothly or until he 'had the answer.' He seemed fascinated by every kind of a machine. I remember that when he was just a baby he used to insist on climbing up in Lizzie's lap to watch her at the sewing machine. She was afraid he'd get hurt, and naturally his presence did n't facilitate the work. 'Oh, Herbie,' she finally said, impatiently, 'you bother me so, and I'm trying to make you some nice dresses. You're just naked!' 'What's the matter with these aprons?' he asked. 'They're good enough. I want to see the 'sheen!'

"Once, after he had started to school, but was still just a little fellow, he came in late for dinner. 'Herbie, it's almost time to go back to school again. Why are you so late?' 'Can't help it,' he answered. 'I heard a woman near the school say her sewing machine would n't run, so I stopped to fix it for her.' 'You!' 'Why, yes! I've got it so it runs fine, too.' He ran mine to good purpose often, especially when I was n't well. I still have a petticoat he tucked for me; and when he was about fifteen he made up several nightgowns on the machine for me.

"There was n't a clock or a lock or a piece of mechanism about the house that he did n't have apart and put together again, to its own improvement. I lay down on the sofa, one afternoon, while he was playing the piano. When I awakened, he had the whole works out on the floor. 'Why, Herbie, what will your father say?' 'Never mind what he says. I'll get it together again and it'll sound better than ever.' And it did.

"Herbie always used to take great interest in my getting things just right. He was very proud of a fine little overcoat I had made him out of his father's old one. It *was* beautiful. At that time, too, it was the fashion for clerks in stores to wear knit coats. Gus had one which he had discarded. I took it apart, stitch by stitch, and made it fit Herbie. Mrs. Angier admired it and asked Herbert where his mother bought it, because she'd like a coat like that for her Benny. 'Oh, Mother made it out of Gus's old one,' he bragged to Mrs. Angier. 'She saves all our old clothes and makes new ones out of them.'

"Indeed, I always took pride in making things nice. So they'd bear the most careful inspection! I took pride in seeing him have the same pride. I made him some leggings once that were equal to anybody's. I put a paper up to his leg and cut out a pattern. I made the leggings of a heavy dark gray pants' cloth; lined them with fine blue flannel. I wanted them so he could go in the snow and not get wet; so when I had finished the sewing — with buttons all along the outside — I sent Lizzie to a German shoemaker to have soles attached. 'Where your mother get her pattern?' asked the man. '*Ach, nein!* no woman ever cut that out without a pattern.'

"Herbert was the most prayerful of all my sons," continued Grandmother Brown with an apparent change of subject. "It was part of his persistence, I guess."

"Oh, really!" I exclaimed. "Well, if he went in for praying, I know he'd do it hard, carrying the thing through with the Lord if he could."

"Gus came home from St. Louis with the typhoid fever," said Grandmother. "He was ill for weeks and weeks. I nursed him myself. It was a terrible time for us. One day the doctor said to me: 'I've done all I can for your son, Mrs. Brown. I cannot give you any hope.' Herbie was in the big closet off the bedroom, while the doctor was there. He had heard our conversation. When the doctor had gone, he came to me and said: 'Wipe your tears away, Mother. I've prayed to God. There in the closet. Gus will get well.'

"He was a strong believer in prayer when he was a little boy. Did I ever tell you how he got his pony? No? Well, there was a man named McCutcheon who used to work for Dan'l, selling sewing machines. Dan'l had added to his bookstore and picture-framing establishment an agency for the Domestic sewing machines. McCutcheon drove around the country with a cart and a couple of ponies selling machines for Dan'l. In the final settlement between the two Dan'l was left with the ponies on his hands. One of them was a very fine little creature, — we called her just Pony, — but the other, named Bronco, was much inferior — a mustang with an ugly disposition. Dan'l tried hard to sell the ponies and get his money out of the deal. But Herbie had set his heart on having Pony for himself. His father would n't listen to him; said he could n't afford to lose the sale; could n't afford to keep a riding horse for Herbert, anyway. But Herbert never gave up hope, and he prayed steadily.

"One night Dan'l came home, saying, 'Well, I sold

the ponies to-day.' 'Don't tell Herbie until morning,' I begged him. 'It will spoil his night's sleep.' The next morning I went through his room before he was up, and said to him, 'Father sold the ponies yesterday, Herbie.' 'Then I'll have to pray some more,' he said, and down he flopped on his knees. The man who had agreed to buy the ponies backed out at the last and refused to take them. 'See?' said Herbie. 'I prayed.' But still Dan'l would n't listen to his pleading. He decided to send the ponies down to Charlie's for pasturage. Herbert took them, riding one and leading the other. It was a distance of about thirty miles. I felt a little anxious about letting him go alone, but the pony he rode was gentle, Herbert was a good rider, and was familiar with the road. He got the ponies there safely and came home again. He went on praying. He had only been home a few days when, one morning, came a telegram from Charlie saying that Bronco had been struck by lightning. Herbert's excitement was intense. 'There, Father, you said that if anything happened to Bronco I could have Pony.' And so Dan'l gave in at last. I guess he thought it useless to hold out any longer, if the Lord was on Herbie's side.

"At first, Pony could n't drive single. One morning, when Dan'l and I were eating breakfast, I looked out of the window and said to Dan'l: 'Look there, will you? That *is* a triumph for Herbie! Tom teaching Pony to drive single!'

"This Tom, a neighbor of ours, was a middle-aged man with some admirable traits of character, but cursed, too, with a fearful temper, which he vented, at times, on any poor animal that might be about. One day, when Herbert was in the alley and Frank in the barn milking the cow, they heard Tom beating his horse. Herbie called out: 'I wish someone would kick *you* behind, sir — kick you till your nose bled.' My, just think how hard anybody 'd have to kick to do that! Would n't that take a lot of kicking? Naturally, Tom was angry. 'Em, hold this horse,' he called to his wife, a nice, gentle woman whom everybody liked. Herbie rushed through the barn where Frank was milking, shouting, 'Tom's after me.' 'That boy, damn him!' cried Tom to Frank. 'I'll tell your father of his impudence.' 'Well, sir,' answered Frank, very deliberately, getting up from his milking stool, 'I don't think you'll get much sympathy from Father. We all think that you are cruel to your horses.' Tom went home. And there, a few days later, I looked out of my window and saw him teaching Herbie's pony to drive single!

"How much that pony meant to Herbert all the years he was growing up!"

"He was an excellent source of discipline, I know," said Herbert, "as anything is that one has to take care of. I remember that one night Father said to me, 'Did you have a drink of water to-day?' 'Why, yes,' I answered in surprise. 'Well, your pony did n't. I found her bucket dry. If that happens again, young man —"

"I don't imagine it did happen again," said Grandmother Brown. "I know that Herbert kept Pony's coat like satin, her stall like a lady's bedchamber. We got a little phaeton, and he used to drive me about town. His one grief in connection with Pony was that I would not let him take her out on Sunday."

"I'm afraid you were too pious in those days, Grandmother," said I.

"She was," declared Lizzie, "but, just the same, she didn't want me to be a Crusader."

"What was that?"

"Didn't you ever hear of the crusade against strong drink that was started in Ohio by women who went around to the saloons praying? It was the beginning of the Woman's Christian Temperance Union."

"Oh, yes. Tell me about it."

"We'd been having a series of revivals here in Fort Madison. They wound up with a Temperance Crusade, a union-meeting affair including women of different denominations. They went from one saloon to another praying and singing. The older women did the praying, the girls the singing. This went on for about two months. About twenty-five women were in the band that visited the forty-two saloons. They didn't go every day, but very frequently.

"Father came home from the store, one day, and found Mother and me arguing about it. Mrs. Angier wanted me to join the band. She was the doctor's wife, a wonderful woman, Mother's friend. 'A good counselor,' Mother always called her. I was much surprised when Mother didn't approve of her suggestion. She said it was casting pearls before swine. But Father said: 'You can't stand straddle of the fence! It's come to the point where you have to show your hand in this town. If she's any girl of mine, she'll go.' I fairly shouted.

"We met at the Presbyterian church. We went first to Billy Pranger's saloon down on Front Street. He was alone. Even the barkeeper was not there. We prayed and sang. Missouri Spatch and I led the singing. We were big strong schoolgirls with big loud voices. Like calliopes. He told us that he did n't like the saloon business; indeed, he later went into the livery-stable business. Then we went to Charley Froebel's saloon. That was filled with the toughs of the town. They stood around in a circle drinking. When Mrs. Coleman knelt to pray, somebody threw a beer glass at her. John Atlee, Father, Gus, and other friends had been following us from place to place. John Atlee caught the beer glass, so that it did n't hurt her. Then the toughs tried to rush us, football fashion, but our men protected us. Some of the boys started a hymn, 'Revive us again.' We took it up, and, believe me, we *did* sing. People pressed in. The street was crowded. Extra police were called out. It was very thrilling. We girls took it as a lark; but I was really very earnest.

"The Crusade lasted from the latter part of January until sometime in April. As a result, ten or fifteen saloons went out of business. That was cultivating public sentiment. A few years later, Murphy lectured here and started the Red Ribbon Movement. Everybody who signed the pledge wore a red ribbon.

"Temperance societies were started in the Sunday schools. We used to sing:—

"'Wine is a mocker
Strong drink is raging
Whosoever is deceived thereby
Is not wise.'

"I remember how old Judge Beck would come in with the bass — Judge Beck, who, Gus said, was 'the right foreleg' and Father 'the main hind leg' of the Baptist Church: —

"For it biteth like a ser-r-rpent
And stingeth like an adder.'"

"Grandfather Brown's animosity to alcohol did n't extend to tobacco, did it?" I queried. "Not, at least, when I knew him."

"Unfortunately not," answered Grandmother Brown. "He never smoked much, but he liked a little quid. He grew up in an age of chewing and spitting. It seems as if habits follow fashions. Now, in colonial days — my grandfather's youth — it was the fashion to take snuff."

"Yes, even the women did it," I reminded her. "Dolly Madison, the President's wife, used to carry a specially big hanky to sneeze into, besides her tiny lace one for show."

"And in my girlhood," went on Grandmother Brown, "all the men chewed and some of the old women smoked corncob pipes. Nowadays, everybody is smoking the filthy cigarette. Even the young girls. I never knew that Dan'l chewed tobacco until we left the Van Vorhes house after our wedding to drive to Amesville. He handed me the lines to hold while he took out a paper with quid tobacco all cut up in it. 'Why, Dan'l Brown!' I said. 'I did n't know you chewed tobacco — I thought I 'd found a man without a single fault. And here you *chew tobacco!*'"

"Why, Father's folks *raised* tobacco on their farm," observed Herbert. "I remember hearing him tell of how sick he got the first time he tried to smoke. He was just a little boy and thought it would be smart, one day when his mother was away, to twist tobacco leaves into a roll and smoke them. He made the experiment in a little outhouse adjoining the kitchen, where his sisters were ironing. He blew the smoke in through the keyhole and laughed to see the girls cough and wonder where the smoke came from. But suddenly he felt very sick, and then they opened the door and had the laugh on him."

"Probably his mother would n't have worried much if she *had* been there," commented Will. "I know that she smoked a pipe herself, both she and her sister, Aunt Betsy Dickey. Perhaps it was part of her advanced ideas to smoke like a man! Anyway, smoking was common practice among elderly women of the pioneer strain."

"No tobacco for me!" declared Grandmother Brown, "Snuffing, chewing, smoking — I think ill of it all. I have always felt about tobacco just the way your Constance felt. Once, when she was visiting us and Dan'l was about to kiss her as he left for the store, she said: 'Hold down here, Grandpa. Not a place I can kiss but on your forehead!'"

"I suppose tobacco chewing did n't seem so much out of place then as it would now," I ventured. "I fancy most of the Fort Madison gentlemen of the seventies had their little quid."

"Indeed, they did," asserted Grandmother Brown. "Nothing about Fort Madison society was particularly elegant in those days. But it was no worse than the other river towns. There was a rough life everywhere along the river fronts. Liquor was plentiful, and that coarsens life on water or land. I tell you there is n't anything to destroy the comfort and happiness of life like whiskey. No one thing in the world ever did so much harm."

"I suppose the river life had its picturesque side," I remarked. "The rivers of those times bore the traffic that the railroads and the automobile roads now bear. It was a phase in this country's development that will probably never come again. I fancy that the bosom of the Mississippi looked quite different then."

"Yes, it did," said Lizzie. "After I was married, I went up and down the river between La Crosse and St. Louis a good many times. My husband, Church, worked for a firm that had a fleet of raft boats on the river, and he used to take me with him until the children came and kept me at home.

"It was interesting to watch the river life. There were sawmills in all the big towns along the Mississippi — in Minnesota, Wisconsin, Iowa. McDonald Brothers of La Crosse, for instance, had a fleet of raft boats bringing down rafts to points all along the river where there were mills that sawed the logs into lumber. Here at Fort Madison, for instance, were the Atlees getting rich with such a mill, and at Burlington the Rands and Hedges. Knapp, Stout, and Company also started a sawmill here about ten years after we moved to Fort Madison, and they sent Will up from St. Louis to have charge of it."

"When Knapp, Stout, and Company sent a raft down from the pineries," interrrupted Grandmother Brown, "Mr. Knapp would n't allow it to be moved on Sunday. It had to be tied up from Saturday night until Monday morning. He got to be worth millions, too."

"You could n't be an hour on the river," continued

Lizzie, "without meeting a steamboat pushing a raft ahead of it — some of them, say, two hundred feet long. The woodsmen used to go into the pineries up north during the winter months, cut down the trees, roll the logs to the nearest creeks, float them down to the main stream when the spring freshets came. They bound the logs together in rafts, floating them endways down the river, using cross logs for binding with logs arranged in cribs at the front of the raft. The logs between were laid in loose, but the men who worked on the raft learned to run over them like squirrels — without a mishap. When they wanted to turn the raft, they would wind the lines around a big spool that was called 'the nigger.' One of the engineers was the 'nigger runner' and kept the raft in the channel. When they wanted to tie up, they made the raft fast to what was called 'the snubbin' post.' All sorts of things could happen coming down the river on a raft boat — collisions, explosions, mutinies. One never knew!"

"I fancy that there was more life and stir throughout the whole valley in those days," I ventured, "than there is to-day. Was n't there?"

"I think so," answered Grandmother Brown. "I know that there were many tramps going about the country. They came to our back doors asking for food, sometimes for work. And there were thieves abroad, too. This house has been burglarized pretty often while we slept. But the worst time was when I distinctly heard them coming, and nudged Dan'l to tell him that someone was in the house and creaking up the stairs. He jumped out of bed and grabbed the knob of the door just as the burglar on the other side of the door seized it. There was a horrible banging and scuffling, and I nearly died of fright, because Herbie, who was just a little boy, was asleep in the room across the hall and, roused by the noise, rushed out there, bumped into the burglar, and, naturally, screamed. I was afraid he would be killed. Fortunately, the man turned and threw himself clattering down the stairs. While Dan'l made a light and looked around, Herbie crept trembling into bed with me. It was all pretty dreadful.

"Several times the town was greatly excited over the escape of prisoners from the State Penitentiary at the end of the street. Fort Madison itself was said to have sent the fewest number of convicts to the penitentiary of any town in Iowa. But at that time there were a number of very desperate characters in the penitentiary — men like Poke Wells, for instance, who had been a member of the famous Jesse James band of Missouri, I believe. Such men did n't care to stay in jail if they could help it, and did desperate things to get out. Now prisoners are treated so well that I 've heard they sometimes contrive to go back, because they 'd rather live there than outside. People's natures are so different! In those days, the townspeople used to visit the prison church and Sunday school frequently. Everybody knew Poke Wells and other notorious characters — by sight at least. Later Poke drugged and killed one of the prison guards whom everybody knew here — little Jimmy Elder. He and three other convicts that did it got away at first, but were recaptured and brought back."

"Yes, we had plenty of excitement in those days," said Grandmother Brown. "Crusades, revivals, burglaries, escapes from prison! Something going on all the time."

"If I remember correctly," I said to Grandmother Brown, "the times were good out here in our Mississippi Valley during the eighties. The West was booming. Many of the boys about here were restless to be off to Kansas City, Wichita, Denver."

"Yes, my boys too," she answered. "Dan'l had sold the store and, in association with other business men, had erected a paper mill here in Fort Madison. They made Gus superintendent, but there was n't room for any more of the Brown family in that enterprise. I watched anxiously to see what prospects in life might be developed for Frank and Herbert.

"Now you know that Dan'l and I had never agreed on the subject of educating our children. I saw that they were always striving to improve, and, as long as that was so, I believed they should be helped. I had been rebellious all the time the older children were growing up that they had had so little opportunity to go to school. After we moved to town, my heart was set on the idea that the two little boys should have every educational advantage that the others had lacked. For a time I had reason to believe that Dan'l would do as I wished. They were such good boys, so faithful in school, so well thought of by everybody, such a comfort to me at home! But Dan'l seemed honestly to believe that he was doing them a good turn when he made them go to work at an early age. Just as if they had n't always — even when in school — done their share of work! Frank sold papers when he was only a tiny boy, and went every summer down on the farm to do his share of labor there. They milked the cow and peddled the milk and cut the grass and hoed the garden and cut the wood and did every chore about the place. If ever they coveted any special thing that boys delight in, they expected to pay for it. I ache when I think of how Herbie begged and begged for an express wagon and how, after he had it, he trudged many miles delivering books and wall paper and picture frames with it. The same way with Pony! I think how he used to hitch a snowplough to her every winter and clear our streets.

"I wanted our boys to finish the High School and be sent to college. I thought Dan'l could afford it. But, no, they must be put to work! Oh, oh, oh! And so, when Frank was in the eighth grade, Dan'l arranged to have him go to work for a paper hanger.

"The idea!" Grandmother Brown's scorn is at white heat whenever she mentions this episode. "The very idea! Just as though any son of mine would be content to go through life a paper hanger. Oh, how blind Dan'l was! At one time he had encouraged Will to be a fireman on the railroad. He had tried to have Charlie be a blacksmith. And now he wanted Frank to be a paper hanger! He talked about the advantage of having a 'trade'!

"For a while the boy could n't help himself. And so he trotted around, unhappily, with a pail of paste, when he should have been in school. But he began, after a while, to study stenography — which was rather a new thing then. He was always studying something.

"It was the same way with Herbert. He was in the High School for a time, but was n't allowed to remain there long. He was sent to work at the sawmill, carrying lumber. I had not words enough then to express my indignation, nor have I now. Oh, Father came to regret his course, but he was obstinate enough at the time. I remember that Herbie earned all of three dollars a week at that mill when he should have been at school, — three dollars! — and once when we were away, Dan'l and I, he paid out those same three dollars a week for his board.

"It wasn't that Dan'l didn't think the boys had ability. He did. He sent Herbert for a while to the business college which Nelson Johnson started here. He fancied that he was disciplining them in a way to bring out their ability and make good business men of them. He thought me incompetent to judge of men and the business world. He talked a lot about self-made men. And then, he was trying, at that time, to get control of the paper mill, and he thought he needed all the money he had for that.

"Naturally, the boys broke away as soon as they could. The opportunities in the booming towns of the West were well advertised among us. But, although I was not one bit reconciled to the programme my boys had to follow, you mustn't think that the atmosphere about here was especially blue in those days. We had many good times, especially during the seven years when Sister Kate's daughter, Jennie, lived with us. Jennie was dainty and pretty and loved to sing."

"There was always plenty of joking and singing and carrying-on, whenever Gus was at home," remarked Lizzie. "You know one of our family pleasures always was to sing. At another reunion, I wish we could get together and sing as we used to do. You remember how we used to sit around the base burner out in the hall, Mother, and sing and sing on winter nights. Negro spirituals: Don't you remember 'These Bones Shall Rise Again' and Gus's favorite, 'Go down Moses':—

> "Way down in Egypt land
> Tell old Pharaoh
> Let my people go!

Gus could sing exactly like an old darky uncle."

"Why, he can yet," said Grandmother Brown. "He busted out once last fall. I rolled my chair out into the upper hall and called to him: 'That sounds mighty good to me. Keep it up.'

"Well, Jennie went, after a while, to Kansas City, where she met her Charl and began living happily ever after. And when he had mastered his stenography, Frank went to Kansas City also, found employment in a bank, and prospered.

"Lizzie and Gus were both married now and in homes of their own. Will and Charlie had been married a long time. Only Herbert was left me. And he began to talk of going to Kansas City, too. Frank, who had always looked out for Herbie and shared everything with him, wrote to encourage him and urge him to prepare himself to take a place in a business office. And so Herbert began to pore over Isaac Pitman's pothooks, too.

"One morning — it was the fifth day of May, 1888 — he went away. He was just a little past eighteen years old — my last baby. I stood at the door to watch him go down the street. I cannot *tell* you how I felt. It was a lovely spring morning, but I felt as if the end of the world had come. No children in my home any more! The last one going from me. Oh, oh, oh! And yet I would not have held him back!"

OLD AGE

VII

INDIAN SUMMER

"When Herbert, my youngest child, left home, I realized that old age was really upon us," said Grandmother Brown. "I used to think often of that poem of Longfellow's — how true it is — called 'The Hanging of the Crane,' which tells of the young people starting to housekeeping, the babies coming one by one, their growing up, their leaving one by one, and then, at the last, the man and woman left together in the house, just two, as they had started.

"Here after all our tug and strain, Dan'l and I were left alone in the old house. Of course, Frank and Herbie kept coming back from Kansas City, — for Christmas and their summer vacations, — but it was n't the same as when they really lived with us.

"Dan'l and I enjoyed going peacefully together to

the Presbyterian church those years. I went faithfully to the Ladies' Aid Society, too. One thing the boys did — the foolish things — was to send me a gold thimble from Kansas City especially to carry in my bag when I sewed at the Ladies' Aid. One year I was president of it, the only time I ever held a public office. Speaking of gifts, the boys sent me many nice things from Kansas City — a handsome black silk that would stand alone, an embroidered shawl, a heavy black satin that I never knew what to do with until I had it made up for Herbie's wedding. They were very generous.

"I was in good health in those years and my housekeeping was simpler than it had been for a long time. I found time to read a book occasionally. About that time I read the *Prince of the House of David*, *Pillar of Fire*, *Ben-Hur*, *A Man without a Country* — all fine books. And I commenced to take the *Christian Herald* then and to read Talmadge's Sermons every week."

"No lighter literature, Grandmother? How good you were!"

"What I really like best to read," Grandmother confessed, "is poetry — Cowper and Longfellow and Will Carleton's things about the farm. The poetry I learned as a child comes back to me as I sit here now. I was thinking just this morning what a fine peace sermon there is in that poem of Cowper's 'The Nightingale and Glow-Worm.'" She threw back her head and recited the long thing through. I marveled as I listened to her pouring forth the lofty sentiments she had absorbed so lastingly, over ninety years before in Grandma Foster's school.

"Dan'l and I had some nice trips together during those years when we were first alone," continued Grandmother Brown. "One time he said to me: 'How would you like to go up to St. Paul this week? The boat gets here Thursday night.' He never had to ask me twice. I was always ready to go whenever *he* was. So that night I heard the boat whistle at Nauvoo and roused Dan'l. We went about midnight. Just across from us at the breakfast table next morning sat a company of young folks from St. Louis. Going up the river for pleasure. 'My wife's a fine dancer,' Dan'l told them. Then they got hold of me and teased and teased me to dance with them. But I wasn't going to show off. All the way up we had the loveliest time. Good company. Fine fare. The Captain invited us to dine with him! And then, on reaching our destination, more pleasure. In Minnesota, we liked to visit the falls of Minnehaha. When I first went with Dan'l to see them, there was a good sheet of water coming over the rock. The cliff extended out so far that children could run back of the falls to play. Now it's just a dribble. Many of the great lakes that were so numerous throughout Minnesota are now dry, their beds grown over with tall, feathery ferns. There were twin lakes we used to drive by once that are now entirely gone.

"In '93, like everybody else, we went to the World's Fair at Chicago. It was wonderful how they thought of all the things they assembled there. I wanted to see everything I could set my eyes on."

"Tell me what you specially remember."

"The statuary was remarkable. Everything in white made the exposition beautiful. It was well named 'The White City.' It had a look of purity that pleased my fancy.

"I said to a friend, 'One thing at the Fair affected me in a way I could never forget.' It was the representation of Jesus being taken down from the Cross, — life-size, — hands and feet puffed up just as they would have been, of course. It was such a perfect likeness of swollen, bruised flesh. It touched a tender spot in my heart. How terrible that must have been!

"I was interested in the performance of an Indian tribe. They had trained ponies that dropped down and pretended to be dead. And there was an Indian girl called Sure-Shot who shot glass balls from off the edge of a man's hat. And then I liked the Village of Dahomey. It is wonderful to think what strides the Africans have made.

"Two years after the Columbian Exposition, Dan'l and I went to the exposition at Atlanta. That was a very special occasion for us. We went to celebrate our fiftieth wedding anniversary."

"Oh, tell me about that anniversary."

"It came on the twenty-third day of October, 1895, and we were having lovely weather. The day before, Dan'l and I hitched the pony to the phaeton and went out to the woods for autumn leaves. We trimmed the house with them — yellow and green and red and brown. One of the neighbors said we should n't have had any but yellow ones. I s'pose she thought we were in the 'sear and yellow leaf,' Dan'l and I. But would n't that have been a dead thing, a flat-looking mess?

"As it was, the house looked beautiful. We provided a good supper. The only special thing I remember was pressed chicken, prepared in a way that I made up myself. We issued no invitations. We just put a notice in the paper that we wished to entertain our friends and that all would be welcome. That brought everybody, and nobody's feelings were hurt through being overlooked. Of course our children were all there and that was the important thing for us; all of them with partners, except Frank and Herbert, who were still unmarried.

"Among the guests was our old neighbor, Charlie Doerr. He was, you know, a justice of the peace. He made Dan'l and me stand up in front of him, and he married us over again. And, by the way, I had a new wedding ring. I had worn the old one out. It broke in two. For a while I went without one, and then Dan'l said it did n't seem natural to see my hand moving among the cups and saucers without a ring upon it, and so, one day, he brought me home a new one."

Here Grandmother Brown paused a moment and then, tossing her head in a mischievous way she had, she said: "Do you know, I've been rather sorry I did n't make him take it back and get me a diamond that time. But I did n't. And I took the old broken ring and an old gold pen and some other pieces of gold that I had, — among them a ring given by my grandmother to my mother, — went with them to Billy Schneider, the jeweler, and asked him to make me a new ring out of them, and then I gave that new ring to *my* daughter Lizzie, and she gave it to *her* daughter Bessie. All of which I think is very nice."

"How about the exposition at Atlanta?"

"Oh, yes. The boys wanted to make us the nicest

present they could think of. The Fair was on in Atlanta, Georgia. They thought we would enjoy it. They gave us a pass and money for all expenses.

"I had to hurry up and get some clothes. I had a gray dress and cape that were very becoming. When we reached Atlanta, we went around together at first. One morning I suggested to Dan'l that we go separate ways, meeting at noon for dinner together.

"I struck the Alabama exhibit. Everything there was so beautiful — the clothing they manufactured, the cloth they made it out of, the fruits displayed. At noon, I said to Dan'l: 'I want you to visit the Alabama exhibit with me. There is a lady there, a Mrs. Russell, who was very kind, and who showed and explained everything to me.' She made him welcome, too, and showed him everything. Then she invited us to go to a fine hotel with her and to visit a wonderful fruit farm the next day. Going along, I said to her, 'This is our wedding trip!' 'That's worth knowing,' she answered. At the hotel a party of young people were dancing. Mrs. Russell and her husband took us about and introduced us to everybody, and they made a great deal of us.

"A guest chamber with bath was assigned to us. We enjoyed it all, the beautiful bed, the lovely bath. But I worried. 'She told everybody that we were on our wedding journey. I wonder if she thought we were just married,' I said to Dan'l. But Dan'l said: 'Let it go so. We *are* bride and groom.'

"On our way back to Iowa, we stopped at Chattanooga. We went up on Lookout Mountain and had dinner there. A car goes up slanting. We stayed until after the sunset of a beautiful day. We walked out to a point of the mountain where there was a house that looked as if it would tumble down into the valley. We saw a great rock where soldiers had scratched their names with a nail. My brother John had been in the battle there. We looked and looked to see if we could find his name. We went down by trolley after the stars were out. The lights in the city below looked like stars, too. Whether we looked up or down, to the heavens above or the town below, we seemed to see stars. I said to Dan'l: 'Are you clinching your toes in? *I* am.' We went down like lightning.

"Altogether, that Atlanta trip was just wonderful — the most satisfactory present our children could have given us. We had that treat as a bridal pair. We went through it beautifully, like newly-weds. I had a nice-looking dress and a gold chain. Dan'l walked with a gold-headed cane. He put on as much style as a French dancing master. That was one of the funny oases in life's desert for me. My grandmother thought if my father had a fault, it was levity. I guess I caught some of it.

"And so we had a few care-free times together again, Dan'l and I, almost like our courting days, in the few years that followed the going away of our last child. But we had our children on our minds all the time. Whenever they were unhappy, it was impossible for *us* to be happy.

"Will and Libbie had built a home in the same yard with us, and their children ran in and out of our door. Carrie was a child of gracious spirit with an intense love of beauty. She had fine taste. If she did n't do anything but tie a bow it was just perfect. When she had come visiting from St. Louis, a tiny girl, she said to me, 'Grandma, have you any pretty clothes?' I showed her my new bonnet with daisies across the top, heavier at each side. 'Oh, Grandma, you can wear *that* to St. Louis,' she cried. As I squatted to look at my tomato vines, I showed the lace on my petticoat. 'Why, Grandma, are *you* a lady?' she exclaimed. I was rather annoyed for a minute, and then I realized that she had been seeing me in my kitchen calico. 'Oh, I'd like you to have a nice black silk velvet dress with a silk lace flounce around the bottom. *That* would be pretty for you to have, Grandma dear.'

"When she grew up she was very skillful with her needle — could probably have excelled in costume designing. She was crazy to make pictures; was always drawing and copying other people's drawings. She showed a talent for music, too, and her father's interest in that led him to set her to piano playing very early and hold her strictly to it. She played extremely well and taught many others to play.

"As a young woman, Carrie meant a great deal to Dan'l and me. She used to run in every evening to see us, and was always so jolly and pleasant. If she was going out, she'd come over to show herself all dressed up in her pretty clothes. She used to tease Dan'l, saying, 'I've come over to close the blinds, Grandpa.' He always wanted them left up. 'I like to pass along and see the lights shining out,' he'd say. Of course, it was once proper, when people carried guns and might pick one off as one sat at one's fireside, to close the blinds, but that time has passed.

"When Carrie was five years old, her little brother came for a Christmas present — the sunniest little boy. He was 'Brother' to everybody and nothing else until the school authorities demanded a name the day he entered school. 'I have n't a name,' he told the teacher. 'Oh, yes, you have; everybody must have a name,' she insisted. 'No, I 'm just Brother Brown,' he contended. He was sent home to find out what his name was. After a hasty family consultation he was told to return and register under his mother's name of Knapp.

"Then, up the street, passing our door every day, lived Lizzie and Church and their nice family of children. Lizzie had had no children for five years. Then she hurried and did her work all up at once; had four babies in five years, and stopped. It was always a happy, noisy household. But most harmonious. No quarreling. Indeed, I never saw a family of children as devoted to each other as Lizzie's four have always been. Whenever one got ahead a little, he always seemed to want to turn and reach out a helping hand to the others.

"Lizzie was a busy woman. Dan, her first child, was never still a minute. When I 'd see her coming with him I used to run and turn my machine to the wall. When his mother lay in bed with a newborn babe, Dan was strangely quiet in the kitchen one day. On investigation, he was found to have climbed up into the sink where he was making 'lazzer' in a baking-powder can and trying to shave himself before the kitchen mirror with the butter knife. ''T ain't mischief,' he declared. 'It 's Price's barber shop.'

When he grew older, he joined forces in mischief with Brother Brown. The two cousins were inseparable in their school days.

"Lynn, the baby of Lizzie's family, tried to tag along. He always wanted to do everything Dan did and have everything Dan had. He is the tallest of my grandchildren, — six feet two or three, is n't it? — and when he was shooting up I used to wonder if there was n't some way to hold him down. But it would have been some job to hold Lynn down long. He was full of high spirits always. I remember how, when he was a stripling, a perfect bean pole, all length and no width, he 'd grab Sister Libbie or me when we were invited up there to supper, and trot us on his knee and not let us down. 'Little Aunt Libbie!' *my* children always called Sister Libbie, but no one except Lynn ever took such liberties with her. Why, Lynn used to throw me around and talk and laugh and carry on with me, when he was about fifteen, exactly as if I was a little girl.

"Of course, in Lizzie's house there 'd be singing. The piano was always going. The children seemed to know every popular song that ever was written. But Bessie really had a serious interest in music. She began to pick out chords as soon as she could reach the piano. When she was only two or three years old, she could tell if a chord harmonized. At seven she began taking piano lessons; later, lessons on the organ, and ever since she has been working with music — studying, playing, teaching. Now she is composing. She has just had a pipe-organ piece accepted for publication. And she teaches her own daughters to sing part songs in duets, and to play. One little one sings the soprano, the other the alto, and then they change about, vice versa. How Dan'l would love to hear that!

"Then there were Charlie's folks down in Missouri. We used to go down there every once in a while for a treat — especially at Thanksgiving time. Dan'l just loved to go over the farm with Charlie and see all the things he was doing. And how Lyde would feed us! I remember one nice time when we got up at four o'clock in the morning. I made coffee while Dan'l fed the pony. We drove through the thirty miles and got there while Charlie's folks were at dinner. We had stopped halfway and eaten our own lunch out in the open. We took out the buggy seat and set it down on the ground, unhitched Pony, and let her rest and eat. Such a pretty day! Such a nice time!

"It was always a satisfaction to me to see how Charlie had worked his way through to independence. He had had to pay such high interest on the money he had borrowed to buy his farm! But he always paid the interest promptly; and by and by he added two more farms and made his place a full square. Charlie's corn was always taller than anyone else's, and his home, his grapevines, his cattle, his fowls, always in fine condition, everything thriving and orderly. Usually he had money in the bank."

"Yes," acknowledged Charlie, modestly, "I had to pay 10 per cent interest on the money I borrowed when I bought my first farm. It was when there was so much talk about resumption of specie payments. The banks were all tight. But that's a way they have, I notice, those Wall Street fellows, of acting scared and hollering, 'Hard times,' whenever they want an excuse for a high interest rate. And they don't get any more decent as time goes on. When we moved to Missouri in 1876, taxes on our farm were $45 a year. They're $230 now on the same piece of land. And that's not so high as in Iowa.

"Still, if I had it to do over again, I'd stick close to the land. I mean that I like to live near the soil. The farmer has a harder time of it part of the year than most city folks do, but then he has the fun of seeing things grow.

"But, oh, Charlie and Lyde have had their share of sorrow," Grandmother Brown told me. "They lost two lovely little children in infancy. And their son Eben, the apple of their eye, died of pneumonia just as he was entering manhood. He and a neighbor's son were about to go away to school when he was taken down. Eben was studious, and Charlie meant to give him every advantage. 'We fear you are in a critical condition,' they told him, when there seemed to be no hope. 'I've known it for two days,' he said, 'but it would n't do any good to speak of it. I wanted to go to school, but now I'm going to a better place.' He was always old beyond his years, with an unusual degree of self-restraint.

"Dan'l was very fond of Charlie's two girls — both so capable and lovable. The winter when Edna went to school in Fort Madison was a nice time for us. She was supposed to board with us — but you should have seen what she brought in her trunk when she came. Four chickens, a sack of buckwheat flour, sausage meat, a slab of bacon, the nicest cakes — oh, what all was n't in that trunk?

"Charlie's Olive was an especially spirited child. She was not given to talking much, but every movement of her little body showed her independence. The way she threw up her head! I was there once at threshing time. Everybody was hurrying to get done by sundown, so that the threshing machine could go to another farm the next day. Lyde asked me to put Olive to bed. 'Don't you kneel down and say your prayers?' I asked her, as she climbed into her crib. 'No, my father prays three times a day, and that's enough for one family,' she said.

"She loved music. When she was a baby, Charlie used to dance her up and down and sing a lively tune, and she'd beat her little feet in rhythm against his legs. But if he sang slowly and made a sorry sound, she'd almost cry. She learned to play the piano early, and then sometimes when she was out in the field with Charlie, she'd suddenly say, 'Wait a minute!' and go dashing toward the house. You'd think that perhaps she'd hurt herself and stop to see what was wrong. But all she wanted was to play a a tune. 'Before I forget it,' she'd explain.

"Preachers that came that way always used to stop at Charlie's. He was somewhat embarrassed, but amused too, one time, when a preacher began picking at the notes of the piano, and, after a while, Olive said: 'Oh, do get away and let me play it!' The saucy little thing! But how she would ring it off, making her head and feet go as well as her hands, vibrating all over as she played. It was a great satisfaction to me later — in 1907 — when Charlie and I could go together to the old college in Athens and see Olive get a diploma in music.

"Gus was running the paper mill in those late eighties and early nineties. He had married Sue Hesser and was keeping house not far from us. When Adelaide was born, Gus was so overcome by the whole experience that he said, 'There'll never be another one.' And there never has been.

"'I don't see how Charlie ever endured it,' he said to me about that time, speaking of Charlie's loss of children. Gus was always wrapped up completely in the mood of the hour, whatever it was. He could rattle away so you'd laugh yourself tired just to hear him, and then he could be silent for hours and days as if there'd been a death in the family. 'Why, Gus, he just had to bear his troubles. There is nothing else to do but endure, when trouble comes,' I told him.

"Gus has always worshiped his one child. I don't think he ever punished her or spoke a harsh word to her in his life. And I don't believe she ever gave him a moment's sorrow.

"As the years went by, Gus had considerable to worry over — as had Dan'l and I — in connection with the paper mill. At one time, after about ten years in the paper business, I thought we had come to the end of all our financial worries, and that an easy old age was assured us. Dan'l had got control of the paper mill and was making money. But about 1893 he sold out to the Columbia Paper Trust. He was offered cash or stock. I pleaded with him to take the cash, but he took the stock. It never paid a dividend.

"Oh, how I wanted him to take the cash — how I wanted it! That meant security. That was something real. I just could n't stand it to have him pass that by and risk nearly all we had in an unknown thing.

I said to him: 'I've worked hard all my life and haven't seen much return for it. I'd like to have a good bank account once, have some cash for all my years of labor.'

"But he said, 'Why, what could we do with it, Mother?'

"'Do with it! Why, you like to travel. We could go to Europe. Think of it! We could build over this old house. We could spend a little.'

"But Dan'l had never cared to spend. That did n't appeal to him a bit. He would n't listen to me. Nor to Herbert, who came home twice from Kansas City to try to influence his father to let the Columbia Paper Company's stock alone. But Dan'l took the stock, saying to me, 'When they pay us out, we'll go to Europe.' Oh, I loved every bone in his old body, but, just the same, I have to say that Dan'l Brown was not a good financier. His penny-wise, pound-foolish ways and his strict integrity did not make him one. Just think! He practically gave away the whole thing, after we had all saved and scrimped for years to accumulate the money that bought control of the mill!

"After the crash came, Dan'l was out of the paper business forever. He put practically all he had left into the purchase of a shoe store. He took in Lizzie's husband to assist him in that, and there he stayed during his remaining days. It gave him the kind of background he had always seemed to like — a village store where neighbors came and went. But it was slim picking for two families.

"In the meantime, Gus felt that he had learned a good deal about paper-making and he tried to turn what he had learned to good account."

"It was expensive education and not to be thrown away," commented Gus. "I got hold of that old mill on a lease. Worked it about seven years. Borrowed money to pay the lease from any one who 'd lend it. I only had the lease from month to month and so I couldn't make any improvements in the plant. But, whenever it broke down, I'd tie the old thing up with string, lamm it across the back, and make it go again."

"In the meantime," continued Grandmother Brown, "I thought constantly of my two bachelor sons off in Kansas City. All the reports we had of them were good. Frank had made friends with an important official of the bank where he worked. And I was never happier in my life than when a letter came to us from Mr. Karnes, senior member of the law firm, Karnes, Holmes and Krauthoff, for which Herbert worked. It was a beautiful letter, saying many fine things about my son — how much they thought of him, and how satisfactory his work was. I began to dream that my Herbie would be a great lawyer some day. The boys were happy, too, in their social relations.

"Mr. Karnes's letter reached me not long before the Christmas holidays. I made up my mind that, some way, I should make the homecoming of the boys this Christmas memorable, make them feel that their good work was appreciated by their parents as well as by their employers. 'Let's give the boys gold watches for a Christmas present,' I said. 'Handsome watches.' And I reminded Dan'l that he had given Will and Charlie valuable horses when they were young men, that he had given Will the lots on which he had built his home and Charlie the farming implements with which he began, that he had given Lizzie more education than the others and helped her husband when reverses came, that he had stood by Gus through his educational experiments in paper making, but that he had made no gifts, so far, to his youngest sons. Dan'l liked the idea when he thought about it, but he thought that gold-filled watches would do! The idea! Something that would wear off! I would n't agree to that at all. Oftentimes, I think Dan'l used to argue that way just to see what I would say. I said a plenty.

"We bought the watches and had them engraved. They were solid gold, heavy and nice. Herbert has his watch yet and Frank has his. And Dan'l said a filled watch would do!

"I was so excited I could hardly sleep. I listened for their coming on the early-morning train. And then I thought I heard just one step on the porch, instead of two. I roused Dan'l. 'There's something wrong, for only one boy's come home!' It was a terrible moment.

"But it did n't last. They were both there, but they had walked together in such perfect unison that it sounded like one step. Under their plates they found the watches. Oh, what a happy time we had that day!

"I remember another time when Frank was back alone, how he said to Dan'l: 'Now, Father, I want you to send Herb to New York to the Columbia Law School. You can afford it easily enough,' he said. And so he could! 'That's the kind of a thing he needs. He will do you credit, will pay you back, many times over.' He argued and argued, and I joined in.

But Dan'l would n't listen. He said that if boys wanted to know any special thing, they'd take hold and find it out for themselves. But I argued that if children showed a proper spirit of industry it was our duty to take hold and help them. I thought that our boys *had* shown the proper spirit. There was *always* strife between Dan'l and me on that subject, and I don't regret it. Not long after this, Dan'l lost the bulk of what he possessed in the Paper Trust, and after that he was powerless to help his children when he would gladly have done so. The trouble was, he lacked imagination. He was close in his dealings, but strictly honest. He wanted what belonged to him, but nothing more. People knew that, too, and he was much respected. He was very generous, in his way, helping many, keeping open house for everybody. He gave credit too easily. I helped him clear out our old secretary about that time, and we actually had a bushel basket of old, outlawed notes. Seems to me honesty ought never to be outlawed. He trusted — trusted — trusted. In my opinion, the cash-and-carry stores have the right principle. People better not buy things till they have the money to pay for them.

"I was very happy over the boys' Kansas City connections, and I was disappointed when they left there. Frank went first. His kind banker friend died, and then he was offered a position in Mexico which he thought best to accept. It filled me with dismay, the thought of his going so far away. It is one of those moments one remembers in life. Frank came home to tell me of his decision. He came around the corner of the house as I was setting out plants in a flower bed. 'I'm going to Mexico, Mother,' he said, coming up behind me. How he startled me! And then, to bring such news! I had to let him go, of course, but I grieved over it. During his first years in Mexico I had many anxious hours, because I did n't always know where he was, and often he was in more or less danger, as I knew. He traveled about from one mining camp to another, alone often, and sometimes to the least civilized parts of the republic. I was afraid he might be killed or come to grief by accident.

"For a while, Herbert stayed on in Kansas City, but he was n't as happy as he had been at first. His special work in the office was to be clerk and stenographer to L. C. Krauthoff, a very able man from whom he learned a great deal. But he had made up his mind that he did not want to be a lawyer. In the meantime, he was offered what seemed to him like an opportunity to get on in railroad circles. He left the law office and became private secretary, first, to the traffic manager of a small railroad, later, to the vice president of a big line. But he was never very happy in that work, and I was much disturbed by such changes — Frank's going to Mexico and Herbie's leaving the law firm for a railroad office. All my fond hopes for them seemed threatened. Such anxieties are hard on mothers. Still, I know that Herbie did n't want to be a lawyer. He said to me: 'I want to understand law, but I don't want to be a lawyer. Lawyers have to take cases against their convictions.' They are bound by tradition. Many of them have their heads on backward. Herbie always wanted to work out new ways of doing things."

As I look over the letters Grandmother Brown wrote that son, I realize how hard it must have been for her to alter her dreams for him. About a month after the golden-wedding celebration, she sent him a newspaper article entitled, "A College at Your Fireside," which set forth the advantages of a certain correspondence school. She urged him to return home. "You could study here undisturbed," she wrote. "There is perfect quiet about the house, and we would be so glad to do anything to help you."

"I could n't persuade Herbert to come home and follow my programme," continued Grandmother Brown. "Frank was writing from Mexico suggesting that Herbert join him there and help him 'turn a trick.' Frank had the idea that, together, they might work into independence, one holding a job while the other prospected. Not long after I wrote that letter, Herbert came home one day, saying that he was on his way to New York, and that, perhaps when he got back, he would resign his position and be off for Mexico."

"I think I know this part of your story perhaps better than you do, Grandmother dear," said I. "Your Herbie came to New York, where I was living then, and told me that he was thinking of going to Mexico — that is, if I would promise to join him there later on. I promised. The year before, I had seen you for the first time. I think you were sixty-eight years old then. Your hair was quite white. But you stood very erect and you walked very proudly. You had on a long white dress and you were walking across the green lawn between your house and Will's, a very queenly figure. I thought I should like to have you for a mother-in-law. I promised Herbert to go to Mexico. The next year we were married, and you were the handsomest lady at the wedding. When we left your home in the early dawn of an autumn morning, 1897, you stood at the door to watch us go. I remember how Herbert looked back, saying mournfully, 'Every time I go away and look back to see her standing there, looking after me that way, I'm afraid it is the last time.' But we've kept coming back, and going away, and coming back again for nearly thirty years now. And, thank God, you've been here every time!"

VIII

DAN'L'S DEATH

"And now, dear Grandmother," said I, "we come to a period in your story in which I feel that I have a special interest. In the last years of Grandfather Brown's life, it was a child of mine and Herbert's who lived with you most intimately."

"How Dan'l did love that baby!"

"I'm sorry that you did not visit us in the years we lived in Mexico," I told Grandmother, "but you see you did not go to Mexico until after Frank married Concha and we had left by that time, so that that part of your story belongs to them. You remember that ill health and financial disaster drove us all home after a couple of years, Frank convalescing from the smallpox. After that, you and I always held on to Herbie's coat tails every time he turned his face towards Mexico."

"Ah, that was an anxious time for us all," sighed Grandmother.

Salvaged through the years I have kept a little package of letters from Grandfather and Grandmother Brown that tell the story of their lives — and much of ours — in the opening years of the twentieth century. Reading them, I realize how vicariously good mothers live. I see how often Grandmother Brown had tried to hold out a helping hand to her children, how she had understood and sympathized with them in situations which they perhaps thought were uniquely their own.

I was grateful for the warmth of welcome she had extended to her youngest son's partner. "I will just mention one remark of Father Brown's about you," she wrote me. "He said a man ought to be willing to serve as long as Jacob did for such a woman as you. It did not make me jealous either, for I loved you too." And again she took my measure approvingly when she wrote: "I heard you say once, 'My father always said that no little bird ever built a nest alone,' and again, 'I am going to break Herbert of thinking he must make so much money. People can be just as happy without it, if they only have a mind to.' I marked such expressions as good and excellent views."

She held me to them, too, when financial troubles pressed heavily on her son and she divined his need of encouragement at home. "A woman's first duty is to make a happy home," she told me. Again she wrote: —

Oh, Chedie, we women do know all about the agonies of childbirth. It is dreadful. But there is an end of it, and it is over with. But we do not know what it is to be the bread winner, to be responsible for the food and clothes and shelter for a family, not for a few months, but for a natural life. And if they have not plenty, the man is to blame before the world, not the woman. Men are in every respect just like we are. They are as easily fatigued; if any difference, their power of endurance is not so great as that of a woman. They need just the same care to protect their health that women do. In truth, we each need the other.

There were times, indeed, when she did not hesitate to remind us that mutual forbearance is necessary to the happiness of the married state. From time to time she admonished us on principles of conduct peculiarly dear to her heart: keeping the Sabbath holy, refraining from strong drink, disciplining children, avoiding debt. "It is not the few big things which we need, and must have," she wrote once, "that bankrupt us. It is the never-ending multitude of little things. The deceiving little things will call out, 'I 'm only a nickel or a dime.' And the very next thing you need that nickel for carfare or a loaf of bread."

Not long after Constance, our first child, was born, Grandmother Brown came to visit us in Buffalo, where we lived two years. Buffalo had harnessed the falls of Niagara and started an exposition, inviting all the Americas — North, South, and Central — to exhibit their wares within her gates. There was much to see, to hear, to write about. With Grandmother Brown to keep a managing eye on the baby and our good German Luise, I made hay as fast as I could, writing for the newspapers about the wonders of that exposition.

With my desire to help mend our fortunes Grandmother was profoundly sympathetic. She spent half a year with us, holding the fort for me at home so that I might labor, gainfully, abroad. Between her and the baby there was complete understanding.

Grandmother Brown told lovely stories. "Look, Constance, what do you suppose this is?" she would say, picking up from the floor a straw that had fallen from a broom. "Once upon a time, this little piece of broom lived in the ground in a tiny, cunning little house they called a seed." Soon the baby was looking for stories in everything. "How does the mahble gwow, Gwamma?" she demanded, standing in front of the washstand to have her soiled little hands washed. Grandmother could always find the satisfactory answer.

Most important of all stories that spring was the story of the waterfall. We all went to see it one balmy day, riding down the beautiful Niagara River in a big boat. Grandmother had heard of Niagara Falls from her earliest days at the knees of her Grandmother Culver. Said she: "My mother went with her father and mother to see Niagara when she was a little girl. She told me that when the falls came into view she buried her face in her mother's lap. The sight was so overwhelming."

Grandmother went to the Exposition too, of course, and lingered long enough in the early evening to hear the rapturous "Ah" that always burst from the crowd when the illuminating lights that outlined the lovely buildings came slowly on, and the dashing fountain in the Plaza seemed to shoot fire, and the music of Sousa's band swept softly across the grounds.

She was especially interested in the concession called

"The Streets of Mexico." Naturally, since two of her sons had lived such momentous years in that Land of the Snake and Cactus! We made her look at everything, including the bull ring and the dance hall. She admired the handsome horses and the picturesque clothes of toreador and matador. She was fascinated by the girl who danced *la jota*.

And then we had a Mexican dinner with *sopa de arroz* and *chile con carne* and hot tamales. But Grandmother never liked hot things — folks were better off without pepper, she always said, "and you need n't put any on my fried egg, thank you."

As the spring days grew warmer, Grandmother began to sigh for her own dooryard. "I must go," she said, "but let me take the baby with me. Grandpa is crazy to see her, and it is only fair he should have her awhile."

"But she's our baby," we protested. Still Grandmother pleaded and Grandfather wrote: "Our house is roomy and cool, our lawn is green and pleasant. The young squirrels have come down to play on the ground. Let Constance come and play too. Our hearts go out very largely to that baby." And I calculated that I could not spend my time writing articles about the Exposition and take care of the baby, too, at home. And so I let Grandmother take her back to Iowa.

The things that were done and said that summer and the next, and the next after that, while two happy old people played with their little granddaughter, were the subject of Grandmother Brown's most eloquent reminiscences. She spent an hour at least on that theme in the course of celebrating her ninety-ninth birthday. It was not that she loved this particular grandchild more than others of her children's children.

It was rather that, for three happy summers, she and Grandfather Brown had her all to themselves.

"When we got home," said Grandmother Brown, "I put her to sleep in the room next to ours where her father had slept when he was a little boy. She had the same bed and the same bureau that he had had and she ate her porridge out of a bowl that had been his. She liked to know about her father. 'Do you know what I'm going to do when I'm a big lady?' she would say. 'I'm going to play the organ and people will come from far and near to hear me. Then they will say: "Who is that making such lovely music?" And the other people will say, "Why, that's Herbie's baby!"'

"The array on the top of her bureau did not suit her. 'Grandpa,' she said one day, 'I need some ta'cum powder an' some witch hazel, an' some 'fumery.'

"'Mother,' said he, 'have you a little bottle that would hold perfumery?'

"I found one and said to him, 'White Rose is nice.'

"When he brought her the 'fumery at night he said to me: 'Would you think, Mother, that that would cost fifty cents, that little bit of scent?' 'Yes, I would,' I told him.

"It was a very hot summer and after one of our warm summer rains I used to let her go wading with her friend, Sarah Hamilton, in the gutter. They enjoyed it mightily. And then she would be all dressed up so sweet and clean and sit out on the porch beside me, waiting for Grandpa to come to supper. When he was within hailing distance, off she'd dart to meet him, bringing him home by the hand. And how he did love it!

"She went to church with us every Sunday morning. And no lady in the congregation behaved better. She looked on the hymn book with me, and always when they passed the plate she had her nickel ready. Lizzie helped me to make her a little outfit to wear to church — a blue dress of soft nun's veiling and a lace bonnet trimmed with blue forget-me-nots. She was a quaint-looking child with her big forehead and slim little neck.

"Once in a while I let her go to the store with Grandpa, but not often. She received too much attention there. Nothing was quite so nice as going down to Uncle Charlie's to see the little pigs and calves and baby chicks. As we got on the train at Fort Madison, the conductor said, 'Let me take the young lady.' As we got off it at Revere, Charlie said, 'Let me take the baby.' She herself said severely, 'The con*duc*tor called me a young lady.' Which amused Uncle Charlie.

"She acted everything out. And she acted it perfectly. Dan'l and I would be sitting here quietly with her. Suddenly she would start up, saying: 'Oh, dear! There's that phone again!' And she would rush to the doorknob and, holding her ear against it, call: 'Hello, Sarah, is that you? No, I'm not going. Yes, we're well acquainted, but — oh, well, you know! Oh, if you're going — well, *perhaps* I'll come. Yes, I think I'll wear my pink.' And then she'd begin to get ready for a party. She'd go through all the motions of putting on each garment and combing out her hair — such *long* hair and so many hairpins to stick in. And she'd do everything in proper order, her collar the last thing on.

"I had given her a little cabinet for a cupboard. There she kept her pewter dishes. And we had a foot rest that I let her use for a table. Around that she would assemble her imaginary family. Almost as soon as she could talk, you remember, she had had two make-believe sisters, Clara and Paystress. In Fort Madison that summer she added a husband named Albert. She was very attentive to him at these make-believe feasts. 'Albert, I knew you did n't use vinegar on your beans and so I got a few olives for you,' she 'd say. And then, perhaps, she 'd suddenly break off and turn politely to Dan'l and say, 'Grandpa, did you ever meet my husban'?' And, perhaps, if Dan'l wanted to tease her, he 'd say, 'Why, Constance, I don't see anyone.' 'Oh, Grandpa, it's just your 'magination!'"

When I went to fetch my child in the fall, I walked in without knocking and found Grandmother sitting in the back parlor with Constance on her lap, looking at a book called *Christ in Art*. It contained illustrations of the Bible by Gustave Doré, and had been a favorite picture book all summer. "She asked me one day," explained Grandmother, "if I had a picture of God. [There seemed to have been a good deal of talk about God in the course of the season.] I told her no, but I had a picture of His son. And then, when she looked at it, what do you suppose she said? 'Oh, Grandma, does n't Jesus look swell in that long raglan?' Another time she remarked, 'Jesus did n't have any luck at all, did he?'

"You remember how excited she was," Grandmother Brown reminded me, "when she heard us talking that evening about the assassination of President McKinley? As you had just come from Buffalo where the tragedy had occurred, it was natural that we should ask you a good many questions about it. Suddenly we all noticed Constance's distress. She was walking up and down the porch, wagging her head and talking to herself: 'Why does n't someone give me a gun, so I can kill that naughty Czolgosz?' Dear me! That was just the way her father acted when he heard them talking about Guiteau having killed President Garfield. 'Why don't they kill him quick,' Herbie said, "'fore he asks God to forgive him? They won't get him into Hell at all.'"

We laughed at this perpetuation of natural depravity, but Grandmother Brown, aged ninety-nine instead of minus three, shook her head and said: "Is n't that dreadful? God's very good to forgive sins. Though they be like scarlet, He'll make them whiter than snow."

Grandmother Brown was very uneasy following Constance's withdrawal from her care. Afraid that mere parents might not be equal to the task that grandparents had long since mastered. Grandfather Brown was quite as anxious.

Reluctantly they reconciled themselves to the thought that their responsibilities for the younger generation were over, that the active work of the world would be carried on, henceforth, in newer homes than theirs. But how sympathetically they looked on at all their children's struggles, whether with babies or with business! All the details of our living arrangements interested Grandmother. "I am so glad that you have concluded to go to housekeeping in the economical way you have done," she wrote us that winter. "You will be blessed in the effort to do the best you can. And I want to remind you, Herbie, that housework is new to Chedie and will be hard at first, and, if she has bad luck with anything, you just put your arm around her and say, 'Don't worry about the like of that! As long as *we* are all right and happy.' I think I can see how your apartment looks with the new rugs and a chair for each of the Three Bears. How I would like to send you some of my canned fruit and jelly to help out on your table!"

And all the time she was following just as sympathetically the fortunes of her other children. She wrote of the difficulties Will and Libbie were having in trying to run a dairy on the old Knapp farm. ("With such unreliable help," she told us.) She was interested in the outlook for Gus, who had moved to Wisconsin, where he was running a tissue-paper mill. ("Business is good, but Adelaide has the measles," she recorded.) She worried over the heat of Hermosillo, to which Frank had recently moved with his young family. ("They are well, however, and have named the baby Edward Augustus," she reported.)

How happy they were when Thanksgiving or Christmas offered an excuse for gathering their children around them! "Indeed, I think I am the happiest old woman in town," wrote Grandmother. "Your Christmas letters do me so much good. I am *glad* that you had such a pleasant Christmas and glad your employers like you, Herbie. I think they ought to. *I do*. You spoke about not measuring your love by the gift you sent me. Now we don't any of us do that. I know you would situate me in a palace if you could, and I would make a millionaire of you. But as these things are not possible, we will have a good time anyway. Oh, I would that these pleasant days might be prophetic of all! Our children's joys and sorrows are our own. . . ."

And all this time, I realize sharply now, they had their own personal anxieties — chiefly a fear of physical and financial dependence. "We begin most sensibly to realize of late," wrote Grandfather sadly, "that the infirmities of old age are creeping on us." Through his mind too ran the unhappy questioning that must weigh heavily at times on all conscientious parents. "If I had managed this or that differently, would my children be now more happily placed?" Seeing how I tried to help when financial reverses came to his youngest son, he wrote me words of appreciation that were balm to my troubled heart: "Chedie, we honor you for the course you have taken in trying to extricate yourselves from your financial difficulties and I have no word of censure to offer because you are less fortunately situated. Always remember you have in myself and Mother sympathizing hearts. We will rejoice with your joys and sorrow with your sorrows, always praying for your success and happiness and hoping soon to see you more pleasantly situated than now." And then he went on to say: —

Within the last ten years I have been compelled to see most of our life savings slip through my hands and pass away from our control forever. I have done the best I knew how, the best I could do, yet it has gone; and I should feel very much hurt, indeed, I should feel very angry if any person should reflect upon my character or integrity because I am worth less than I might have been under more favorable circumstances. What charity, forbearance, and sympathy I demand for myself I willingly accord to others. I console myself in the fact that I do not owe a dollar to any man.

But I am old and useless so far as making money is concerned. With you and Herbert it is different. You are both in your prime, both possess more than ordinary ability. Only keep in good heart; do not be discouraged; resolve to pay the just claims against you; pull together; make a long, strong pull together, and we believe a brighter day will dawn upon your pathway. Just wait and see the cloud roll by.

Herbert and I decided to enter the Government service. The following summer saw Constance again with her grandparents while we were carrying on an investigation in Cuba. In the closing years of the nineteenth century momentous events had occurred in the history of our nation. The Spanish War had been fought and now our Government was beginning to extend its activities beyond our own shores. Among the Iowa boys who had marched up San Juan Hill Grandmother Brown had had no sons, but a call came afterward from our War Department, while it was administering the affairs of Cuba, that reached Herbert and me. We were anxious to respond. But how about the baby? "Leave her with us!" cried Grandfather and Grandmother eagerly.

The day was just breaking as the Santa Fe train pulled into the sleeping town. Through the quiet streets Herbert walked the few blocks to the old house, as he had done so many times when coming home on vacation, into the front hallway, up the stairs to his parents' bedroom, leading his small daughter by the hand. Recognizing familiar landmarks at every step, her excitement was intense when finally, without a word, he popped her into bed between Grandpa and Grandma!

"One could really *visit* with Constance," declared Grandmother. "Grandpa would get so interested sometimes that he'd almost forget to go back to the store. She liked, as he sat resting after dinner, to take the pocket comb out of his pocket and comb his hair. Perhaps she'd put a wreath of clover on his head or a chain of dandelions around his neck. And how her tongue would run on all the time! Dan'l used to laugh sometimes until the tears came.

"The troubles her imaginary family made her! Her sister Paystress got sick frequently and had to have a hot-water bottle at her feet. And how she did worry over her baby! 'What's the matter with the baby?' I'd ask. 'Oh, she's got the tapiocas,' she would say. Or perhaps it would be the 'amelias.'

"But I think the thing that Constance did that tickled Dan'l more than anything else was making friends with the policeman. When we did n't know how else to quiet her, if she 'acted up,' we'd tell her that we intended to call the policeman if she did n't stop; that he came and took away people who cried and carried on and locked them up. One day, when we were sitting out on the porch, Dan'l said to her, 'There's Mr. Kessler, the policeman!' Without a word she started up, ran out of the gate and down the street to him, took hold of his hand, and walked back with him, talking as fast as she could and looking up into his face. You could see that he was surprised to have her take hold of him that way, but that he was pleased, too. She asked him if he locked up little girls. He said he liked good little girls, but had to lock up bad ones.

And he showed her his star. Then she said, 'Do you know what I've been doing to-day? I've been planting maple seeds to make trees. I'll plant two for you.' And she did. Later, after she'd gone home, Mr. Kessler called here and said he'd like to have the little trees. But after that the word 'policeman' had no terrors for her. 'He's my *friend*,' she told Grandpa impressively. Grandpa laughed about that story until his death. 'How Constance made friends with Mammon,' he used to call it."

At last the happy summer had to end. Grandmother and Grandfather had to give her up again. Constance wailed: "I don't want to go away from here. I'll tell you what we'll do. We'll have Father and Mother come live here, Grandma. There's plenty of room. And I'll take care of you, Grandma, when you are old, so you won't die. And by and by we'll all put on our hats and go to Heaven together — Grandpa and Grandma and Uncle Will and Aunt Libbie and Aunt Lizzie and Frankie and Henrietta, too — and won't Jesus look pleased when he sees us coming? He'll think it's a surprise party."

"He'll sutn'ly be s'prised to see my ole black face," grunted Henrietta, while the rest of us laughed.

When Herbert stopped in Fort Madison on his way West, the following January, he was distressed to find that his father was not so well as he had been the previous summer. On the Sunday before New Year's Day he had suddenly collapsed while sitting at his ease in the family circle.

"Lizzie and Church had come in Sunday evening after meeting as was their wont," Grandmother Brown told me. "Father sat in his big chair by the stove, telling how Charlie was to bring a turkey up for New Year's dinner. All at once he turned and looked at me with the most peculiar expression. 'What's the matter, Dan'l? Can't you speak?' He shook his head, and then his head dropped over on his breast. We thought he had fainted. Church jumped on his bicycle and flew for the doctor. Before the doctor came, Father had recovered consciousness, but his mouth was twisted, his speech was thick. He rallied, however, and on New Year's Day, when Charlie came with the turkey, he was able, with the help of his sons, to walk to the table.

"Gradually he got better, but he needed crutch and cane to help him about. Do you remember what Constance said when you told her that Grandpa was ill and could hardly walk? 'He can lean on me!' she said. You wrote us that and Dan'l was so pleased — oh, so pleased — that I've always thought it helped him to get better. And then in the summer she came again, and he *did* lean on her."

It was a happy change for all of us at the end of a winter of discontent. Herbert's Government work had taken him, the previous fall, to field service in the West. Month after month went by with no sign of his being able to come home again or have us join him. It was the winter of the anthracite strike and much of the time we suffered for lack of fuel. When my house was in its most cheerless state, my child took the whooping cough. But for good old black Maggie, who cooked and stoked for us and entered tirelessly, with song and dance, into the make-believe of my sick baby, while I bent, shiveringly, to an endless task of editing, I should have harbored black bitterness in my heart against the cruelties of life.

When the spring came I took civil service examinations. I tried every examination I thought I had a chance to pass. I think I tackled something like seventeen tests; I know I spent a week at it. Result: I was appointed to a "permanent" position as an editorial clerk. Temporarily, for the summer, I was detailed to follow my husband through Iowa and Minnesota. Renting my house and seizing my child, I took the first train possible for Fort Madison, knowing that Grandfather and Grandmother Brown would be only too delighted to look after my baby while I followed their son around the country.

The third year's idyll in Fort Madison began with Grandfather Brown and Constance both below par. Grandfather's huge frame looked sound and stalwart, but he had difficulty in moving about and was dependent on his crutch and Grandmother Brown's assistance. Constance was pale and puny after her winter's whooping and hung on Grandmother, too. But it was the month of May. The trees were full of singing birds and all Fort Madison was sweet with the scent of locust blossoms.

"We used to have a locust tree at the farm," began Constance, addressing Grandpa and Grandma the morning after her arrival, as we all sat together blissfully under the grape arbor, "and it grew and grew until it made a beautiful bower. Albert and I used to sit under it, and one night he plucked a blossom and gave it to me and when I went to bed I put it under my pillow and kept it there and it smelled so sweet."

"But did n't it wilt?" asked Grandmother.

"Oh yes, but when I'd sprinkle it with water the flowers would pop right up again. Well, the years went by and the years went by" — with a large wave of her hand — "and Albert did n't come any more." She was very sad and mused awhile, then suddenly smiled and jumped up, ecstatically. "But one morning I opened my eyes suddenly and there was Albert. And he said: 'Will you marry me?' And I said, 'Yes, I will.' And so we were married the next day. And I looked under my pillow and there was the locust blossom. I wore it in my hair. Is n't that a pretty story?"

I left them to their stories and their plays and turned to my Government work.

"Grandpa did enjoy her so that last summer," sighed Grandmother. "Of course she was older, and more interesting than she had been before, and then, too, he was physically more helpless and sat at home with us more than he had done in other years. I remember one afternoon, when he had gone to the store and we were waiting for him to come to supper, Constance said: 'Don't you think it would be nice if we'd hear someone come crutchin' along, an' crutchin' along, and he would crutch up on the porch, an' it would be Grandpa?'

"When we'd start up the stairs for bed, Grandpa first with his crutches, I next with the lamp in my hand, Constance following behind, she'd sometimes say, 'I want to be carried.' I'd say, 'No; Grandpa can't carry you and I can't. You'll have to walk alone.' 'I'm coming,' she'd call very gayly after a moment. And then, when we got upstairs, she'd be so busy helping. 'Now, Grandpa, you sit down on this box and let me take off your shoes and stockings,' she'd say. 'Grandma says it isn't good for you to stoop your head.' And it wasn't.

"She 'acted' more than ever that summer, but 'acted up' rather less," continued Grandmother Brown. "Dan'l was *so* amused one day when we were coming out of church and Constance whispered to him: 'That's the best sermon I ever heard.' 'How so, Constance?' asked Dan'l. (Dr. Stewart's text had been: 'Be not weary in well doing'!) 'Well, Dr. Stewart said it was hard to be good all the time. I guess he knows.'"

When the time came to leave Fort Madison, it was hard to say which mourned the most, grandparents or child. "All I want is Father and Mother and a farm!" was her passionate declaration when told that she was going to live in a beautiful city called Washington.

Settled in Washington, we invited Grandmother Brown to spend the winter with us. No one was, at that time, seriously concerned about Grandfather Brown's condition. While considerably crippled, his general health and spirits seemed to be good. He said that he would like to go up to Lizzie's for a change, if Grandmother wanted to visit Washington and we needed her help. She came a few weeks before Christmas and stayed until April.

How wonderful life seemed that fall of 1903! To have a steady job — meagre, perhaps, but certain — with a fair outlook for growth and advancement! To have a neat little house where we could be together! Modest wishes, but how hard had they been to realize! Now, at last, we had earned the right to stay in Washington, each of us with a job, my husband with the hope of a place in the newly created Bureau of Corporations, which promised to make such interesting investigations in fields with which he was familiar. There was the possibility, too, of his being able to go to the law school after office hours.

Whenever we could get release from our various duties, we showed Grandmother the wonders of Washington. She was nearly seventy-seven by this time, but as unjaded in her appetite for sightseeing as any girl of seven-and-ten. For the emblems of her country's majesty she had great reverence. The Capitol and White House she approached as if they were the seats of liberty, the shrines of greatness. As for the Library of Congress!

"I think often," she told me on the day of her ninety-ninth birthday, "of what Constance said once after we had been there: 'Grandmother, do you suppose that Heaven is any prettier than the Liberry?' I said to her: 'Why, yes, we are told that eye hath not seen nor has it entered into the heart of man to know how beautiful Heaven is.' And then Constance said, 'But they *couldn't* make anything prettier than the Liberry.'"

A spring day at Mount Vernon raised Grandmother Brown to the zenith of enthusiasm. For Grandmother Brown no halo had a lustre comparable to that of George Washington's. The correctness of his deportment and the elegance of his manners, added to the high integrity of his character, always appealed to her particularly. To visit his home was a memorable experience for her, and Mount Vernon has few visitors in these careless days who observe its details with the enthusiastic understanding that Grandmother bestowed on it. Every iron crane, copper kettle, and pewter plate in and around the kitchen fireplace reminded her of similar implements in her own childhood home. The spinning room where yarn was spun and cloth was woven for General Washington's slaves moved her to recollections of spinning wheels and looms she had seen in action. The old carriage in which General Washington and his lady drove to his Virginia church was unlike the Ohio vehicles in use in her day, but interested her, therefore, all the more. As we stood on the lawn in front of the mansion regarding the noble river below us, she exclaimed: "Oh, what merry junketings must have gone up and down this stream! Can't you just imagine what interchange of hospitality there was between this house and that of the Custises and Lees at Arlington?" But there was one thing at Mount Vernon that Grandmother Brown did not approve of, and that was the cat hole in the bottom of Martha Washington's bedchamber door. "I would n't want a cat coming into *my* room at night," she said, inclined to be critical of Martha for allowing it.

"We went to Arlington twice that spring," said Grandmother Brown. "The view from that terrace is worth many trips. But the great pillars Lee put up in front of his house are too big. They look as if he had tried to show off. I remember that on either side of the hall that runs through the house is a large wall tablet which gives the history of the land and tells what it sold for originally. I remember it was *so* cheap.

"Of course, I enjoyed the wonders of the Capitol and liked sitting in the galleries of Congress. One day, when I was in the Senate, I remember hearing a debate between Senator Tillman and another senator who was, I think, Senator Dolliver of Iowa. 'Pitchfork'

Tillman, you say! Yes, I thought he acted kind o' like a — well, *like* a pitchfork. He'd shake his mane and get *so* excited. They were discussing the Isthmian Canal. I got very much excited myself, listening to them. It looked so nice to me to have ships going through from one ocean to another. Dolliver came out away ahead in the argument, I thought. I looked for our other Iowa Senator, too, Mr. Allison. Dan'l always admired him so much.

"In the House of Representatives I soon picked out General Grosvenor, representative from Athens. With his heavy head of snow-white hair he was easy to identify. But then, I had known him all my life. He always came to see me when I went to Athens."

"Do you remember the New Year's Reception we went to at the White House?" I asked. "It was a lovely, mild winter day and as you and I were walking down Pennsylvania Avenue, past the White House, we noticed the line of people going in to the reception. 'Let's fall in,' I suggested."

"Yes indeed, I remember," answered Grandmother Brown. "Before I knew it, I was shaking hands with Theodore Roosevelt, President of the United States. I thought he was rather a homely man. He might have been a man of strong mind, but he was n't good-looking like *my* boys. There were some things I'd have liked to say to him, but people were crowding along and I did n't like to stop. I would have liked to mention that I had a husband and five sons, all Republicans, and that my daughter had married a Democrat but had brought him around into the fold. It did n't please me when he took 'In God We Trust' off our money. I wanted that left on for the good of our government. But I often think of what Dan'l used to say when Gus would be scolding away about Roosevelt: 'Well, I don't suppose Roosevelt *is* perfect. Fact is, I don't know of anyone who *is* perfect, except myself.'

"I saw President Roosevelt quite a number of times that winter. You remember he used to go riding from Park Road and take his horse down into the park not far from your house. One evening when Herbert and I were coming from the city we met him just as he was going to mount his horse. He spoke to us.

"Oh, all of Washington was interesting to me. I had had a life of toil. It was a great change. I kept lingering on and on. It was hard to leave.

"Dan'l had been writing, you remember, that he was enjoying himself so much with the young folks at Lizzie's. He wrote what a fine time he'd had on Halloween with pumpkins and things, cutting up with the young people in the barn. But after a while he began to get tired of so much singing and going-on. 'Bessie and Frank are nice girls,' he wrote, 'but it's beau and go, and go and beau, all the time. Better come home soon now, Mother.' I was beginning to pack up when I got another letter that made me hustle, sure enough, as fast as ever I could. He wrote that he had rented the house, furnished, to some people who wanted it very much, and that he had arranged to have us board with them. The idea! I hurried home, stopping in Athens only long enough to attend the Home-Coming Reunion. Very uneasy I was every mile of the way back.

"And yet I had such a good time, too, in Athens. That home-coming week of 1904 was wonderful. It was organized by George A. Beaton, who had become a rich man, the grandson of a neighbor of ours. There was a tent in front of the college with seats and food for three thousand people. Tables covered with muslin. Sister Libbie, Sister Kate, and I were guests of honor. We came in by a separate door and sat with Mr. Beaton's sister. That's something — to be the guest of honor among three thousand people."

To Grandmother Brown her home had always been the centre of her life. That anyone else should take possession of it and be able to lay rough hands on her household goods filled her with dismay. She went hurrying back to Iowa with blood in her eye. One of the characteristic things about Grandmother Brown that always delighted me was the way in which, when she thought it worth while, timid as she was, she would put her back against the wall and defy all comers.

In her absence, members of her family had been thinking that she and Grandfather Brown ought not to live alone, that they had more house than they needed or could comfortably take care of, that it would be a good idea — and profitable, too — to have others living with them.

But their ideas did not meet with Grandmother Brown's approval. On July 24 came a letter giving a delicious recital of her trials, all happily past by that time, accompanied by a neat little drawing of her plan for remodeling the house for the use of two families.

I had heard so much about the money I was throwing away, and that I did not need so many rooms, that I determined to make one more desperate effort to get the house into shape so that the rooms could be rented. We have applicants for rooms all the time. But they always ask the same questions: Have you a bathroom? And how is the house lighted? Finally, I decided where and how a bathroom could be made and telephoned Mr. Vollers to call and give his opinion of my plan, which he did. He said it was a fine one.

Now I will borrow that money which your father calls *sacred* for our burial purposes and put in the bathroom and the gas and pay it back with the rent. I will make a diagram of my plan so you will know how it is.

Since I have got the snarls and tangles all straightened out, I am going to tell you that I had a *hot* time at first when I got home. Father was down at Charlie's, had been there several weeks. From the time these people came in here he had given no attention to how things were going. He was so perfectly happy with the arrangement that he made them feel that the house and all that was in it was theirs, with himself in the bargain, and he had won all the children his way, except Gus, who said to him, 'Mother will not stand this when she comes.' Well, I cannot give it to you in full detail, but the whole house and the warehouse and grounds about it were Chaos. I had looked around what time I had before starting for Charlie's that morning and I went away heartsick. Of course when I got down there I tried to tell how I found things. Well, I might as well have tried to put out a fire by pouring on coal oil. Finally, Father swelled up and declared to me that I could just set my heart at rest, that he had made this arrangement and it was a good one, and that he would never keep house again while we lived. I told him he could live with them without me, or with me without them.

But just as soon as we got home and Father began to look

around he went at once and told them that we would have to have the house, and he said to me that he was sorry he rented it, also that he was sorry for the way in which he had talked to me, and that he would never do it again. I cannot take time to tell the half. But poor old Father, he does feel so chagrined. He told Libbie to-day that he had been completely hypnotized. I think this is why he feels so willing to fix up the house. So when you write do not refer to any of the unpleasant things I have mentioned. My ill feelings have passed, and when one is sorry for his mistakes and errors he should be forgiven. So, too, I wish you and Chedie to forgive me for losing my patience sometimes and acting foolish. And do not forget to praise Father for fixing the house. . . .

And so Grandmother and Grandfather settled down for their last two years together in quarters snugly suited to their needs. In numerous letters — usually addressed to Constance — Grandfather described the new arrangements with satisfaction. He wrote: —

Grandma and I sleep in the sitting room now because I cannot go upstairs. The base-burner sits in the front room where we can hear the doorbell and our friends find us at home. My big chair stands by the south front window. While we have given up most of the chamber rooms to the Thomases, we are quite comfortably settled. The Thomases are very quiet people and have everything nice, so they suit us to a T.

We are keeping your little bedroom as near like it was as we can, so it will be ready for you when you come back next summer with the robins and worms. We have not let them cut your little maple trees down, either.

Grandma has things pretty well placed and regulated again. She says she wishes you could just see her brass andirons and brass doorknobs now that they are polished until they are as bright as gold! She has worked awfully hard, too hard for one of her age, getting things straightened up but she will do it. I am so crippled that virtually I can do nothing, though I do make out to get a bucket of coal now and then.

This has been one of the loveliest falls I ever knew. And now we are having beautiful Indian summer. Then perhaps comes winter after election. You may say to your father that your Uncle Will is running for county auditor with a fair prospect of election. Three days more and I guess we shall elect Teddy for four years more. Well, I like Teddy — I do!

On the opening day of 1905 — a day "as pretty as May, clear and bright," he wrote: "I went over to the Court House to shake hands and wish all the new incoming county officers a happy new year, Will among the rest. All Republicans — for once!"

Drawing closer and closer to each other in those last intimate days and yearning towards their children, Grandfather and Grandmother approached the sixtieth anniversary of their union. Centred in their own destiny, they yet looked around them thoughtfully, taking note of how the world wagged. Roosevelt's tiltings with Big Business interested them, especially when their son Herbert was assigned to help in the much-advertised investigation of the Oil Trust. "Herbert must tell us all about the Government investigation and what is going to be done," wrote Grandmother. Having a lively memory of how the Paper

Trust had picked *him* clean, Grandfather regarded Roosevelt as a just avenger of the Little Business man.

Grandmother regarded her son's part in the "trust-busting" programme very seriously. But she was anxious, too, that he should get that law degree. And she wondered, uneasily, how he could manage both. "My only fear is that you are loading yourself too heavily," she wrote.

She had perfect faith in the outcome of the Government's inquiry. Of course righteousness must triumph — in the nation as in its small component units. Writing on her seventy-eighth birthday anniversary, she said: "This is a beautiful, bright April day and the first Sunday after our Gus has taken the office of Mayor of Fort Madison. I am happy to say that every saloon and poolroom and all that sort of thing in the town is closed to-day — from eleven o'clock last night until to-morrow morning. Now that Will is Auditor, and Gus Mayor, and Church President of the Board of Education, I think Herbert should be here. He might be City Attorney. How is that? Oh, I do want to know all about Herbert's progress in the law college and everything."

Every letter that year of 1905 breathed a longing to gather her children around her. She was rebellious that Government work held us in Washington, even during the hot summer. "Oh, if we could only see your whole family come walking in!" was her cry.

As the year wore on, she wrote: "Father has even suggested taking enough out of the little money we have at interest to go to Washington and return. He would do it at once if I would give him the least encouragement. That is how childish he is. My opinion is that he is deeply regretting not having kept our boys in school, though he does not come right out and say it in so many words. He sees how well Lizzie's children are doing. The boys are saving money to go to college. Father often makes the remark that he has made many mistakes, but that he did the best he knew how, and that it is too late now to help the matter. When he talks that way, I feel very sorry for him, because I see my own mistakes in the same way and there is no help now. I can only try to do my best in the future."

Some weeks after their sixtieth wedding anniversary Herbert was able to join them. "We would have been glad to celebrate our anniversary," Grandmother had written, "but all things seemed to go against it, with Sue's mother buried that very day, Will and Libbie short of help on their dairy farm, Charlie overburdened, Lizzie doing her work alone. But they all came in that evening, some of the grandchildren with them. Lizzie went to the kitchen and made chocolate, the best we ever tasted. It was a little quiet surprise, altogether pleasant." When Herbert arrived, soon after, he took comfort in seeing how actively his mother's lithe figure flitted about her small domain, and what satisfaction she found in ministering to her Dan'l. He carried away with him a pretty last picture of them sitting before a cheerful fire, touched with the sorrows of life but delicately happy too.

"After Dan'l got sick, I used to wash his feet," Grandmother told me as she gathered up her century of memories. "He could n't do it himself. I'd bring in the little foot tub and set it before the base-burner.

He said to Lizzie, 'Since Mother's taken charge of my feet they're just as smooth as a baby's.' But he would say to me, 'I hate to have *you* wash my feet.' And I would answer, 'Why, that's according to the contract, Dan'l.' And he would say other nice things to me. He told me he was a better man for having lived with me. Dan'l seemed sort o' mellowed all those last years."

Grandfather's last Christmas came. "Oh, I had the best joke on Dan'l," said Grandmother, recalling that happy holiday. "He was in need of a new suit, and I thought I would n't let him know I had saved the money for one. I went to Ben Hesse, the tailor. I selected the kind of goods I wanted — dark blue. I said to Dan'l: 'Mr. Hesse wants to take your measure for a man about your size who lives in the country and can't come to be fitted.' I told Mr. Hesse to leave the suit in the hall on the settee Christmas morning. Mrs. Thomas found the box there and came bringing it in. 'Aunt Maria, what's this?' she asked. 'Let's see,' I said, and opened it. 'Now, that's Gus!' exclaimed Dan'l. 'I do wish he would n't do such things.' 'Gus nothing!' said Mrs. Thomas. 'It's Aunt Maria!' I said, 'Now, Father, go out and get into that suit and let's see how it fits.' He looked fine in it. But suddenly he said, 'Are these things paid for? Now, Mother, what did you do that for?' 'I wanted you to look nice,' I told him. He died before it was worn out. But we had had that happy Christmas time. And our children all remembered us so generously!"

Grandfather died in May 1906.
The year had opened auspiciously for him, and

Grandmother's letters had glowed with satisfaction in his apparent improvement. "Father is very much better," she wrote in January. "He can walk about the room without his crutch, with just his cane."

Confident that Grandfather would be himself again "when the nice warm weather" came, Grandmother even thought it might be possible for her to make some summer visits. "I am thanking my Heavenly Father now every day that he has blessed me with such good children. I want to see them all. I want to visit Charlie's folks. They have been so nice to me these last two years. And then I want to come to your house again or have you come here. Ah, Herbie, I am so happy to learn of the work you are capable of doing for the Government.

"The first years of a person's life," she told us, "the advance is rapid. Likewise, the last years, the decline is swift. So, dear children, let us all try to make the best of the time allotted to us. I have now entered my eightieth year and your father will be eighty-four in August."

We planned another visit to them, but Grandfather Brown's summons came before we could get off. On April 24, Grandmother wrote to tell us that he had had "a return of that old paralytic trouble," and that his right arm and hand had become entirely helpless. "I hope my own strength may hold out, so that I may be able to wait on him," she wrote. "He could never get his clothes off or on alone, or cut up his food on his plate. In many ways he needs help all the time. He has wanted to write you, but put it off. This morning he says, 'Now it is impossible.' The children here are all very attentive and kind to us. And I hope, as the weather grows warm, that things may move on comfortably with us and that we can yet have one more visit from you and your family." But, alas, a few days later she wrote to say that Grandfather was much worse, had become entirely helpless and unconscious. "The boys have their business which they are compelled to attend to," she told us, "but they and Lizzie take turn about with the nurse at night, taking care of him. The doctors think he will recover. But it will be very slow, many weeks or perhaps months; so the outlook is a sad one at best. All our pleasant anticipations of a visit from your family this summer are at an end, I fear. To see him is only to make the heart ache!

"That last fatal stroke came on Easter Sunday," Grandmother Brown told me, "while Father was eating his supper. He had been looking for Charlie all day, wanting to see him. Charlie did not get there until after Father had been stricken, but he thought that Father knew him. Dr. Stewart had been in, late in the afternoon, and had prayed. When he had finished, Father had said 'Amen' in a clear voice. Then he wanted his supper. Henrietta was late, so I hurried to the kitchen, and I quick made some biscuits. They turned out to be fine, and I poached an egg and opened some Grimes Golden Jelly. Sue had come in and she said, 'I'll sit here and wait on Grandpa.' He ate awhile, and all at once he could n't swallow. From that time on, he was confined to his bed. We got a nurse. He never seemed to suffer. He died in a few weeks."

All of his children lived near except Frank and Herbert. From far-away Mexico Frank could not come to the funeral. From Washington Herbert hurried as soon as the news of his father's death reached him. He came into Fort Madison on the early morning train and walked, as he had so often walked at that hour, the few blocks to his old home. He entered the front hallway of the quiet house where all were still sleeping. Turning into the parlor at the left, he found himself standing, unexpectedly, beside the body of his father, lying on the old sofa where for many years he had been wont to take his daily nap. But for the telegram which had brought Herbert, that morning, to that place, he would have fancied that his father was only sleeping. Numb and shaken, he stood alone there in the twilight of the early morning and looked, with startled eyes, upon his father's face, knowing that his gaze could never be returned.

"It shook me so," he told me, "that I had to go out in the air again and walk up and down the porch awhile before I could go in and speak to Mother. If you could have seen how majestic he looked! Like a fallen tree! So tall and symmetrical, larger, stronger-looking than any son he has. He lay there, smiling pleasantly. Just as if he had lain down for an hour's restful sleep."

"On the hillsides the peach trees were in bloom when we laid him away," Grandmother Brown told me sadly.

IX

GRANDMOTHER BROWN'S TRAVELS

FOLLOWING the death of Grandfather Brown, there were seven years when Grandmother Brown spent considerable time on railroad trains. Nearly every summer she went to Athens. One year she spent long periods in Chicago. She visited Boston and Washington. Once she got as far away as Mexico.

"Put me on a moving train if I'm sick," she used to laugh, "and I'll get well. It's good for mind and body to get out and see the world. People who stick at home all the time grow narrow-minded. Once a friend of Herbert's wanted to buy me a magazine to read on the train, but I did n't want it, and Herbie said to his friend, 'Oh, if that train should pass a tree Mother did n't see, it would have to back up.' It's true. When I'm traveling I wish for eyes on both sides of my head. I've always been glad I had those trips around. It serves me with pleasant things to recall as I sit here now."

But in the year after her husband died Grandmother Brown was dazed and tired, and her first journeys were visits of sorrowful duty. Soon after Grandfather was laid to rest she had another loss to mourn in the death of her oldest and dearest sister. How appropriate it would have been if, after all their years apart, after their separate joys and sorrows, those two, who had shared everything as girls, even their wedding day, might have had the comfort of being together again for a few years at the last, as they had been at the first! But such satisfaction was not to be. Grandmother rushed to "Sister Libbie's" bedside and sat there sadly for weeks, watching the life that was so precious to her ebb slowly away.

Difficult as were the first months after Grandfather's death, they were perhaps not so hard as the time that came later. For at first there had been much to do to rearrange the house so that Gus's family could share it with her, much to do to minister to her dying sister. Whenever there was something to be done, however difficult, Grandmother Brown was in full possession of her powers, girded up and moving forward. It was not until after she found herself established in her old home again, but under changed conditions, that she began to feel fully that age-long tragedy of the old, that her work was done. She wrote: —

Oh, my dear Herbie, They are pleasant and kind to me, and I know it all looks as though I ought to be as happy as a queen. I have not one word of complaint to make. The fault is all my own, that I cannot settle down and feel at ease and happy. Maybe, after a while, I shall get used to it. But, here in this house for over thirty years I was *housekeeper*, in every sense of the word. My charge was outside and in. From the coal house to wood house and wash house, and you might say the barn. How we worked out there at different times, you and I, even to cleaning out the cistern there! With waste planks we made a good platform around the pump. And here around the house is the pavement we laid. Also it was mine to see to every repair necessary to keep the old house from tumbling down. I had pride and pleasure in seeing the premises in good order as well as all things inside comfortable in a sanitary way. Clean beds and plenty of good bedding, clean and plentiful if not elegant. So with my family's clothing! Made at home and mended and darned. Or I made some extra effort, now and then, to get a piece of plain furniture for the house, such as seemed indispensable. At present some of these self-same articles serve to furnish a servant's house and some are at Lizzie's, some at Charlie's, some at the secondhand store. Anything to get rid of them! All is changed. All looks strange to me and gives me a feeling which I would rather get away from, although I know it to be the carrying out of natural laws. And I am not complaining. I am doing the same as many old people have done, I suppose, who have led an active life and suddenly find themselves living without a purpose. Oh, my heart is so full. I could write a big book on the subject of going out of this world gracefully.

Gradually she responded again to the demands of life. Once more she felt the thrill of "looking nice," the joy of seeing contentment in the faces of those she loved. She told about how rich the gifts in her Christmas stocking had made her feel: "Oh, I am getting awful hoggish. I went right out and spent the money Charlie gave me for a fine leather handbag. I could never get my spectacles into my little leather pocket-book. Now I can put in specs, gloves, kerchief, comb, pocketbook, and then some, and it is pretty, too. But I feel sort of mean about it. And I am having my fur cape made into a collar and muff. I don't suppose I shall ever wear these things out, but Lizzie, Libbie, and Sue have all just put me up to getting them. And good things always do make me feel comfortable when I go out."

But despite all the tender care with which she was surrounded, and her satisfaction in her family, that first winter of her widowhood was hard for dear Grandmother Brown. Her health was delicate, her spirit lonely. "I get along all right, only I am so lonesome, *so lonesome*," she wrote her youngest son. "The folks here are just as good to me as they can be. But, Herbie, you are my baby boy, and you are more in sympathy with me, I think, than is anybody else in the world. I am so afraid you will not have time to come here." On his birthday, in 1907, she wrote him: "I thought of you the first thing this morning. I feel just as anxious for you to-day as I did thirty-seven years ago this day. When you were a few days old I was distressed for fear you would be left without a mother. I thought at that time I had a great deal to live for. Now, I cannot see that I have. I don't see that I can do any good; yet I live on, almost eighty.

"I do enjoy living in some respects as much as ever I did. I am interested in all the great improvements that are going on in the world. And my interest in my children and grandchildren is all it could be. It is this: my usefulness is gone, and about all the friends of my youth have gone; in fact, all the nearest and dearest have gone, and the situation in my life has come to such a sudden change that it overwhelms me. If I were young and had before me the duties, the hopes and cares, that I once had, it would be quite different. But I am *through*. Just sitting, waiting to be called. Nothing to complain about. I am situated, I suppose, more pleasantly than the average person eighty years of age."

And so she had her hours of darkness. But, with her usual fine reasonableness, she soon tried to adjust herself to changed conditions. Toward the end of her first year of widowhood, she began to plan to take some of the journeys which had been urged upon her. In another year she had found new "duties, hopes and cares." She discovered that she was not yet "through."

She came to Chicago to see us. When, discouraged by the slow advancement in the Government service, Herbert decided in the fall of 1906 to accept a business offer in Chicago, she had been rather disturbed. She knew his interest in the Government problems on which he had been engaged. And, while she realized that Government salaries were small, she reminded us that they were certain: "My dear children, while you were in Washington I always have felt so comfortable in regard to your getting your pay for what you did — as Uncle Sam is not so liable to fail, or, for any reason on his part, to bankrupt his employees. Oh, the foolish vanity in a mother's heart! How I have dwelt upon the thought of Herbert being promoted to some high Government position, when, at different times, he wrote me how the reports he sent in were highly commended. Truly I ought to be thankful if my sons are *good* men. Men have sometimes been called great when they were *not* very good."

When she came to Chicago she saw, for the first time, our little Beatrice, now three years old. "I am anticipating great pleasure in being with you children," she wrote before setting out. "Constance tells me such nice things about her little sister playing hide and seek, and about her golden hair all over her head. It makes me want to see her."

Beatrice was asleep when she came. "Ah, what a beautiful little girl!" cried Grandmother, when I brought the baby to her, warm and pink and dazed from her nap, but sweet and loving, as was her wont. Later we all walked down to the shore of Lake Michigan. Hand in hand, Grandmother and Beatrice went on ahead — the straight back and proud white head of the slender old woman moving on beside the fair, dimpled body of the little girl in her white dress and white hat.

Happy days followed, when Grandmother sat looking out over the blue expanse of the great lake while two little girls gathered stones and shells, paddled in the water, or, barelegged in the sand, played at her feet with spades and pails. And then came school days when Constance trotted off, reluctantly, to daily lessons and Beatrice was consoled at being left behind when Grandmother would let her help to make a pie or stir some "ginga bed," or, since she liked to help the little girl with her buttonings and fastenings, would assist in putting on all the accessories Beatrice could find — beads, rings, fan, purse, and "hanksha," which must never be used or "mussied up," for Beatrice was an orderly little soul, her grandmother's true spiritual heir in that respect. Greatest adornment of all, an old compass attached as a watch!

If perchance anything went wrong and a little chastisement seemed in order, even Grandmother had a hard time knowing what should be done about it, for Beatrice had kissed the Blarney stone. She put a conscientious elder completely in the wrong by leaning her soft little body up against one and crying, "Wock me, Dwamma, wock me! Wipe my teahs away! I lud you, I lud you, *tho* much. Wock me. You have n't wocked me long time."

Finally Grandmother thought she had to go, although Beatrice tried to coax her to stay longer: "Atta file, the snow 's tummin', Dwamma! An' Santy Twawse tummin' too." "I 'll come back then," promised Grandmother. She kept her word, coming in as Herbert and I were setting up what Beatrice called the "Twitten Twee," after having got the family stockings hung across the mantelpiece and the children prayed to sleep.

The joy of that wonderful Christmas day when each had all of happiness his bursting heart could hold! It is true that tears stole at times down Grandmother's wrinkled cheeks as she watched Constance's ecstatic rocking of her big Brunhilde doll and turned at Beatrice's shout of rapture: "A new toat for Teddy!" but they were not tears of sorrow. Countless "tups o' tea" she drank that day with Teddy Bear and Beatrice, with Brunhilde and Constance, at the party that went on, interminably, with the new dolly dishes around the tabouret in the bay window. So many things to be tried on and tried out and all to pass Grandmother's inspection, especially the work of the toy sewing machine which would really sew when "Herdie deah," as Beatrice always called him, "made the wheels doh woun'." It was no wonder that, by the time the festive turkey, which I had, somehow, managed to roast and baste amid all the excitements of the morning, was attended to slumber should have hung heavily on every eyelid. It was eighty-year-old Grandmother who best survived the day. While the children welcomed, for once, a nap, and Herbert and I, curling up together on the sofa for "just a minute" fell into the sleep of exhaustion, Grandmother put the house in order. Seeing the state we were in, she stole softly into the kitchen and washed up all the dinner dishes while we slept.

Other kinsfolk came in the course of that Christmas week — Aunt Mary and Uncle Gus and Cousin Nellie, and so on. Every night there was someone. And every night after dinner we lighted the candles on the Twitten Twee and gazed in admiration, Grandmother the happy centre of the group, little Beatrice on her knee, her fair curls with their blue ribbons crushed against Grandmother's sweet old breast. And so the year 1907 ended in a lovely Christmas, such a Christmas as was never to come again for us.

On Grandmother's return home, she wrote briefly: "My dear Children, I am here safe at home again — I had a delightful trip to-day. Oh, my precious children, I hope this will find you all well and happy, *happy*, HAPPY."

During the whole of that next year, Grandmother was eager to help us in any way she could. To use her skillful old fingers in the fashioning of little garments gave her keen delight. Each month came one of her surprise packages. In January we received panties. It was before the evolution of the blessed rompers, and painstaking mothers still dealt in countless panties and petticoats. "At the time you were having so much company while I was there," wrote Grandmother, "I was always asking myself: 'What can I do to make up somewhat for all this work and expense?' when one day it occurred to me that I could make your children some panties." In February came holders. "It is your birthday, my dear Son," she wrote, "and I wanted to send *you* a present, so I made three little crash holders for Chedie. You can call them your present, and she can pin one to her belt when she is cooking, and so have it at hand to take up anything quickly if necessary." In March came a little black silk jacket for me. She had bought it for herself but wrote: "It is a little too jaunty for a woman of eighty-one years. Oh, I do love to do something to help you save a few dollars." And then in April came a little cloak for Beatrice — looking like a beautiful new garment, although made out of an old one that Constance had outgrown. "I hope it will fit all right," she wrote. "I have enjoyed making it. It took me back to the time when Herbert was little and told Mrs. Angier that Mother saved all the old clothes to make new ones of, which was true, for there was never new bought until every old dud was worked up. I put a hanger in, for Beatrice will enjoy taking care of the cloak that Grandma finished on her eighty-first birthday."

She wanted to help us too in other ways, to give advice in matters of education and discipline, reaching deep into her reservoir of experience. "I wish you children would n't bother Constance so much about her spelling and the multiplication table," she wrote more than once. Again: "Is Constance learning to help do the work? Constance, you write and tell me what all you can do. The more you have her help you, Chedie, the better it is for her. Everything pertaining to housework is much easier learned at her age than later. It gives recreation a better relish to have first accomplished something. It is healthful for children to feel themselves useful. Of course you will have to exercise a lot of patience. But don't scold her, and *don't* tell Herbert of any mistake she makes, no matter *what* it is — a bad report from her teacher or whatever it may be. *You* settle it."

On the subject of what she called "the better method of governing children" she waxed eloquent. "Among all of King Solomon's mistakes," she wrote once, "I think the greatest was when he said: 'Spare the rod and spoil the child.' Better have said: 'Spoil the rod and save the child.' Jesus, our pattern, never said anything like that. When the children were chided in His presence, He forbade it, and gathered them around Him and took them in His arms and blessed them and loved them. At another time, He set a little child in the midst, and said to them, 'Unless ye become as a little child, ye cannot enter into the kingdom of heaven.' I do not mean that a child *never*, under any circumstances, need be punished. But that should be the last resort, after all other methods have failed. Just listen to your little Beatrice when she says: 'Don't 'pank me. Dwess *lud* me an' pat me.' It's a very good way.

"As I sit here alone in my room, thoughts like the above occupy my mind much of the time. As I near the end of life's journey, I can look back and see my mistakes and I have a longing, oh, so great, to make others see where a world of trouble may be avoided. And as I think of our children and how we, the authors of their being, have them in our hands to mould their natures, I see how our example has far more to do with the case than our precept."

All this time Grandmother's thoughts seem never to have centred on herself, but to have dwelt continually on the prospects in life for her children. "I have had many happy and hopeful thoughts about Herbie and you, as to what may come of his work in Washington — since they seem to want him back there," she wrote us that spring. "A mother has high hopes for her children. I wish I could come in and sit a while and talk it over with you, and, at the same time, help some on the buttonholes."

But a few weeks after our return to Washington, we traveled sadly down into the Valley of Death, where, for a bitter month, our little Beatrice lingered before she passed on beyond. Before the end came, and afterward, we turned to Grandmother. With great simplicity, but unerring instinct she comforted us: —

My dear children, Your telegram bearing the sad tidings is just received. Our dear little Beatrice is gone. The tears blind my eyes. I cannot see to write. Would that I could take you in my arms and comfort you as when in your infancy little troubles came! But, alas, in the carrying out of

God's laws, how helpless we are! Although it is among the first things we learn in this world, and we are daily reminded of the fact that, sooner or later, this sorrow is sure to come in one way or another to every one, — none is exempt — yet I have never known a person who seemed to be prepared for it. It comes as a terrible shock, an anguish of soul that cannot be understood until it comes into our own home, and it is beyond the power, even of a mother, to soothe. She can only weep and mourn with you, having but one thought which may bring a ray of comfort. That is, that we shall meet again never to be separated and where pain and sorrow will never come. May God sustain and comfort you, and guard, guide, and direct you.

Mingling her tears with ours, she suffered again the sorrows of her own heyday. In a few days she wrote again : —

My dear children, Herbie, Chedie, and Constance, my mind has been with you every moment since I received Chedie's letter — that was the 8th — except when I was asleep, and then often dreaming about you. I think there is no one who can so fully understand the extent of your sorrow as myself. I know what it is to put away all the little clothes and the playthings. I had all of that to do. Although it was over forty years ago, it is as fresh in my memory as though it were but a day. I remember how I felt, how I thought I never *could* become reconciled. I tried to think how much worse it would be if the children were left without a father, or if I had been taken away from them. And I would think about a neighbor whose husband died and left her with nine children, and they were very poor. And I would think of another neighbor with whom we were very intimate who had two nice little boys drowned in Skunk River, about two weeks before our little Lottie died.

Well, I tried to think of other people's sorrow and so, in a measure, forget my own. Besides, I had plenty of work to keep my mind busy, which was no doubt a good thing for me. Yet, with all the effort I had made, grief would overcome me, especially toward evening, and I would give way to weeping. Finally, one day when I was feeling so distressed, I went out to take a little walk. I took Gus with me. He was then eight years old. We were walking along and suddenly he stopped and spoke more like a person of eighty than one of eight years. "Mother, you must stop feeling so bad. You must not do so any more. Lottie was so good and so handsome. You love to think about that. We don't know what might have been her lot. It might be good or it might be bad. As it is, every recollection of her is pleasant and we *know* she is happy. So you must not worry and grieve any more."

This little lecture did me good. It was beyond his years. I was surprised. Had the same words come from an older person, they would not have affected me as this did. It seemed to me almost supernatural, and I had great control over my feelings from that time on.

As I think about your sorrow, I have wished *I* could have taken Beatrice's place. I would have been glad to have done so and spared her to you.

In the meantime, in far-away Mexico, Frank and Concha were in sorrow also. A promising baby boy, named for Grandfather Brown, had suddenly sickened and died. Grandmother yearned towards that stricken household also. She was urgently invited to visit it and so, as soon as she had seen her granddaughter

Bessie married, she was off. "The church is handsomely decorated and presents of the bride are coming in by the wholesale," she wrote. "All things for the young couple look most lovely. My prayer is that they may continue so. They would be the first in the world, however, to pass without *some* trouble, *some* time. Oh, I have a yearning in my heart to do something for my dear children whenever they are in sorrow, and so I want to go to Mexico this summer. And there is no good reason why I should not do so."

Reviewing that experience in her hundredth year, she said: "It was all of a sudden. I heard that Johnny Henderson and his wife were home from Mexico. I thought that I might go back with them. And so, in a few days, I was off.

"We had a very pleasant trip," she told me. "I enjoyed seeing the strange sights on our journey and the many wonderful things in Mexico. It was queer to have the sun shine in on the north side of the house, instead of the south, as it does at home.

"We crossed the border at Laredo," she said. "The Hendersons left me there and I went on alone in an old Mexican car. The nastiest, dirtiest car I was ever in! I reached Aguascalientes in the night. Frank and Concha met me. 'Mother, I expect you're all tired out,' they said. I was n't. Traveling always rests me.

"I was there ten weeks and returned to the States alone. I did n't go anywhere except to Aguascalientes. I should like to have seen Mexico City, but the revolutionary disturbances made it seem unwise to travel about. I saw enough. Oh, those poor people!

"'Why, this is Jerusalem!' I said to myself the first morning when I walked out and looked about me, seeing the flat-topped houses and the women carrying their water jugs on their shoulders, wearing sandals on their feet. 'Jerusalem or jail!' I used to think, as I looked out through barred windows at long, solid rows of wall. One night, when Frank and Concha were going out and I was staying at home with the servants and children, Frank said to me, 'You are perfectly safe here, Mother — as safe as in the Fort Madison penitentiary!'

"Sometimes, when I sat at those grated windows, I saw terrible sights of poverty and cruelty. One day a poor girl stopped there and asked Concha if she would take her as a servant. Concha told her that she had three servants already and could n't take any more. The girl was lovely-looking. She stood there a moment, gazing up and down the street, and her eyes filled with tears. Mine did, too. But what could I do? Frank gave me a piece of drawn work one day, a beautiful thing. 'I expect the girl who made that never had enough to eat in her life,' he said. Think of it! A girl came one day with doilies to sell. Concha could make them herself and needed none. But Frank said, 'Buy them. She's hungry,' and then he explained to me, 'She says she's had nothing to eat all day.'

"And yet the whole state of Chihuahua, I heard, was owned by one man!

"The hungry children! That was the worst sight of all. They used to make tamales at Frank's house. They would take corn and boil it up until it was soft, then mash it on a great stone under a roller. What's that you call it? A *metate*? Yes, I guess so. They would cook up the corn, some of it with hot stuff, and some without, for me, and wrap it in the husks. Such an awful sight of work! And then our children would sit in the doorway eating their tamales out of the corn husks. The hungry little Mexican children would come crowding around, picking up the husks from the street. Shame on the rich people of Mexico! To me it was *terrible* to see little children so hungry that they'd grab for husks.

"I suppose that hunger and poverty make people hard and cruel. Certainly one sees cruel things in poverty-stricken Mexico. I used to feel so sorry for the poor little burros. Half-starved things nibbling and gnawing at the green stuff that would come up between the cobbles. Once I saw two great heavy fellows riding on one poor little burro. And they thought nothing of strapping a saddle on to a burro's sore back.

"The fleas and the lice there are terrible. Even nice people get them.

"And once I got a louse on me. A louse! I went to try the mineral baths for which Aguascalientes is famous. Two Mexican women washed out the tub before I got in. I bathed and left refreshed. But before I got back to the house I was most uncomfortable. I stripped as soon as possible, and there upon my body I found a fat gray louse. Think of it!

"One wonders, all the time, about the religion of those people. They are devout church-goers. Everybody goes to Mass. 'What are those bells ringing so fast for? Ding-dong! Just like our fire bells!' I asked Concha the first Sunday I was there. The church bells were making a fearful clatter. 'To make the people hurry up,' she told me. In front of the church I saw a mass of people all kneeling and holding up their hands. And once I saw a pitiful sight, a woman creeping along on her knees in the rain, groaning and weeping as she hitched along. Concha said she was doing penance. Poor thing!

"Up around the smelter, things were very pretty. There was a big park kept in order by Mexican gardeners and a vast array of pretty flowers, especially one great vine like a climbing pink geranium that grew against a wall. Oh, Mexico is a rich country. The mines are n't all. It will grow wonderful fruits and plants. But the natives are the most unhappy people I ever saw. Some of our American friends there seemed to see only the pretty things. One of them said to me, 'Oh, you're wasting your sympathy. The Mexicans are a happy-go-lucky set. They don't mind being poor. They won't work anyhow, unless coerced.' But, during my ten weeks in Mexico, I saw things that put me entirely on the side of the peons, poor souls. If the revolution is really a fight for control of the soil, as you say it is, I hope that those poor people will keep at it until they get what they should have. I suppose conditions will right themselves in time, but it will take time."

Grandmother's first reason for going to Mexico was not to see the country, but to become acquainted with the household in it where were children of her own blood.

"They were pretty little things," she said, "and they wanted to talk to me and would chatter away, but I could n't understand a word they said. The very first day, little Marta told me something with great earnestness. 'What is it?' I asked Concha, seeing how serious the child was. 'We had a little brother that died, did n't we, Mother? And Father got flowers!' That was what she was trying to tell me. Little Chita could say 'Grandma,' but that was all. They would come up to me and put their arms around me, and smile, and show that they loved me, but I did so much wish they could talk to me.

"I came back in September. My health was greatly improved by the change. It was an interesting experience, but nothing would tempt me to stay there any length of time except a mint of money and the chance to come home, afterward, to live."

After the summer in Mexico, Grandmother Brown settled down contentedly to a sheltered winter with Gus's family in her own old home. Her mind was occupied with travel plans for the future.

But as the Christmas holidays drew near, her heart grew heavy with the realization of how irrevocable was the happiness she had shared with us but a year ago. She wrote me words of great wisdom which, at the time, I was hardly strong enough to digest. They were the wisdom that sorrow had taught her, that she tried to pass on to me.

Jan. 11, 1909.

You say that Herbert never speaks of little Beatrice. Experience has taught me to know and feel that that is the proper thing to do. It is not that our dear ones are *forgotten*. Their memory is in our heart, just as dear, but more peaceful. To keep our minds wrought up on any distressing subject does, in a measure, wear us out and disqualifies us for meeting the demands of life, which are the same under all circumstances. And without benefit to the one who is gone. I am in almost continual warfare with my own nature against the inclination I have to worry over things. It has done more to shorten my days, has been the cause of more doctor's bills, than all the hard work I ever did. What Herbert has said to me on this subject has done more to help me break down this unfortunate disposition than anything I have read, or than anything any friend has ever said to me. And yet, too much remains.

I know, oh, I know so well, what you feel in the loss of little Beatrice. I have passed through the same loss, and more. I lost, besides my children, my mother, my only brother, and my husband, who was the only man in all this world to me. Now I am alone. All the friends of my youth are gone. I have lived to learn all the lessons there are in life. And I know that the sorrows that are common to all mankind such as the loss of those who are dear to us are not the greatest sorrow. For, with it all, there is the beautiful hope and assurance that we shall meet again where all will be harmony. We shall no more be left to unconsciously do things which will bring regret to our souls.

It is now evening, or night rather, as it is after nine o'clock. I am alone in the old house. The family have all gone to a ball. I do not go out anywhere now at night. I am too old. And I would not be so unreasonable as to expect any-one to stay here on my account. I am not afraid. But there is a loneliness I feel which cannot be described. Nor can it be understood until it is known by experience. All are gone. The children that I loved and hoped to see have a pleasant life have each had to toil and meet with reverses and disappointments and sorrow. In their childhood troubles I could always give them some relief. But the trials that come to them now are beyond a mother's power to avert. If laying down my life would do it, how quickly would your darling Beatrice be laid in your arms in perfect health! I can do nothing but sit here alone, and think. The clock ticks loud and it is late. I must go to bed and try to sleep. Good night.

But for the most part the four years that followed — from the fall of 1908 until the fall of 1912 — were among the sunniest of Grandmother's many seasons. Who shall say that the ninth decade of life may not be the crown of all? "Everybody is so nice to me," she wrote. "Here came Nettie Doerr, the other day, to invite me to dinner. Well, they had a grand spread of good things served in state. I don't know why it is, but I do receive so much attention. A few weeks ago, Mrs. Tanjore Hitch and Mrs. Fred Dodd had a fine party at Mr. Hitch's new home. I was there, the only old person invited. I looked about from room to room among all the company and discovered that I was old enough to be the mother of any one of the guests. And, to make it still more gratifying, on my taking leave at the close of the evening both of the hostesses took my hand and remarked, 'Mrs. Brown, you don't know how *glad* we were to have *you* at our party.' I felt embarrassed, thanked them as well as I could, and told them that I felt myself highly honored. I would have thought nothing of it, if some other old ladies had been invited. Children, don't think I am boasting. I only mention this to have you know I don't go about with a long face and a dear-me-suz or people would not want me around."

In the summer of 1909, Grandmother made a visit to Boston, and then sailed down to see us at Washington. Said she: "Nellie persuaded me to join her in a visit to

Boston. To see Sister Kate's daughter Jennie, who lives in a beautiful suburb at the end of a chain of lakes. Oh, I've been so glad I did."

It was a sizzling hot day when Grandmother and Nellie arrived. Cousin Charl, going to meet them at the Boston station, found Nellie in a wilted state, with her hat pushed back from her hot forehead and a jaded look in her eyes, hunting a soda fountain. "Where's Aunt Maria?" he asked anxiously, fearing that if Nellie was so overcome by the heat her poor old aunt would be quite prostrated. But he loves to tell how he found Aunt Maria waiting on a bench, looking as prim and pretty and fresh as a little white daisy. Sitting there with her feet together and her gloved hands neatly crossed, a brand-new bonnet poised precisely where it should be above her white locks, a piece of folded white lawn at her neck, white bands at her wrists, everything in order and immaculate, her expectant old eyes beaming with enjoyment.

"How many beautiful things I saw on that trip!" said Grandmother Brown. "Things to enjoy thinking about the rest of my life! Jennie's garden slopes down to the edge of the lake. It is a little garden, but just perfect, with stone seats and bordered walks and terraces and a pergola. Beautiful scenes from every window! And inside all is charming, too — the fireplace, the inglenook, the way the stairs come down, the little fountain in the dining room, and, in the butler's pantry, the marble top of one of Sister Kate's old walnut tables cemented into the woodwork to make a place for rolling out the pie dough on. Oh, Jennie always did know how to do things. Not a thing out of order!

"She and Charl took us everywhere and showed us everything, and made a big fuss over us from the first day to the last. Of course, I enjoyed seeing Boston Common and the State House and the interesting old streets, but the city itself did n't interest me so much. What did I care for shopping — especially when my corns hurt? What I liked best was the long drives — seeing the thing as a whole.

"They took us for a delightful drive out Middlesex Fells. That is a large section where the ground is not tillable, but is grown up with various kinds of trees, and between them is a beautiful growth of huckleberries. A good road winds through, but people are not allowed to pull up any flower by the roots. We passed a man and woman picking huckleberries. The huckleberry pies were so good. They're unknown to us in the West.

"They had other good things to eat that were strange to my Western tongue. Fresh mackerel and halibut steak. Every Saturday night they had baked beans and brown bread and onion salad. Very good indeed, but I like my kind of beans better — baked in a broad dish. Oh, I know how to make good baked beans.

"They drove us down the road where Paul Revere rode that night he hung the signal lights in the Old North Church, — 'one if by land, and two if by sea,' — out through Lexington Common to Concord Bridge, past many historic places.

"We went some place nearly every day. One day we drove along through Salem; drove to Witch Hill, where they hung the witches. Just think of that awful time and the terrible things our ancestors did! The poor old women of that day! I tell you what — it is modern dentistry, perhaps, that saves old women now from being considered witches. Without our false teeth we look like witches, sure enough. In those days old women would have, maybe, a few old snags saved to scrape an apple with, and the rest of the face fallen in so that nose and chin would almost meet. My mother had the first false teeth I ever saw. They were on a gold plate. People did n't know they could use anything else but gold.

"Well, the poor old Salem women were probably toothless, and that's how their troubles began. My great-grandfather was born in Salem and several generations of Fosters before him. I'm not sure but that one of the poor old women put in jail there for witchcraft may have been a relation of mine. Here, read about her in the *Foster Genealogy!* See, she was Ann Foster and confessed to having ridden on a stick to Salem Village, having bewitched a hog, caused the death of a child, made someone sick, and so on. She was examined four times. Poor old thing! 'Finally dismissed to the sheriff to be taken care of as guilty,' the book says. And her sons all the time telling how pious she was! Those men just worked upon her and frightened her, until she was ready to confess anything. Well, they did n't kill Ann Foster, you see. She died in prison before the law could take its course. But they did hang Mrs. Rice's grandmother. Mrs. Rice was a woman we knew in Amesville. Her grandmother was a dear old lady who never harmed anyone.

"We drove with Charl and Jennie to the House of Seven Gables. How charming that was! A guide showed us around, and when we left she told Nellie that I was the most interesting visitor she'd ever had there! I remember she took us into a closet and said: 'Now, there's a way to get up the stairs from here. See if you can find it.' I found a sliding panel. You see, there is no lime in that country, only granite. So the houses were paneled instead of plastered. We went up the hidden stairway and saw the room where witches were tried. Hawthorne was always offended that his grandfather had been one of the judges who tried the witches. Of course he would not like it.

"One day we drove down to the shore and just looked and looked at the beautiful ocean. We decided to take a boat and sail to Chesapeake Bay, and thence to Washington. We left Boston in a steamer that took us close around Cape Cod and then on down into the harbor of New York. It was one grand thing to sail into New York Harbor and see that Statue of Liberty holding out the light there. I wanted to take off my hat.

"We reached New York on the hottest day of the year. Nellie was so worried about me. I said, 'When it's very hot, just keep cool.' She laughed, but it's true. It just adds to one's heat to fret.

"We soon put to sea again and then all was well. I can't *tell* you how I enjoyed the sea and the moonlight. I just looked and looked. Nothing but water, and yet so much to see! I was never tired of watching the rippling waves. And the phosphorescent lights — like glowing coals in the water. Oh, those were three perfect days and nights. And when we reached your house, there was another happy period of sight-seeing. When I went back to Fort Madison that fall, I had a headful of lovely and interesting things to remember and think about."

Grandmother Brown's letters in the next two years bespoke the contentment of her spirit. She was busy counting her mercies and hospitable to new experiences. The general serenity of her mind was shot, from time to time, with anxiety for her different children, but she never succumbed to it. When adversity touched them, her spirit sank and yet she would rally and write bravely: "But I am happy anyhow, for all my sons are *good* men. Thank the Lord!" Whenever the world passed judgment on one of them approvingly, pride leaped high within her. "I had no feeling of vanity as I read the article about you," she wrote her youngest son in December 1909. "I immediately shut the door, knelt down, and thanked God from the depths of my heart for all his goodness and mercy to me."

She went on to tell other things that made her happy: of how her grandson Knapp, home for Christmas, had come hurrying up to see her. "His whole appearance shows he is a man of good habits. He is in favor with the company he is employed by and has offers from others." Of how Lynn and Stella were home too and had come to see her. "They keep house and are saving money," she noted approvingly. Of how Dan and Zetta had come in too, "both looking fine and doing credit to themselves. Dan bought and paid for a piano for a wedding present for his wife," she rejoiced. Of how her son Charlie had sent her a Christmas check, how her son Will had been over for a good gossipy visit, how her son Gus and his family had been "so good" to her — "they could not be better." And how she had had such a pleasant surprise in receiving a check from a young woman who had once had a room at her house and who wrote: "This is no gift. I have owed it to you all this time; you were so good to me." How much she found in everyone around her to admire, how much to praise and be thankful for! No wonder she lived a hundred years, an inspiration to those who knew her!

She had praise for all our gifts, expatiating particularly, with a fellow craftsman's enthusiasm, on the needle case that Constance had made her: "Especially the sewing being so even and so neatly done for a little girl, I am proud of it." So glad to get the money! "Well, if I come to visit you, I will try *not* to come looking shabby, also will try to behave as well as I look. I have just finished a beautiful silk dress for myself, cut it out and made it all by my lone. Just think of that for my age! Have n't I much to be thankful for? How can I, indeed, ever be thankful enough for the lovely way in which I am situated in my old age? I can say with the Psalmist: 'He anointeth my head with oil, my cup runneth over.'"

But in the spring of 1910 a tiny cloud on her horizon began to loom large, though she would not let it darken her spirit. "Last week," she reported, "I went to an oculist and he told me that a cataract was growing over my left eye, and the right one, having most of the seeing to do, I'd better save. He said I should not do much sewing or reading. Well, this is what I will do: Just make the best of it, and be thankful for one good eye. It is a lot better than none. And I am so thankful that it is me, instead of any one of my children, or grandchildren, so I am happy to think it is as it is. I have one eye and can walk around and enjoy every good thing."

She came to Washington that summer and saw a great oculist, hurrying home in time to be the honored guest at the pretty wedding of her granddaughter Carrie. What became of her cataract I do not know. Seventeen years passed after that time, and, beneath her eyes, many yards of beautiful embroideries blossomed and many miles of New Testament texts were scanned.

As the year 1910 came to a close, severe illness visited our particular household and Grandmother indited some precious missives in which she enunciated the rule of conduct which is the explanation of her triumphant old age. "Now, Constance," she wrote, "do your best in taking care of your mother. Comfort her and your father too. If you practise the little play sermon you preached here when you were just a baby, and your grandfather and I were the audience, and, with your finger raised as much as to say, 'Give full attention!' you said, 'If you wish to be happy, make others happy,' *then* you will be happy yourself. At the close, your grandfather said: 'The little child preached better than she knew. That is as good a sermon as I ever listened to.' If we would live by that rule, we would have Heaven here to a very great degree. The more you practise it, the more convinced you become of the truth there is in it."

And so, loving and consoling, trying to make others happy and to be cheerful herself, Grandmother Brown accumulated the years.

The year 1911 is memorable in Grandmother Brown's travelogue as the year when she visited Rutland and beheld with her own reverent eyes the home of her great-grandfather, Lieutenant Foster, and the home of his friend General Rufus Putnam. With awe she told us about it when again she came by boat from Boston to Washington.

She was like a bird of passage in those travel years. With the first smell of spring in the air her thoughts were off to scenes of her childhood in the Ohio country, and she began to preen her feathers. This year she took flight earlier than usual, alighting, happily, in her beloved Hocking Valley on the day before her eighty-fourth birthday. "I had the pleasure of spending it in the old town where I was born," she told us. "If I could tell you of the warm welcome I have met from every old acquaintance you would be pleased. On Monday, after my arrival, Nellie was called to the phone, and a lady said to her: 'We learn by the paper that your aunt, Mrs. Brown, is at your house. Be *sure* to have her come with you to our meeting of the D. A. R.'s on next Saturday. Tell her, also, that we want her to give us a little talk.' During this week Nellie spoke to me, several times, about the matter and suggested my making some little notes to help me out. Again, on our way to the meeting, she said to me,'Now, Aunt Maria, do you know what you are going to say?' I said I thought I could make out. Well, after the business of the meeting had all been attended to in the most parliamentary order, we heard a fine address by Mrs. Chubb, the wife of one of the college professors, on 'The Evolution of the American Flag.' Then music. Then I was introduced, and did my little talk, and when so *many* ladies came forward and shook hands with me and praised my talk and said they enjoyed hearing me, I felt greatly embarrassed. On our way home

I asked Nellie if she thought they meant all they said. 'Why, Aunt Maria, it was fine!' Well, I did not go to book or paper and take to myself the credit of some sentence or thought belonging to another person."

Her cup of contentment ran over a few weeks later when Herbert joined her in Athens and visited with her the sacred shrines of their ancestors. "If you would come," she had written him, "we could have the pleasure of looking at the old hills and going over the ground where your Father and I were born and spent our youthful days. It would be a joy to me to point out to you some of the old landmarks. Every old hill and rock and rill is dear to me."

But with all Grandmother's effort to meet life cheerfully, it could not always have been easy. The year 1912 brought her suffering and sorrow. All around her, she saw her contemporaries dying. "Grandpa Knapp died last Tuesday," she wrote while struggling herself with illness. "I'll not be here long. I feel sure of that. All I have done in the last two days has been this little amount of bad writing."

She was well enough, however, when Knapp brought home his bride that same month, to take enthusiastic note of Marguerite's charms. "I was very favorably impressed," she told us. "They are going to housekeeping in Sioux Falls right away. Knapp's marriage makes my family number thirty-six." As spring approached, she did her best to rally her forces and do her part to make Adelaide's wedding day a happy occasion. "I have had a pretty hard pull," she reported. "It is a harder matter for old people to recuperate than it is for the young. But there is to be a wedding here about Easter. Sue and Adelaide left Sunday night for Chicago, taking with them an empty trunk in which to bring back the bridal robes. Adelaide is having the finest outfit I have ever seen. A church wedding, too!

"Adelaide was married on my eighty-fifth birthday," went on Grandmother Brown, recalling that event happily as she gathered up the recollections of her ninety-nine years. "She looked lovely. She had orange blossoms and a veil. But it made me vexed when I went into the room where she had dressed and saw how the hairdresser had snipped off the orange blossoms. Bits of blossoms all over the carpet! Such a waste! Flowers that they had sent South for!

"Everything was very fine. A canopy to walk under from the carriage into the church! Music! Lovely decorations! But Gus looked as if it was a funeral. And then they all came back here and had a reception.

"Yes, everybody made a good deal of fuss over me too — since it was my birthday. That was the time Mr. Timpe was proud of me. I went into his dry-goods store a few days after, and he came forward, saying, 'Why, Mrs. Brown, I was proud of you when I saw you come in to Adelaide's wedding.' Well, if one of my boys said that, I shouldn't be surprised, but when an outsider flatters me that way I'm embarrassed.

"If I should live to my hundredth birthday, I want to be dressed just as I was at Adelaide's wedding. I still have that black satin dress with white silk fichu. The way I came to get that fichu was this: I saw it in the store and wanted it. I told Dan'l. He said: 'Why don't you get it? Have it charged.' But right after dinner, without saying a word to me, he went to the store and bought it, and told them to tell me it had been sold. When I went to get it I was *so* disappointed. Then, when he came to supper, what do you think? He was wearing it spread over his old, dusty coat. Well, I wore that pretty thing to Bessie's wedding, and Olive's, and Edna's, and to Adelaide's. Then I thought I was going to die, and so I gave it to Adelaide. But, if I live, I'd like to wear it again. If I live — well, it's all right if I do, and all right if I don't.

"Oh, I don't know why I went to Ohio that summer," went on Grandmother, recalling with deep sadness the death of her oldest granddaughter. "I left immediately after Adelaide's wedding. Carrie walked to the gate with me when I was starting away. Oh, I felt so distressed when I heard of her death. It knocked my brains awry. To have her go that way! Her little baby only lived an hour, but Carrie lived four days longer. She made a happy exchange perhaps; but, oh, it *hurts* us so. The baby was buried with her. Before she died she said to her mother: 'Has the baby been laid away yet?' 'No.' 'Are they keeping it to bury with me?' They were."

In Washington, we looked for Grandmother Brown that summer, but she had lost all heart for visiting. She hurried home from Athens back to her sorrowing children in Fort Madison. "I want to go home," she wrote. "While I am perfectly well, I *am old*. It hurts me to be worried. Maybe, too, if I am at home I can comfort poor Will and Libbie."

Grandmother's trip to Athens in the summer of 1913 ended disastrously. She broke her hip, and during the last fifteen years of her life was unable to walk.

In the winter before this event, though greatly depressed by Carrie's death, she set herself resolutely to work to appreciate every benefit she had. "Let us be happy while we may, and make life as pleasant for each other as we can" was her Christmas message to Constance. Events were stirring among the third generation — and the fourth — to hold her interest that winter. There were three grandchildren now in Lizzie's family, each to be inspected when brought home from time to time. Two little girls almost finished with the business of getting teeth and beginning to attempt conversation that winter. One small boy just finding the use of his legs. And there was Frank's boy Edward, come up from Mexico to spend the winter with Lizzie and Church and go to our American schools.

All of which pleased Grandmother. Nothing interested her more than to watch the development of her offspring. And it was their custom to lay all their works before her, sure of her hearty approval. School reports, Camp Fire honors, poems and pictures of their making, anything that was accounted meritorious was likely to be sent to Grandmother.

When the summer came, Grandmother went to Athens, as usual, and flitted about among her old friends in her independent way. She went to Lancaster and she went to Logan, visiting cousins' children almost as light-footedly as she once went visiting their parents, long since dead.

"I came back alone from Cousin Barsha's — her real name is Bathsheba, —" she told me, "starting back just before sundown, though they wanted me to stop overnight. 'No, I'll be back just in time to eat supper with Nellie,' I told them. On reaching Athens, I hurried to get the bus. There is a curb around the station house. The shadow of a telephone pole fell across it, so that I did not see it. I struck my toe against the curb and fell.

"I didn't know that I was hurt, but I found that I couldn't get up. Two men lifted me and dragged me to the bus. I felt faint. When we reached the house and Nellie came running out, the driver carried me in and laid me down on Nellie's bed.

"Will was summoned from Iowa and Herbert from Washington. After a few days I was put on a stretcher, and Will got me safely to Fort Madison. Four times they put my stretcher through a car window. It was a hard trip, but everybody was most kind. I remember that once a porter said: 'Now, Grandmother, don't be afraid. We'll not hurt you.'

"It was good to be at home in my own room again. But, oh, what suffering! For weeks and weeks. The Fort Madison doctor put a weight on my foot. If I could have endured the pain, my hip might have healed with my legs not drawn up as they are. But I couldn't stand it. They had to take off the weights. I had a long, hard sick spell. I got well, but I can't straighten out my legs. I'm a cripple now for the rest of my life. I couldn't use crutches, because my arm was hurt and my hands got rheumatic and I was liable to fall. Once, when Herbert was a boy in Kansas City, I had had rheumatism in my hand and arm. Herbie got passes and took me to the Hot Springs of Arkansas where I had the baths and drank the waters. The rheumatism never troubled me again until I broke my hip.

"At first I thought I could not endure it to sit here, day after day, until the end comes. Just think! I took my last step on almost the very spot where I took my first ones. The Baltimore and Ohio station at Athens is built on what was once my father's farm. I saw that I'd have to make the best of it. So I said to myself, 'This is nothing. If any of my children should go wrong, now *that* would be trouble.' I have so much to be thankful for. A good meal set before me three times a day! And everybody so good to me, so good. Just as nice as nice can be!"

X

SHUT-IN

WE had no letters from Grandmother Brown in 1914. For many months she was completely helpless and in the care of trained nurses. There was a feeling in the family that, having a broken hip and being unable to walk even with a crutch, she would, of course, at her advanced age, need constant attention. Nothing could have been more abhorrent to her than such a situation. Before the year was up, she had not only dismissed all professional nurses, but had devised adequate means of waiting on herself. She wrote us about how she had contrived it: —

On the fifteenth of October, Gus and Sue left for El Paso. Henrietta, my old colored girl, came to give me my usual bath. I said: "Now, instead of a bath, I want you to go to the woodhouse and see what you can find to lengthen out the legs of this kitchen chair." I saw that if it was high enough so I could get from it back on to the bed, and if it had rollers on it so I could push it around the room, I could help myself. Well, she brought a pole which I think a rug had been wrapped on. "Now bring the saw, the hammer, and nails." I sat up on the side of the bed and directed, found just how much must be added to the chair legs. "There! Saw off four pieces! Now start your nail right in the middle of the round piece and drive it clear through so you can see the point of the nail. Now, put that point right in the middle of the bottom of the chair leg and drive it in. Then some smaller nails round it to be secure!" So all were done. When Gus came home he said: "Well, Mother, after this, when there's house cleaning to be done, you can just take hold and help!" He had ball-bearing castors put on my little chair. And now I wait on myself, night and day. The expensive wheeled chair Gus had bought for me was not satisfactory in any way. The seat was so high it took two persons to get me into or out of it. But this little kitchen chair on rollers just the height of my bed serves me almost as well as my own legs. You ought to see how I can fly around my room on it. I had to invent my own walking machine, you see.

I have the chair by my bed at night. In the morning I roll myself into my lavatory, wash my face, neck, and hands, clean my teeth, and back out into my room again, get into a kimono and into a rocking-chair, and am ready for breakfast. But I comb my hair straight down. I cannot get my lame hand to my head to do it up.

Before long she was persuading her lame hand to do its old work. Gradually she compelled it again to dress her hair, to sew and embroider and knit once more. But it took painful persistence on her part to get the recalcitrant member to obey her will.

It disturbed her greatly to think that her infirmities might, in any way, curtail the liberties of other members of the family. "I am glad that my condition has never kept Sue from anything she wanted to do or any place she wanted to go," she wrote. "Now I do everything for myself except to bring my food upstairs and sweep and dust my room. I get Henrietta to do my washing and ironing, and once a week she gives me a bath. The rest of the week I take a sponge and do it myself. I don't like to feel myself an encumbrance. They are all good to me, and I make as little as I possibly can for them to do. At first they seemed to think that, because I was crippled, I must not be left alone. I've broken them of that idea. There's never a week, now, when I am not alone in the house two or three nights. At first, they'd insist on having Frances, the colored woman, to sit with me. I did n't want any colored woman — or white woman either — sitting there watching me. One of the nurses I had here for a while annoyed me so, listening for trains. 'Just go to sleep,' I used to tell her, 'and don't lie awake listening for trains to keep you awake.' The best way for a person to do is to make the least trouble possible. Sometimes they forget to bring me a little knife, — on account of my lame hand, I can't wield a big one, — so I just use the spoon handle to spread my bread, then lick it off, smooth and clean, so they won't know the difference and feel bad about it."

She spent a great deal of thought in working out all the details of her living arrangements with the end in view of making herself independent of others' assistance. About this time, Gus bought from her the old house and remodeled it. Various alterations made in her own quarters added to her comfort, especially the addition of a bay window extending beyond the line of the house in such a way as to enable her to look up and down two streets. From one window she could look up to the bluff behind the town, from the other down to the river that washes its shores. Seated in this bay window she was easily discerned by all passers-by, and few there were who did not wave to her as they went by.

One of the first essentials she demanded as an aid towards dressing herself was a pole with a hook on it, wherewith she might, herself, reach down the hangers from her closet pegs. Below her windows she had places conveniently arranged to hold her books and magazines and sewing basket. Nothing must be too high for her to reach from her little roller chair. With great pride she showed all her little efficiency tricks. Talk about Taylor's motion studies! Not a lost bend or turn in Grandmother Brown's system of locomotion about that room!

"See that cupboard over there between the windows. I must tell you about that," she said. "You know, when we first came to the farm there was n't a closet or cupboard or shelf in the house for holding anything. The first time Dan'l and I went back to Ohio, we left directions with our boys for that cupboard to be made while we were gone. The walnut log out of which it was made grew on our farm. Will and Charlie hauled it to the sawmill at Denmark, then hauled the lumber to a carpenter, where the cupboard was made according to a size I had left marked on the bedroom wall. When we moved to Fort Madison, we brought the cupboard with us. When Gus remade the house he put in closets, and this was set out in the warehouse. After I broke my hip I had it cut down so that I can now reach into it from my chair, without bothering anybody. I told Will that when I got done with it he was to have this cupboard. It does n't look as if I were ever to be done with it."

In that cupboard, easy of access, Grandmother kept such treasures as she liked to show to company — the handiwork, for instance, of different grandchildren. For my contemplation she produced from the cupboard a china plate with the picture of Ohio University on it. "That's a souvenir of the home-coming week at Athens in June 1904," she explained. "Oh, here's something else I want to show you. See this chocolate Easter egg. Two strange little girls brought it to me last Easter. I was so pleased. I did n't even know them. Pretty little things! That's what you get for being old!" said Grandmother Brown smilingly.

Certain anxieties connected with disturbances in Mexico, in Europe, and in Washington bore heavily on her spirit at this time. The revolution in Mexico grew more and more acute, and most Americans in business there thought it prudent to leave the country. Frank remained until the spring of 1914, and Grandmother felt uneasy about him. When, at last, he and his family fled from Aguascalientes and, after a circuitous journey by way of Mexico City, the Isthmus of Tehuantepec, and New Orleans, arrived safely in Fort Madison, she was much relieved.

"What a sight they were, poor things!" she told me. "They were only allowed to bring out what they could carry in two suitcases. They had to leave their furniture, their cows, everything except a few clothes. You see, our Navy had fired on a school of Mexican cadets at Vera Cruz. All over Mexico arose the cry, 'Death to Wilson.' On account of the revolutionists, it was impossible for Americans to get back to the States by way of El Paso or Laredo. But, with the help of the British and by payment of a heavy sum to the people who controlled the railroad, our folks at the smelter and other Americans in the neighborhood of Aguascalientes managed to hire a train that took them to Mexico City. The train was guarded and run with the shades all down. Even then, they did n't know but that they would be stopped any minute and held up by bandits. But they got through. On the transports they were packed and crowded together. They were almost a whole month on the way, and on rations all the time. With all those little children! Think of teaching a little two-year-old to chew a piece of corn beef, suck the juice, and then spit it out! They had always been used to good Jersey milk; but they had to lose two fine Jersey cows and a male calf. One of the little girls broke out badly with prickly heat, and when they reached the quarantine station at the mouth of the Mississippi an ignorant official insisted that she had smallpox. But finally they reached Fort Madison, all of them alive and well. Now all the children are in school, except the baby. The very *prettiest* children you ever saw. Just think! all had to be clothed from the skin up, and they are well clothed, too. The two youngest, Carmen and Elizabeth, could not speak a word in English. Now they talk everything. Oh, we cannot *estimate* the loss and worry all this revolution in Mexico has been to Frank."

In the meantime war was declared in Europe and the world was in turmoil. Constance was spending the summer with friends in Thuringia. To provide for her safe conduct home after war was declared was no easy matter. Grandmother Brown shared the anxiety we felt on her account. It seemed best to leave our child in Germany until some trusted friend could be found to escort her back to America. Thirteen months elapsed before a satisfactory arrangement could be made. But, in the meantime, the possibilities of disaster were haunting. Once she was started home by way of Switzerland and Italy, and just then Italy forsook the Triple Alliance for the Triple Entente and plunged into the conflict. Italian trains were requisitioned for soldiers, Italian frontiers closed to foreigners. She had to travel back to her German friends and await more favorable opportunity for passage home. Worst of all, perhaps, was the fact that the postal service was uncertain; letters getting lost; coming through irregularly; mutilated, often, at the hands of the censor; written, for a while, in German only. The cable service was unreliable and expensive. There was a ghastly month when we did not know exactly where our daughter was, whether in Germany, Switzerland, Italy, or on the high seas. We tried to keep the details of our worry from Grandmother Brown.

But in May, just after the sinking of the *Lusitania*, she wrote anxiously: "I want to hear from Constance.

I *wish* she were at home." In June: "Thoughts about her are on my mind day and night." In July: "All Constance's letters have been greatly enjoyed. Thank you for translating them. What an experience for a child! I pray she may reach home in due time, all safe and well. Then, how I would love to hear her tell all about it!" When, in midsummer, Constance was returned to us, Grandmother's rejoicing overflowed: "Oh, my precious child: I wept tears of joy over your card this morning. Our family are all glad. Old black Henrietta came to give me a bath. I told her you had come and she shouted, 'Oh, that's good!' I want to know all about how it was with you after you left Germany, and how long after that before you started home, and about your ocean voyage. Oh, Constance, I have slept better since I don't wake up and wonder where you are."

While watching over the safety of her dear ones in Mexico and Germany, Grandmother Brown's spirit also brooded anxiously, that year, over the affairs of her son in Washington. She knew that he was often subject to attacks from individuals and organizations within and without the government departments who opposed his efforts to introduce business methods into the administration of the public service. Hampered by those who should have helped in the good work instead of hindering it, he asked Congress to make his office — an office which he himself had originated — an independent establishment. Congress honored his request. And then his detractors besought the President not to reappoint him to that office. President Wilson disregarded them and reappointed him. But such battles take their toll of body and spirit, even though they end victoriously. He tried to keep harassing details from Grandmother Brown, but she divined that her son was neither well nor happy.

"My boy Herbie," she wrote, "does he not know that Mother would like to know how business goes with him? I am just as much interested in my children now as when I put them to bed every night and heard them say their prayers. Yes, even greater is my anxiety now than then."

When recognition came at last, she wrote: "I am glad, and I am thankful, too, for all the good fortune that comes to you. I went carefully through the papers you sent until I came to the part about my Herbie. Then I read that over and over. Herbie, I think your business must be *very, very* trying. But do right and fear not. Keep close to God.

"And now I have a little poem that comes just right in your case: —

> "Perish policy and cunning!
> Perish all that fears the light!
> Whether losing, whether winning,
> Trust in God and do the right.
>
> Some will hate thee, some will love thee,
> Some will flatter, some will slight,
> Cease from man and look above thee,
> Trust in God and do the right!"

It was a pleasure to pass on to her every bit of encouragement that came our way. "The newspaper article of November 30 about your work is at hand," she wrote Herbert, as the winter of 1915 was setting in.

"Truly I have reason to be proud of you. But not more than when you were a little child and stood beside me when I measured out milk for you to take to a customer. When I had filled the quart measure, you would always say, 'Now put some more for good measure.' Or, weighing butter, 'Now put on some for good weight.' That spirit pleased me. And when you would rather go without oysters than go into a saloon to get them, I took delight in telling it to my friends. And never a night, while you lived at home, that I did not know where you were. You always sought the best company. How happy I was when I received that letter from Mr. Karnes about you when you were in his law office! He could not praise you more than he did."

On she swept to an estimate of her other sons in this same letter: "And Frank also has been a credit to himself. When I was in Boston, Jennie said to me, 'Aunt Maria, I never think of Frank when a little boy as anything but a little *gentleman*. He is the same this day, and well informed, too.'

"Then there is Gus, who has held the office of mayor six years. He is often called upon to make a speech," she said, "and from all I hear does credit to himself. He has the finest paper mill in all the country, a good ice plant, has made the old home beautiful, and I guess is worth a plenty too, as worth is counted at the bank.

"Then here comes Charlie. The last time I was at his house he had just received a letter from the Agricultural College at Ames, Iowa, inquiring about his method in certain things and saying they would be there, the next week, to take some photographs. I said, 'Charlie, that is a compliment.' 'Oh,' said Charlie, 'they have written to me a number of times, asking about things.' I wanted to know how they found him. He said, 'I suppose they passed by and saw my farm.' Well, Charlie has struggled along, using his own common sense and working hard. For more than twenty years now he has been quite independent.

"And there's your brother Will. He always had the credit of keeping the best lumberyard on the Mississippi. He was county auditor at one time and could have had the office as long as he wanted it. So all my boys have been able to get along without the education which I *longed* so much to give them. May God bless them every one and lead them in the paths of righteousness for His name's sake."

It seems to me, as I read over the letters Grandmother Brown wrote us in 1916, that her spirits were at low ebb that year.

The sadness of life pressed in upon her more, that year, than before or after. She missed Will and Libbie, who had moved to South Dakota to be with Knapp. On February 16 she wrote: "When Will Carleton said,

> Old folks sorrows, aches, and pains,
> Are ofttimes o'er much for their brains,

he told the truth. I have been feeling depressed much of the time during the winter, hearing of many deaths among my relatives and friends. I am thinking that I would like to cross the river and be with the rest of them. But perhaps if anyone were to point a gun at me I would dodge it."

This was the year when Grandmother definitely abandoned all hope of ever being able to walk again.

It was not easy for her to be reconciled to such a sad inevitable. There must have been many times, at that period, when she would even have preferred not to make the effort necessary to go on living, and living cheerfully.

She had taken such pride during 1915 in the way in which she had been able to overcome her minor disabilities — to recover the use of her hand in writing and to steer herself, unaided, about her room. She confidently expected to walk once more. In July 1915, she had written her first letter after the accident. "Until the last two weeks my hand has been perfectly helpless. For many months it lay in my lap, palm up and swollen badly. Now see what I am doing — writing to you! *This* has been given me in answer to *prayer*, and although this writing looks *bad*, I am *oh, so happy* to be able to do it. I write a few words and then rest." A few weeks later, she reported: "I go down stairs by sitting down on the top step and sliding on to the next one, and up by sitting down on the bottom step and putting my hands on the step back of me and boosting, and up I go." And so she set to work with determination early in 1916 to recover the use of her legs also. "I have what Constance used to call 'a surprisement' for you," she wrote. "I believe I am actually learning to walk, even though my legs are drawn up and one shorter than the other. Gus cut the crutches off the right length for me, and when Henrietta gives me my bath she helps me practise. When we began I could bear no weight on my feet at all. My legs were like strings. Now she just goes behind me and holds on to the crutches so they can't fall and lets me walk. I can go five or six steps and then rest, and go another five or six. I think that is wonderful for one almost 89 years old."

But, in November of that same year, she wrote sadly: "For two months I took a treatment to straighten out my legs, hoping by that means to be able to walk. True, it did get my legs almost straight, but I cannot stand alone."

With equal patience, however, and better success, she persevered in compelling her hand not only to writing, but to all of its accustomed tasks. "I put in six hours yesterday doing what I have done in less than two when I had the use of my hand," she wrote. In time it recovered most of its old-time cunning with a needle. But how few there are who, at age eighty-nine, would enforce such self-discipline!

She closed the year on a note of happiness with expressions of satisfaction for our various gifts to her. First, for *The Soul of the Bible* which I had sent her. "I know much more about my Bible," she wrote, "than if I had never broken my hip. I have taken the *Home Department Sabbath School Quarterly* and have, the last two years, studied all the lessons. Thomas à Kempis says it is vanity to desire to live long and not care to live well, and that we all desire knowledge, but what availeth knowledge without the fear of God? I would be willing to live my life over again if I could make it better." Next, she told Herbert that the lace collar he had sent her was beautiful, but added: "It is made to wear with dresses cut low in the neck at front. Now your mother is an old woman, Herbie, and must dress as becomes her age. She may be ever so elegant, but *not* too young. I do appreciate it that Herbie does not think I am old, that he thinks Mother will stay just the same always. Well, I have not grown old at heart."

In 1917, Grandmother celebrated her ninetieth birthday. "The party was a complete surprise to me," she wrote. "I had called it off because I thought it would make too much work. But on the morning of the ninth I was called upon by a reporter from the *Gem City* to tell something about myself. Then came the reporter for the *Evening Democrat*. Then flowers began to come in, and I have never seen so many and so beautiful. Potted plants and cut flowers. Not one *ordinary* bunch. I was quite overcome. I wanted to cry. I asked myself — what can this be? I never did anything to merit all this. In the afternoon, callers commenced coming. Sixty-two were registered and many regrets. It was quite a hand-shaking. By companies the guests were invited to the dining room and served to coffee and good things."

The reporter from the *Evening Democrat* described how Grandmother related interesting anecdotes of happy childhood days, telling her guests that it was just as much fun then to take a ride in an oxcart as it is now to ride in one of the high-power motors. "Mrs. Brown enjoys doing things and keeping busy," he said. "Aside from much reading, she has found time to make four quilts since last July, each composed of 1223 pieces."

One of these quilts Grandmother Brown bestowed on Constance. It is a beautiful thing put together with Irish chain stitch. She apologized to Constance for a little irregularity in the piecing of one corner, — which no one would ever have detected, — saying that she was rather out of practice as she had n't made quilts since Charlie was a baby. As Charlie was then approaching seventy, we thought it not at all strange that she had forgotten just how she made the last one.

Grandmother had two parties that week. The second one was in honor of her chapter of the Daughters of the American Revolution. "I wanted to make the chapter a present," she told me. "I thought it would be nice to give it a facsimile of the old-fashioned tin lantern — 'lanthorn' they called it in those days — that was hung in the Old North Church the night Paul Revere made his famous ride. I wrote to Charl and Jennie about it. Charl hunted all over Boston to find one of those old tin lanthorns for me. Nobody had any. Finally he heard of one up in Laconia, New Hampshire, a lantern that is certainly over a hundred years old. You see it has perforated sides through which the light of the candle inside shines out. That's what Longfellow means by his verse — 'The *checkered* light the lantern makes.' There was candle grease in the bottom of this lantern when it reached me. It had n't been used for years.

"Well, I got dressed up nicely. They put a flag over the entrance to the parlor. The house was beautifully decorated with blooming plants and cut flowers. Among other things was a bowl of ninety yellow jonquils which the chapter had sent me.

"After the business part of the meeting, I asked one of the ladies to read Longfellow's poem, 'The Ride of Paul Revere.' Then the lights were all put out and Sue brought in the lantern and set it in the middle of the table." The reporter for the *Evening Democrat* informs us that "Mrs. Brown made a short talk in which she pointed out that the war in which Paul Revere made his famous ride was waged for the same reasons that we have declared war to-day — Liberty and Freedom. She closed her talk by repeating the Sixty-seventh Psalm, and the words seemed to have acquired beauty from the sweet simplicity of the speaker and the quaint surroundings."

"The chapter decided to have the lantern hung in the Library," Grandmother went on. "One of Gus's men at the mill, who does beautiful lettering, copied what I wrote, and that hangs beside the lantern. I have a picture of Paul Revere's house. I want to have that framed to hang beside the lantern. Maybe, when I'm dead and gone, some of the children will say, 'Mother did that.' I think it's nice to remember how things used to be. That does n't mean I don't want things to change. I believe in progress. But it's well to note what strides we've made."

The two parties took place a few days after the momentous sixth of April on which the United States entered the World War. Like everybody else, Grandmother Brown was stirred by the declaration of war to forgetfulness of her own affairs. She was absorbed for a time in "doing her bit." Lucky the doughboys who wore *her* well-knit socks!

More, probably, than her children was she moved by the emotions that swept over the land. Exposed to the preachments of the press, it was natural enough that in her patriotic soul endorsement of the war as a righteous action should have followed. But she was far less warlike, I am sure, than were most citizens of the Mississippi Valley. True, her simple soul was horrified by what she read of "German atrocities."

She spoke often, with feeling, of a little child whom some visitor had "seen" somewhere near there on a railroad train. Could it have been a Santa Fe train? Or was it, perhaps, a "Q" train? Anyway, "a little Belgian child whose hand had been cut off by the Germans." The child seemed to appear in many places, flitting on ahead always. It is hardly strange that it should have almost crossed dear Grandmother Brown's troubled way.

The worst sorrows of the time were spared her. Strange as it may seem, none of her large family was of age to be affected by the draft. All were either too old or too young. They had all been born, apparently, when Mars was in eclipse. In the Civil War, her husband and son had been rejected. In the Spanish War, her two sons of military age were living in Mexico.

And now, for a third time in her long life, war had passed her softly by.

But she saw how, nevertheless, the World War took its toll of her children in different ways. She saw the added taxes, the higher prices, the new anxieties about health and freedom, about manners and morals. All these things wore on her. As the year 1917 drew to a close she felt despondent, and wrote that she was not making any Christmas presents and hoped we would send none to her. "My temporal wants are well supplied," she said. "There is but one thing I wish to do before I cross the bar. That is to talk or write to you at length — but I have not strength enough now."

With the coming of peace, however, in 1918, she felt happier and stronger. As did all the world.

SHUT-IN

The year 1919 was a difficult one for the families of two of Grandmother's sons. When Frank's wife and oldest daughter lay ill in a Fort Madison hospital and Gus's wife had to go to a Chicago sanitarium, Grandmother considered anxiously how she might lighten the family cares, fearful always that she herself might be a burden. Characteristically, her strength responded to the need. With others around her ailing, we found her alert and cheerful, trying in every way to preserve the balance in the afflicted households.

"I am about the *wellest* one in the family," she wrote us. "The warm weather agrees with me. I have got now so I can use my thimble, and I have crocheted some, too. I have made two white dresses for Frank's little girls, Carmen and Elizabeth — made them as pretty as could be with fine tucks and ruffles, lace and insertion. It was what they were much in need of, and I could help them in that way.

"Sue's illness makes me feel myself a great encumbrance," she went on. "Only a few little things I can do like seeding cherries, shelling peas, stringing beans when they are brought to me. So, considering all things, when I lie down at night I pray that I may awaken on the other side, but I still find myself here, and the family just as pleasant as ever. Gus brings fresh flowers for my room, and here on my little table is a thermos bottle of ice-cold water, and there is the electric fan. In fact, I want for nothing. Everybody is *so* good to me. All things around me are beautiful too. Our yard is a beauty spot with the hedge around it and flowers, flowers, flowers. People stop to look as they pass by."

This was the year when Grandmother found a new

theme for her admiring pen. Having long celebrated her children's and grandchildren's merits, she began to get comfort from dwelling on the good points of her great-grandchildren. She closed the year with an enthusiastic review of her wealth and standing as a great-grandmother. "Adelaide and her husband were here for Christmas dinner," she wrote. "After we were all seated at table, their little boy, David, called out: 'I want to sit by Grandma.' So the move was made and all was lovely. I enclose a picture of Edna's two boys and Olive's youngest girl. (Poor Charlie and Lyde! Olive's death left them broken-hearted.) I have fifteen of these great-grandchildren now, besides my fourteen grandchildren. (Seven of my grandchildren have died.) All these children are above the average in good looks and equal to any in intelligence. No deformity in mind or body. Have I not something to be thankful for? They will all be well educated too."

And so it was that she took satisfaction in gloating over the merits she saw in each generation — in child, grandchild, and great-grandchild — even as a connoisseur might turn over his treasures, calling attention to a fine point here and there, proud of the collection. To others her jewels might seem lacklustre; but she would stake her life on it that they were genuine. It was partly this fierce pride in her handiwork that kept her going beyond the ordinary span.

The year 1920 will always be remembered in the annals of the Brown family as the year when dear Grandmother almost crossed the bar. That anyone, at age ninety-three, could have a severe case of pneumonia, followed by erysipelas, could recover, and, after a while, seem more vigorous than before would certainly be accounted against probabilities. But that is the record that Grandmother left upon the books of 1920.

"Yesterday, Gus and Sue left for Battle Creek," she wrote us on January 13. "They are to spend several weeks there at a fine sanitarium, as Sue was not improving. Then they go to Florida to spend the rest of the winter. Gus is not well either. I shall be lonesome."

The next word we had was that Grandmother had pneumonia. We feared that, at her age, it meant the end. "Gus and Sue were at Battle Creek," said Lizzie, telling the story, "and Rebecca had gone to Waterloo to see a sick brother. It was impossible, at first, to get a nurse. Frank summoned me. He said that she would die. But when Gus got here, he said, 'Not yet.' She seemed to be coming through when erysipelas set in. Her eyes were swollen shut for several days. Her ears were abscessed. Her eardrums burst. The poison of the pneumonia went all through her. She was in a terrible state. She could hardly hear. All her hair came out. She was quite bald and had to wear caps."

All hastened to do what they could for poor Grandmother. But it was a hard pull at age ninety-three. "When she began to get better physically," said Lizzie, "she decided that she did n't *care* to live any longer. That was the hardest time. We had to all help then and coax her back."

"Well, for some time," said Grandmother, "I could neither see nor hear. I would think, 'Now, if I could just wake up on the other shore!' But here I stay still. It was Lizzie pulled me through. She is better than any of the professional nurses with their caps and things. Oh, my hair just combed out, just shed off till I was hairless. Then it came in as curly and nice as could be."

"I should like to have seen you then. Bobbed at ninety-three! They all said it was so becoming. Why did n't you keep it short, Grandmother?"

"Not I! I sent for a barber when it needed trimming. He bobbed me all up, but as soon as my hair grew a little I tucked it up."

Gradually Grandmother Brown got well. But then poor Lizzie came down with pneumonia and had to be sent to the hospital. After everybody was restored, up from bed and back from hospital and sanitarium, the idea began to travel from mind to mind that, in the nature of things, not many years could pass without a break in the family circle. Everybody began to plan for a reunion while there was yet time.

But before that took place another outstanding event occurred in the family history. The Brown paper mill was sold to an Eastern company, owner of a string of paper mills. A good day's business, perhaps, for Gus, but one that made him mournful and sentimental. "When I sold that mill," said he, "I was making a ton of paper the cheapest of anyone in the country. I was sick or I would n't have sold it. If I had n't sold, though, they would probably have built a mill somewhere around here. Competition would n't have bothered me if I had been well, but where they might have had me, of course, was in getting straw. I had a lot of fun making that a good mill, the finest ever. Now I've sold out and have no business.

"I can't bear to go near the mill now. It makes me homesick. You don't know how often I've wished I could show Father that mill as it came to be. When it was n't breaking down every day or two, or when we did n't have to shut down, as we once used to do, until we could lay in another load of straw! When it was just banging along in fine shape, turning out the best possible paper of its kind, turning it out at the cheapest possible price. Well, as Mother is always saying, everything has to come to an end *sometime*."

During 1921, Grandmother seemed stronger, even, than before her illness. She complained of finding it hard to read or write, but at ninety-four had no difficulty in sewing. "Reading hurts my eyes more than sewing," she wrote. "It is difficult for me to see to write and to steady this old jerky hand. But I am fond of my needle, and now that I am compelled to sit here it offers a pleasant pastime. How many lunch cloths I have made I cannot tell, but the largest and finest was for a round dining table. It was for Adelaide. Would that I could show it to you! It was fine indeed, and Gus takes so much interest in my work. It pleases me. This is the way I do. Saturday afternoon I put my work all away, never see it again until Monday; then after I have read a chapter or two and eaten breakfast, made up my bed, put all things to rights about my room, it is nine o'clock. I work until eleven, then lie down until twelve. I belong to the Christian Herald Prayer League which takes a few moments at noon for prayer. My children are not forgotten. After dinner, which is at half-past twelve, I work again. Oh, I forgot one thing. I always take time to look over the morning paper, the *Chicago Tribune*, to see what the contemptible 'Hinglish' are doing to Ireland."

As she sat over her beautiful embroideries, her thoughts were busy planning a reunion of her children in the old home. To have them all visit her again together instead of straggling in at different times was her dream. The more she thought about a reunion, the more she wanted it. Why not a birthday party? She began to tease for it, like a little girl "going on" five instead of an old lady approaching ninety-five.

When Gus's automobile ran into a railroad train one day and he was nearly killed, she was more than ever desirous, after his recovery, to gather her six children about her, and see them once more all together. "When they picked him up, they supposed he was dead," said Grandmother. "Oh, it is my hope and prayer to be the *first* one taken. Of course, *some* one has to go first. Just a little while and we're all gone. No one will even know we've lived. How many know about my grandparents? That was made to be so."

Grandmother's first reunion birthday party took place finally on April 9, 1922, as planned, except that Lizzie was unable to be present. "Such things do not come about often," wrote Grandmother afterward. "That I, at age ninety-five, should sit down with five sons at table, all of us in good health! I did thank God silently. Now, if we should all live another year, I want all my sons' wives to be here with them, *sure*."

Thus began the series of wonderful birthday reunions which gave Grandmother Brown a new lease on life. Through her letters, after the institution was established, ran a genuine purr of contentment.

"I have been sitting here now almost nine years," she wrote a month after the first party. "It does not seem so long. I have so much to be thankful for. Where is there another mother who has so many good children and grandchildren and great-grandchildren? I have had the pleasure of seeing all of them. They are all bright, intelligent children. Then, I have a host of friends who come often to see me. I have a pleasant room and flowers all the time, never less than two or three vases, and the best the market affords to eat, and a good appetite, and everyone is pleasant. To sit here is nothing, after all. I believe I have about the best time of anyone I know.

"Yesterday was Memorial Day. Fort Madison made a greater demonstration than ever before. Old war vets and soldiers with flags, bands of music, scouts, and school children marched past my window. Everybody had their flags out. How thankful we should be that we are Americans."

But, before the time for the second reunion came, Grandmother Brown's heart beat apprehensively for her oldest son. Would there never be a reunion with every child present? "About six weeks ago," she wrote, "your brother Will had a slight paralytic stroke. But a letter from Libbie yesterday says he is much better, has on his clothes and is sitting up. You can imagine the strain of anxiety I have been under."

He improved and was able to attend the birthday party of April 9, 1923, when Grandmother Brown celebrated the ninety-sixth anniversary of her birth. Gus and Sue came hurrying home from a visit to California in time to order the birthday cake. When the great day actually dawned with all present, some instinct of rejoicing made Grandmother don a white summer gown instead of her customary black. So was she photographed sitting among her children. A few weeks later, radiating the bliss that the occasion had brought her, she wrote: "Herbie, my dear precious son, God's gift to me in my old age! It was kind of you to try to do something to help my hearing. Though the apparatus did no good, I thank you just the same. I don't worry about not hearing so well, I think about the multitude of things I have to be thankful for and be happy about. My family well disposed, all provided with their own homes with plenty of everything to make them comfortable. I can do no less than thank God and be happy and busy myself with embroidery. I love to make pretty things for people. They seem so pleased with them, and it keeps me out of mischief."

Among the pretty things that came to being under Grandmother Brown's skillful fingers before the next reunion was a gift for the President of the United States. She wrote on November 20, 1923:—

HERBERT AND FAMILY,

I am writing to tell you that I have embroidered a dresser scarf for President Coolidge and his wife, Mrs. Coolidge. I will send it by express to you and wish you to take it to the White House. It will be enclosed in a wrapper to you. Remove the outside wrapper and find the inside directed to the President and Mrs. Coolidge. The following is what will be written on the package:—

My friends think it is wonderful that I can do work of this kind at my age. I am ninety-six years old. My father, Eben Foster, was born in Sudbury, Rutland County, Vermont, your native State. I have five sons, all Republicans. I am sending this in care of my youngest son, Herbert D. Brown, resident of Washington, D. C.

Sincerely,
Maria D. Brown.

This pen writes along sometimes good enough. Then it refuses to make a mark and with my shaky hand I make bad work. I hate to send my writing to the President. Perhaps the pen and I are both worn out, but I will not give up until I have to.

Mother.

"How did you happen to think of making something for President Coolidge?" I asked her.

"Why, a friend told me that she had read of a woman who had knitted a wash rag for President Wilson. She was eighty years old and her friends thought it remarkable that she could knit a wash rag! I thought that if a woman of eighty could knit a wash rag for a Democratic President it behooved one of ninety-six to make something more than a wash rag for a Republican President. Besides, most of my Grandfather Foster's children were born in Vermont."

When, in 1924, Grandmother Brown celebrated the ninety-seventh anniversary of her birth, it was my very pleasant privilege to participate in the celebration. Writing to Constance, I said: "As we alighted from our train, Gus and Will stepped up to greet us. 'I'll have to kiss you old fellows,' I told them, and that's the way they looked — like 'old fellows,' though it was hard to realize that Gus is now seventy years old and Will nearly seventy-eight. Remembering how alert and vigorous Will used to be, I could not help but notice how much more slowly he moved, his once-aggressive shoulders a little drooping. As for Gus, the old melancholy drollery dropped from him in familiar fashion.

"They drove us up to the house. There on the curb, awaiting us, stood Knapp and his bright-eyed little girl, Carolyn — Knapp whom I had last seen as a boy in his early teens, smiling 'Brother Brown.' Still smiling, but with deep lines in his face that the smiles had carved. 'Forty-three I am, by golly!' he acknowledged.

"As we entered the house, Libbie came down the stairs to greet us — 'Will's Libbie,' as Grandmother so often called her to distinguish her from 'Sister Libbie.' Not far behind came Becky, mistress of the establishment in Sue's absence. Seeing her silvery hair, I suddenly realized that Libbie is now an old lady.

"Greetings exchanged downstairs, we went above to see Grandmother. There she sat in her rocking-chair, facing the door, a look of expectancy on her face, an expression of dancing happiness in her keen old eyes. As far as I can see, she is mentally as alert as at any time since I have known her, and physically, except that she is lame and her hearing is less acute, she has changed very little in a quarter of a century. A little thinner of form, a little more spirituelle of face, a little more tender of phrase perhaps.

"That evening, as we sat in Grandmother's room, came 'Frank's folks.' And then Lizzie's family, three generations strong. And then the train brought Charlie, but alone and unattended, since Lyde is not well and Edna too busy. Charlie is the youngest for his age of anyone in the family. Living all his life outdoors, he is weathered to a beautiful slim hardness. Instead of his family, he brought with him a mammoth turkey, which Edna had been fattening for some time against the joyful celebration. Sue had sent to Kansas City for a fillet of beef, so there was an abundance of provision for the birthday feast. While we were having an exciting political discussion in Grandmother's room — Lizzie, Charlie, Will, and I being the chief disputants — Libbie came to the door and beckoned me out to ask which I would vote for: Turkey or Beef? I cast my vote for the Turkey, and Turkey it was. After the callers had gone, Herbert and I heard noises in the kitchen that tempted us to peep in. There stood the housekeeper with Libbie on one side and Becky on the other putting the finishing touches on that Bird. I never saw such a fowl. I am sure it must have weighed thirty pounds. When it was stuffed and trussed, Libbie smeared it all over *thick* with lard and then encased it in waxed paper, so that it needed no basting and came on to the table a beautiful golden brown. When the birthday party came off we did full justice to that wonderful bird.

"The next morning there was good news. Another great-grandson had arrived in the night for Grandmother Brown. Gus greeted us smilingly, and told the long-distance tidings just received from Harry —

Gus who, up to that hour, had been most of the time rather restless and obviously distracted. Adelaide, who was married on Grandmother's eighty-fifth birthday, has now given her a great-grandson on her ninety-seventh birthday. Would more courteous efficiency have been possible?

"Happy with relief, Gus got out his Packard and drove us down to Keokuk to refresh our Washington and South Dakota eyes with a sight of the Big Dam that is one of the great power projects of our country.

"'Just think of having the washing, ironing, sweeping, baking, all done for you by electric hands!' commented Grandmother with awe. 'So different from the housekeeping of pioneer times.'

"There followed, the next day, inspection of Gus's pig farm in the Green Bay bottom lands.

"'Do you know,' said Grandmother, 'that pigs *like* to be clean if they have a chance? Gus is very proud of the tiled wallows he has installed for his pigs.'

"And a third day we went to see the new High School in which Frank and his family have such pride, because Frank is a member of the School Board that brought it into being. A fine little plant it is, too.

"'You'd think he'd built it, brick by brick,' laughed Grandmother.

"And another day we inspected the penitentiary and the ten-cent store and the paper mill. And every day some of us sat, knee to knee, with Grandmother, sewing and gossiping and talking politics. With a presidential campaign pending, subjects like Farm Relief and Prohibition kept coming into the conversation. I asked Grandmother Brown about her voting.

"'I never was a suffragette,' she answered. 'I never wanted to vote, would rather not. I thought that if there was anything the men could do by themselves we'd better let them do it. I have always felt this way, that it is a woman's duty to make a happy home and teach her children to vote the Republican ticket. If they keep their homes right and teach their children well, they have enough to do. But, since women can vote these days, I always exercise my privilege. I see to it that there's one vote right, anyway. They always come here and get my vote. They think I'm worth it, you see. Two men, one a Democrat and one a Republican, come and give me a ballot to mark.'

"'And how do you mark it?' I queried.

"'Well, since Dan'l has gone, I have no one to direct me in political matters. I don't read enough to judge about affairs. I don't feel capable of deciding, so I vote the way Gus does.'

"'Why not the way Frank does or the way Will does? Or you might ask Herbert.'

"'Will and Herbert are too far away. I have n't asked Frank, but I suppose he's a good strong Republican. He naturally would be, because he belongs to that kind of a breed. I'm a dyed-in-the-wool Whig-Republican myself and so was Dan'l. Now, let's leave politics out of it!'"

The momentum of that wonderful birthday party carried Grandmother Brown contentedly through her ninety-eighth year. That year closed also with a family party attended by all her children.

When we assembled on April 9, 1926, to celebrate the ninety-ninth anniversary of Grandmother Brown's birth, she and all her children were in fair condition. The "in-laws" too were all there. With great joy and gratitude we gathered around her. "Is it possible I have started on my hundredth year?" she said to us. "Just think! Dan'l would be a hundred and four. We would have celebrated the eightieth anniversary of our wedding day. Maybe I'll have to keep right on staying. I don't know what God is going to do about me. I said to Libbie, 'I don't see what I'm being kept here for,' and she said, 'They haven't got Heaven in order for you yet, Grandma.' Libbie is always teasing me about my love of order."

I stayed on awhile after the others had gone, and Grandmother and I talked things over.

"Perhaps my broken hip has been a blessing," said Grandmother. "Certainly my life has been prolonged through this disability. I have had to rest and take things easy these last thirteen years. I was getting *so* tired. I would be just done out after making griddle cakes for Nellie. Breaking my hip, I was forced to sit down and behave. You know what James Whitcomb Riley said: 'This world would be all right if folks would only behave.'"

I looked around Grandmother Brown's room and marked how it showed where her loyalties had been centred. From her windows I saw the views of bluff and river, of church spire and garden. On her walls I noted her pictures. Her mother. Her children. Her granddaughter, Carrie, blithe and gay as she once was, looking at us over her shoulder. Pictures of Constance at the time when Grandfather had such joy in her. Gus and his first grandson.

I saw Grandmother looking at the picture of her

oldest son taken in his early manhood. Suddenly she exclaimed: "My boy Willie! He was a nice-looking young man." Then, proudly: "All my sons are good-looking. That picture was taken in Milwaukee when he was working there with Charlie Stevenson. I recognize that coat with the velvet collar. Here I had a card on my birthday from Charlie, an old man now, eighty-three years of age, living in California."

And I saw her look up to the enlargement of her youngest boy's scowling baby face. "How Herbie hated to have that first picture taken! But Lizzie was so proud of the pretty little coat she'd made for him."

Here, pictures of her first and last-born sons! Over there, reminders of the first and last-chosen Presidents of her country. George Washington on his knees at Valley Forge! The letter that Calvin Coolidge wrote her in acknowledgment of the bureau scarf she embroidered for him, framed and hanging up. The slender shaft of the Washington Monument. A picture of the McGuffey Elms on the Athens campus. A view of Jennie's cottage beside the Mystic Lakes near Boston. A painting of the D. A. R. spinning wheel done for her by my Constance. Joyce Kilmer's poem, "I think that I shall never see a poem lovely as a tree," embossed and framed for easy reading. "Charlie copied that," she told me. "He liked it." And a framed essay of Lucy W. Peabody's called, "From a Carpenter's Shop."

I watched Grandmother as she moved about her small domain. It was hard to catch her off duty. When I opened her door softly in the morning I would find her up and dressed; sometimes with her bed made and the room in order, though the sun was scarcely up; waiting for her breakfast. "I can't eat breakfast when my room is in a tumble," she said. "I only have to go round the bed twice to make it, but it takes practice to do it right, sitting on a roller chair." One morning I found her staring into the cherry tree outside her window. She said: "Oh, when the leaves are out, I think how beautiful the trees are; when the trees are bare, I think how nice it is to see the houses and the people coming and going."

After breakfast she would lie down again. About nine o'clock, just as others were settling to work, she took a nap. "Well, by the time I've made my bed, and combed my hair, and done all my primping, I'm tired," she explained. "You see, all my young days I had to get up early, and now I can't forget it." In her little chair she would fly across the room to her couch. "No, there can't anybody help."

"Yes, I slept as sound as a nit," she would tell you when she wakened. Refreshed by her nap, she would rise and read a chapter in the New Testament. "I've started several times to read the Old Testament, but before I get very far I see such dreadful stories in it about war and other terrible things that I give it up. I like the Psalms, though. My favorite is the Sixty-seventh. That takes in all the nations of the earth. I'm interested in them all having a good time. I committed that to memory. I'll say it for you if you like."

She said it.

"More people have committed the Twenty-third than any other."

She repeated that.

"In the New Testament I like the twelfth chapter of Romans. Adelaide committed that to memory when she was a little girl. Here, read it aloud to me, beginning with the ninth verse. 'Let love be without dissimulation. Abhor that which is evil; cleave to that which is good.' There! That's the whole story," she said with emphasis as I finished with 'Be not overcome of evil, but overcome evil with good.' That's a funny expression: 'in so doing thou shalt heap coals of fire on his head.' You've heard of the darky who said, 'I 'se tried hot water on his head. I never has tried coals o' fire.'

"I study the lessons in the Westminster Home Department Quarterly. The lessons are all explained — as they understand it. Oh yes, I like the Quarterly. It all agrees with my childhood teachings. The greatest blessing of my life was my early Christian training. But I'm not sectarian. What that early training was can all be summed up in the words: 'Do right and fear not.' Hard to know what is right? Well, in my little narrow way of going I have n't found it very difficult to determine what was right. Have I never felt any doubt? No, I never had the least feeling that way. It seems to me so simple. Just 'Love God and keep His commandments.' Why, if you love God, of course you will *want* to keep His commandments.

"And the greatest of all commandments is Love. No need for a Ku Klux Klan then. The Klan was a good-for-nothing thing in Civil War days. It is now. It tortured and killed our soldiers. It worked under disguise. I have no use for them — the dirty set. They must put on those masks. I think that is contemptible. Why, we never worship God behind a mask. They try to terrorize everyone. I hope they'll fade out. People that pretend to be patriotic — how can they belong to the Klan? A friend told me that out in Oklahoma City every single minister belonged to the Klan. Is n't that dreadful? We don't want secret things. We want all to be open and above board. Things done on the sly with a hood over your face — no, no! I don't approve of that in government or religion or anything else.

"I belong to the Christian Herald Prayer League. At noon every day we take three minutes to pray. There are so many things to ask for and so many things to be thankful for that three minutes is n't long enough. What do I want to ask for? Why, dear me, with all my big family, can't you see how much there is to pray for?

"Prayers do avail. We must have faith. That is the hardest thing for me. George Washington had faith, even in his darkest hour at Valley Forge."

Sometimes, when callers came, the talk swerved to the costumes and customs of the modern world, its manners and morals. Extremes annoyed Grandmother. "I never wore a large hoop skirt," she said. "I had a small one once. I never had a bustle. We used to gather our skirts in the back in deep pleats so that the material stood out a good deal. That's all the bustle I ever had. Corsets I never liked. Those I did wear were homemade — had bone eyelets made by punching the goods with a stiletto and drawing the cloth smoothly around the bone."

"What's the matter with women nowadays?" she would burst out sometimes as she looked over the photogravure section of a Sunday paper. "Having their pictures taken with nothing on but what would be a clout around their middle or something that shows their shape! Makes me wish I could be a cow instead of a woman!

"And how the girls sit nowadays! How can they *bear* to? A lady should never cross her legs in company. If immodesty is n't immoral, what is? I don't understand.

"As I look over my life," said Grandmother thoughtfully, "I see many things I would change if I could. But in the main I feel that I have kept the faith. I 've done the best I could with the light I had. Nothing great to boast of — just my proper duties as they came along. What's that to anyone? Why are you putting all these things down, child?

"I 'm proud of the family I 've reared. I wanted my children to go to the finest schools. Dan'l and I were in harmony on all subjects except that one. I wanted to give the children more education, but he said that if they wanted it they 'd get it. They 've made out somehow. Pretty well, too! As Herbie said to me one day, 'Five sons, Mother, and none of them in jail!'" She laughed, and then said soberly, "I feel very sorry for mothers whose sons go to jail. Poor, poor things! Most of them can't help it if their sons go wrong.

"Then all of my grandchildren are nice. Not a black sheep — no, nor even a lame duck — among them. Oh, I have to brag a little," she said, laughing and tossing her head proudly. "All my children and grandchildren and great-grandchildren are very remarkable. If they 've not been to the finest schools, at least they 've been reared in good homes. Circumstances have much to do with our lives. But character has more. And character is made in homes. Every child should be made to realize that he has his own character to make, that no one else can make a name for him. There are certain things no one can hide — his financial condition and his personal character. Not for long!

"You want to know how I explain my length of years? A good inheritance, I guess. I've never had any particular rules of health. I have always avoided extremes — that's the main thing. In eating, for instance. But one of my worst faults was overworking. I was ambitious. I never said, 'I can't do it'; I just took right hold. Down to the time Herbert was born I worked too hard. That was n't right, especially at childbearing time. I began that pretty young, too. I am less than twenty years older than Will. And then, in twenty months, there was another baby. Birth control? Babies more widely spaced? Yes, that should be so. Just think! I was washing, ironing, cooking, and having babies too. That was too much. I'd just shove the tubs aside and get dinner for the men. And then always ready for company! Dan'l was always inviting home to dinner someone who came to the store. We can use ourselves up too early just as we can wear out a garment. When I went to Ames a neighbor said, 'If ever I saw a picture of health, it was you as a bride.'

"Just think! Dan'l never had but two pair of pants after we were married, until we moved to Fort Madison, that I did n't make. I was married Thursday and the following Monday I began to make him a pair. The cloth was so thick that I had to go through it three times for each stitch. I'm not bragging. You're asking for information and I'm telling you. I said to Gus one time: 'I'd like to have a cord stretched to hold all the clothes I've made; I think 't would stretch from the prison to the mill.' 'Yes, and back again,' he said. At any rate, the garments I fashioned were always well made. I like to make things look comely. I did fairly good housekeeping, too. I'm sure I've baked enough biscuits to make the Great Pyramid. To keep house well, too, is to know where things are. Each article in my house had its place. I never had to hunt for things.

"I soon learned that if I wanted to keep well while I was working so hard I'd have to be careful about my diet. I learned not to eat when worried or tired. That time Gus was so sick with typhoid I couldn't digest anything heavy. I lived on milk — we had plenty of it. When I had worked overmuch I'd go to bed without my supper. Then in the morning I'd get up ready for breakfast. I learned to stop eating before I was full. I made it a habit, after I got Henrietta, to lie down about half an hour before eating, so that I could come to my meals rested.

"I have never eaten much meat. When very young, I couldn't eat it at all. At the Brice House old Mr. Brice used to be very nice to me. He would sometimes eat with us. Once he cut up a piece of steak for me, but I wouldn't touch it. Mr. Hatch called me back to the table, saying, 'Eat that meat.' I ate it, but my mother said to him, 'Let that be the last time you demand such a thing. A child shouldn't eat meat if his stomach does n't call for it.'

"We had a great advantage in our youth from being

out of doors so much. We had a healthy start. Our playgrounds were so roomy, our swing such an invitation to other children. We had apples the year round. We grew up in freedom.

"Mental attitude? Yes, that's most important for health. At times I've grieved too much, I know. Things took me pretty hard sometimes, but what can't be cured must be endured. And at such times I have had a habit of going off by myself to think things over, to turn to God. On the farm, I used sometimes, when tired and discouraged, to take my baby and go to sit among the cattle, smell their sweet breaths, try to breathe deeply and calm myself.

"I don't know about staying here another year," said Grandmother. "As long as I can help myself, it's all right. But if I can't make my bed or comb my hair I shan't want to stay. Now, I've lived ninety-nine years. That's none too long to prepare to live forever and ever. We can hardly think what that means.

"They talk about Heaven being paved with gold. Who knows anything about it? I'd prefer green grass. It says in the Bible, 'In my house are many mansions.' That means something for homes. No marriage or giving in marriage? Well, I'm glad of that, too. I like that idea. We shan't know how it is till we get there. But I believe it will be better than we can imagine. Oh, I don't imagine that things will be so different there. We'll not be all messed up together, but live in families, with interests, too, such as we had here. That's the way, at least, it appears to me.

"Some people believe in baptism as essential to salvation. I don't worry about babies not being baptized. Jesus said, 'Let them come unto me!' There is nothing in the Bible to warrant a belief in infant baptism. Jesus was n't baptized until he was a man, and then he was immersed. You can think of your baby and I of mine as waiting for us, wherever they are. Do you remember how Beatrice told you, when she was dying, that you must brace up?"

"Yes — only she said 'brave up.' 'Don't weep, Muddy. It's nuffin about.' She meant, 'There's nothing to cry about.'"

"I 've thought of this so many times," went on dear Grandmother Brown. "I wonder if my little ones and Beatrice get together and know their relationship."

As the day drew to a close I used to watch Grandmother's preparations for the night.

Getting undressed and getting to bed were a ritual. Every article in the room had to be just where it belonged before she began to retire. The blankets were pinned together according to some scheme that prevented slipping. The spread was doubled back just so, the extra blanket folded in its destined place. Her nightcap awaited her under her pillow, the *proper* pillow. Her handkerchief, her bed shoes, her little shawl, all were disposed in a certain reasonable order against all possible contingencies of the night. "No one can help me," she would say gayly. "I know how every strap and button goes. Bessie's little girl said, 'Did n't Grandmother look nice with her teeth out and her night bonnet on?' Well, good night, everybody!"

XI

THE CENTENNIAL

NUMEROUS interests claimed Grandmother Brown during the last year of her great century. Unfortunately, one dear solace of her days had to be relinquished — her needlework. Her precious eyesight must be saved for reading and for occasional letter-writing. At first she mourned her lost occupation, the joy of working for others and seeing something beautiful grow beneath her skillful fingers. "How long do you suppose I'll have to sit here?" she would sometimes ask with a patience that went to the heart. When the suggestion was first made that she could knit without taxing her eyesight, she seemed indifferent, but later, in conspiracy with Santa Claus, she knitted five lovely white shawls — a very considerable chore for a woman on the eve of her hundredth birthday.

"See, I wore a corn on the end of my forefinger," she said. "Fifty balls of yarn I knitted into shawls last winter. And I did n't drop a single stitch!"

"No, nor get a single spot on all that white wool," I told her with appreciation.

In her hundredth year she developed, for the first time, an interest in the radio. "I must tell you that Gus has put a radio in my room," she wrote, "and I went to Sunday School this morning and shall hear good sermons now." A previous attempt to interest her in radio entertainment had failed; she had been oversensitive, in the earlier stages of the invention, to the disturbing "static."

Before Grandmother Brown was crippled she saw two movies. She talked about them with enthusiasm, crude as they doubtless were to what has since been developed. "One was the story of 'The Prodigal Son,' she said; "only he did n't come back home in rags, but driving in a splendid coach. The other was a series of sacred pictures. I remember, particularly, 'The Flight into Egypt.' There were Joseph and Mary, and the cow looking as natural as life — pulling out the straw and chewing away — with the baby looking on."

During her hundredth summer Grandmother enjoyed several long automobile rides. "When Nellie came," she told me, "we drove down to Charlie's. What a fine time we did have! Why, that thirty-mile drive just shook me up enough to make me feel good." But she was not to be weaned away for any length of time from her own bay window in town to residence in Gus's cool summer home on Black Hawk Heights. "Yes, I know it's beautiful up there," she would tell you. "I love the view of the river. And they have more birds on the bluff than down here. But I have to be waited on up there. The beds are a different height from my chair and someone has to lift me up and down. No, I'm better off down here where I can do things for myself."

And so she sat, summer as well as winter, content in her old homestead, with doors wide open to the town. "People don't need to knock," she said. "My friends just walk in the front door and up the stairs to my room. I'm always glad to see them. If they find me asleep they go away. And if no one comes I can sit in my window and watch the people pass. At all times I can help myself here, except only that someone has to bring my meals to me. When the housekeeper took her vacation, last summer, Marta and Carmen came to stay with me. Their young friends kept coming in and all were good to me."

"And you did n't go to the circus last summer?" she was asked. "No, I have n't seen a circus for two years," she answered. "Gus wheeled me down to Front Street, in 1925, to see the parade. I told him that there were just two things I wanted to see — the Indians and the elephants. I love to look at elephants, though when I look at their loose dark skin I always think of Herbert's disappointment at the first one he ever saw. When they brought him home from the circus he was plainly downcast, and when I inquired the reason he burst out: 'What for do they keep those dirty overalls on the efalunt? You can't see his hair at all.' "

Even without the circus, Grandmother — thanks to visiting and knitting, radio and reading — got through the summer very pleasantly. At times, however, what she read grieved her greatly. The daily papers brought tidings of disastrous floods. On September 16 she wrote: "The present situation here at this time is *so* distressing. I can think of nothing else. We have had *rain, rain, rain,* until the whole Mississippi Valley and all east and west of it are afloat. Where the Des Moines River empties into the Mississippi, the river is twenty miles wide, covering thousands of acres, destroying crops, and wrecking homes, and it is so cold — oh, *so* cold. Perhaps you have read about it in your papers. But to be in it is to know it. It will cost Gus thousands of dollars. The levees five or six miles below his farm broke and hundreds of men worked there all day last Sunday. Oh, I cannot write. The present state of affairs here makes me nervous, I guess, or maybe I am getting old."

Later in the fall, Grandmother became uneasy on another score. "I don't see why I don't hear from Willie," she fretted. "I wrote him on his birthday and not a word has he answered. It is n't like him."

And then they had to tell her. That, on the eve of his eightieth birthday, Will had had a second stroke, that he had rallied and was slowly but steadily improving, and planned to be with her on April 9, when she would celebrate her hundredth birthday.

Grandmother took the news sadly but philosophically. "Willie is an old man," she said. "Perhaps his time has come. If he improves, it will be wonderful to have another reunion. But if he dies I do not want to celebrate my hundredth birthday. I do not want to see an empty chair in the circle."

Throughout the winter Will continued to improve.

With help, he was able to move from bed to chair and chair to bed. He dwelt on the thought of the family reunion. He talked about it in the happy hours of visiting with the kinsfolk who made the long journey to Sioux Falls to see him again while yet they knew that visiting was possible. Charlie, who so seldom left his own dooryard, went to see him, and the two old brothers — only twenty months apart — lived over again their youth together. Herbert went from Washington and Gus from Fort Madison. The younger generation went, too, — Dan and Zetta all the way from Topeka and Adelaide's husband up from Marshalltown, — all eager to cheer "Uncle Will," the first of Grandmother Brown's adult children to whom Death had plainly signaled. And, best of all, came Lizzie, good old scout that she always is, anxious to give a lift over the hard ruts in the road, expert in helpfulness.

"Those two were always so harmonious," sighed Grandmother Brown, thankfully. "And Lizzie's such a splendid nurse. I'm glad she could go to Will."

"We've had the best visit, Will and I," Lizzie told us, later, when she joined the family at Grandmother's birthday party. "I went to him, last fall, as soon as I heard that he was ill. And since Christmas I've been with him continuously. Oh, we've talked over all the days of our childhood and youth. 'Do you remember this?' he'd say. And 'Do you remember that?' I'd ask. We have n't missed a thing."

When the first week of April came, Will was preparing for the journey. "If I must die, why not in Fort Madison?" he would say if ever anyone suggested that it was not wise to make the exertion. Lizzie went on ahead. And then, on April 6, another stroke put him to bed. Even then he made them understand that he wanted to go to the reunion.

In the meantime, Grandmother was happily making plans for the celebration of her birthday. Informed only that Will had decided it would be imprudent, in view of his uncertain health, to attempt a long journey at that time of the year, she accepted the situation hopefully, saying, "Yes, it will be pleasanter for him to come in the summer. That is something to look forward to."

"Will's not coming!" was almost the first word we heard as we tumbled off the long train that brought us from the East. Kinsfolk rose from all sides to greet us, to convey us to Grandmother's side. Constantly, during the next two days, her old face was turned, expectantly, toward the door. "My precious boy! My little Constance! Cousin Angie — how nice of you to come all the way from Woodbury! And Jennie and Charl from Boston! And Nellie from Athens! Lizzie's children from Kansas and Illinois — every single one coming, even her four in-laws and her eight grandchildren! All Frank's children will be here, too, even the two college girls and the first grandchild, Edward's baby boy. And you must see John, Adelaide's second boy, born three years ago, on my birthday. If only Will's folks could be here now! And Charlie has to leave Lyde and Edna at home, — neither of them is well, — but he'll bring Olive's daughter Ruth with him."

Her room filled up, and everybody visited — with Grandmother and with each other. Calmly at times; more often with excitement and exclamation, as cousins who had not met since childhood clasped hands again.

Grandmother the centre of it all, extending greetings, receiving gifts, exchanging caresses, talking, laughing, explaining! "No, Will's not coming now. He did n't dare undertake the trip. He'll come in the summer. We'll have a good visit then." Then, "This lovely thing for me? How good of you!"

"How well you look, Grandmother!" we told her. "And how pretty your room is with the fresh wallpaper and the new rug and the spick-and-span white curtains and all the lovely flowers!"

"Just look at my bedspread!" she proudly urged. "I made it myself. The pillowcases, too! All my work!"

That night before the great day there was a buffet supper at Bessie's little house, with much music and merriment and practising of songs for the next day. For the benefit of their elders, Lizzie's various grandchildren showed how they were keeping up the family tradition of song, Dan's children playing the piano with the *sang-froid* of veterans, Bessie's three girls singing their mother's compositions as if such performances were a matter-of-course obligation. "Why did n't Ruth bring her violin?" asked someone. "Robert's learning the violin too," piped up another child.

The cold April showers held back for Grandmother's centennial. Her day dawned clear, if not bright, amid a week of heavy downpour. One could believe that spring, at last, was on the way.

Birthday greetings began early. Although one of the oldest towns of the Middle West, Fort Madison had never before had an opportunity to honor a centenarian. At ten o'clock, the hour when Grandmother was born, the city bells and factory whistles proclaimed, by order of Mayor Tower, their joy in wishing her a happy birthday. Church bells added their jubilant clamor, Protestant and Catholic bells alike. Dear Grandmother got a big thrill, as did we all, from the three minutes of riotous sound. "But then," she said, naïvely, "I really don't believe I have a single enemy in all this town and I know that I have many friends. The people of Fort Madison have been very good to me. Their loving-kindness makes me very happy."

First, a radio concert came through the air from Davenport, the announcer telling all listeners that in Fort Madison a sweet old lady was celebrating her centennial and listening in at the morning concert. And then the boys of the high-school band called at her home and were escorted upstairs to the hall outside her room, where they played several selections. Afterward they crossed her threshold and each shook her hand. "I made them a little speech," she told me happily. "Such nice young boys!"

Presents poured in. Telegrams and letters came also from old friends, tributes from business associates of her sons whom she had never met, greetings from clubs and associations. "Just see!" she exclaimed. "Here's a letter come by air mail. Is n't that wonderful? I think of the rhyme about Darius Green and his flying machine. They laughed a good deal then, because flying would n't work, but they would n't laugh now. And here's a note from Charlie Stevenson, recalling days at the farm. That long table, and Dan'l asking the blessing! And then, just as soon as he had finished, Sister Ann shouting, 'Amen! Who'll have the biggest potato?' Oh, Ann always *was* a case! Oh dear, oh dear! A telegram, too, signed 'Barsha's boy' — his grandmother was my cousin."

Rapidly the room took on the aspect of a débutante's boudoir. The Ladies' Aid, The Missionary Society, and the Social Union of the Presbyterian Church each remembered her with floral tributes. The King's Daughters sent her a hundred sweet peas. The Daughters of the American Revolution gave her a potted plant. The laundryman wrote his felicitations, and a watchman at the ice company sent her flowers. The man who cuts the grass contributed a piece of delicious cake from his own lunch basket. A colored messenger in the departmental service at Washington bestowed on her a picture of the Lincoln Memorial. But of all the gifts and greetings none meant so much to her as the telegram from South Dakota: "Dear Mother and All: Congratulations on one hundred summers to you. Wish we could have all been with you on such a rare occasion. Your boy Willie and family."

She might, not unnaturally, have forgotten her nap that exciting morning. But she did not. When the time came, she shooed everybody out of the room and composed herself for slumber. When she awoke, she dressed herself handsomely, unaided, in black lace for her birthday party.

"Why, Grandmother," I said, "I thought you wanted to be dressed in the black satin you wore at Adelaide's wedding! And she's brought the fichu for you to wear."

"Yes, I know," she answered. "But I found that I would have to have the black satin altered if I wore it again. What's the use of bothering people?"

And indeed it would have been a carping critic who

could have found any fault with Grandmother's appearance when she was fully dressed. On her feet the new slippers with their smart tulle bows which Adelaide had given her; at her breast the lovely corsage of orchids which Cousin Angie had brought her all the way from Philadelphia; about her shoulders the rich silk shawl with its lavender embroideries which Cousin Frankie Golden had sent her from Indianapolis. "The Fosters are all proud. They like their Sunday clothes," Grandmother once told me. And at age one hundred she herself had her pride in looking nice.

"You are beautiful, Grandmother," I told her.

"My child, you've kissed the Blarney stone. Beautiful — with all these wrinkles?"

"Yes, your bones are beautiful, Grandmother — the bones of your skull and brow and nose. The way your head rises from your shoulders is beautiful. The expression in your eyes is lovely, too."

About one o'clock the guests began to gather in the lower rooms of the house. Six tables were spread for the birthday feast. Children, grandchildren, great-grandchildren, cousins, and in-laws, we made a company of forty-two.

When all was ready, a son and grandson picked up her chair and bore Grandmother down the stairs. At the foot, she was carried between an aisle of great-grandchildren who sang, kindergarten-fashion, "Happy Birthday, Dear Grandma, to You!"

She was seated at the centre of the long hostess table in the dining room, her own born children grouped around her, their wives attending; Gus presiding at one end, Sue at the other; Grandmother's one daughter sitting opposite her, the oldest son present at her right, the youngest at her left; the three visiting cousins having seats of honor beside Gus and Sue, the rest of us mixed in between. The decorations followed a scheme of pink and white. The centrepiece was a gift from a noted candy manufacturer of Boston, a fragile ornament made to look like a great rose, its graceful petals stretching halfway across the table, a single pink taper rising above the bloom. "Lift the petals and there's candy enough to supply a multitude!" explained Grandmother with appreciation. "And just think, with all its delicacy, Jennie and Charl conveyed it a thousand miles in perfect condition!"

In the bay window of the dining room a long narrow table was laid for the nine youngest guests, all under twelve. There Bessie's pair of little girls kept company with three brace of small boys, Dan's two, Lynn's two, and Adelaide's two, with Frank's seven-year-old, Billy, thrown in for good measure. And at the other four tables in the parlor the guests were grouped according to their generation, the great-grandchildren of high-school age at one table with grandchildren of college age and of middle age at other tables. And so it was that, seeing so many, Grandmother had hardly a chance to dwell on the thought that her first-born was absent. "Herbert said to me," I afterward heard her tell a friend, "'Just see, Mother, what you have started!' And I want to tell you that, as I looked over the company, I was not a bit ashamed of my work!"

As soon as all were seated, Herbert asked his mother to say the blessing and to say it loud, so that all could hear. The admonition was scarcely needed, for the strength of Grandmother's voice was one of the marvels of her personality. A moving prayer she made, with thanks to God, first of all, for music — the children's singing having stirred her heart; then thanks for family and friends, for favors of the past and future; a plea for "guidance in ways of righteousness"; a prayer for reunion in Heaven, where, nevermore, partings shall be. When she had finished, all sang, some of us with parched throats and wet eyes —

> "My country, 't is of thee,
> Sweet land of liberty!"

The merciful reaction followed. Delicious food. The cheerful din of many voices and dishes. The fragrance of savory meats and steaming coffee.

Between the courses we sang, under the skillful leadership of Bessie, who, with a pitch pipe in her hand, was seated at a table whence she could survey all the rooms. Grandmother liked her singing without accompaniment and thus it was we gave it to her. Old songs she and her Dan'l had been used to sing together in singing school, songs they sang with their children in an Ohio village, on an Iowa farm, about their Fort Madison base-burner.

A joy it was to watch Gus at the head of the long table — to see how the years dropped from his shoulders and his countenance, how his back straightened, his head came up, his voice boomed out, and his tongue carried on the words trippingly, though the younger voices sometimes halted.

> "Say, darkies, hab you seen ole Massa,
> Wid a moustache on his face?"

Grandmother beamed her approval. Opposite her, Lizzie, who had said, "At another reunion, I wish we could get together and sing as we used to do," sang lustily until Grandmother exclaimed, "I wish they'd sing 'Swing Low, Sweet Chariot.' Then, as they crooned,

> "Swing low, sweet chariot,
> Gwine for to carry me home,"

I saw Lizzie's eyes fill with sudden tears, her throat quiver. Though she sang bravely on, I knew that her thoughts were with the absent brother in South Dakota whom she had been attending all winter, for whom — as Grandmother did not yet realize — the chariot was bending low, "gwine for to carry him home."

Bessie had written a three-part song — words and music — and dedicated it to Grandmother. Standing between the double doors, her trio of daughters sang it charmingly.

I Come to Thee in Prayer

> I come to Thee when morning light is breaking;
> Lord, hear my prayer and keep me through the day;
> Teach me to do Thy will when the world is waking —
> I come, O Lord, at dawn to pray.
>
> I come to Thee when midday sun is shining
> And life is full of promises so fair;
> The day is bright, each cloud has a silver lining —
> And still I come, I come to Thee in prayer.
>
> I come to Thee, the sun is slowly sinking
> Into the purple shadows of the west;
> What sweet content for me to just be thinking —
> Lord, I come to Thee, I come at eve to rest.

Devoutly we listened, our hearts melted, but before anyone could sink too deep into melancholy we all fell into the tune of "Auld Lang Syne," carrying it along with words that Bessie had also written for the occasion.

A Hundred Years

Now Grandma Brown's lived a hundred years
In the good old-fashioned way —
And if we'd follow in her steps
We might prolong our stay.

It was after this, I believe, that the cakes for the two birthday children were borne triumphantly in: a big, big glistening angel food blazing with a hundred tiny lights (made for Grandmother by Chita — twenty-four eggs, if you please), and a smaller cake for little John lighted by three bold tapers.

And then, when all the food was disposed of and we were, temporarily, too full to sing, utterances of another kind were heard. Cousin Charl read the gracious poem which Dr. James H. Dew-Brittain, rector of the Episcopal Church, had written in honor of Grandmother, a tribute to her and to the hundred years of proud achievement which she had seen. Next I made bold to review briefly the family history, not forgetting to mention Lieutenant Ebenezer Foster and Captain Benjamin Brown; and then short shy tributes were paid to everybody by Gus and Herbert. At the end came the composition of telegraphic greeting to Will, the absent eldest son.

The photographer came then to take a picture of Grandmother completing her hundred years. She sat before the fireplace and was *so* anxious that the andirons should "take" well. Also that the enormous basket of flowers with which the Bureau of Efficiency had expressed its pride in her should be shown. Next she wanted all her family photographed in a group around her. And we all waited until Edward and Alice flew home to get Jimmie, their baby, for the picture.

Before the picture-taking was over, neighbors were at the door crowding in to greet Grandmother Brown. Some of them lingered to join in the singing which started up again. All afternoon one heard "Let my people go!" reverberating, at intervals, through the house. And after Grandmother had been carried upstairs for a late nap groups of people kept on singing excitedly, standing on tiptoe and stretching their arms up: —

"We're from Ioway! I-o-way!
That's where the tall corn grows."

"No trouble telling the age of people who were here at different hours," remarked Sue whimsically. "The vintage of the songs they sang gave it away."

Refreshed by her second nap, Grandmother enjoyed the evening. She did not again go downstairs, but callers ascended to her. First of all came a handsome white-haired woman, who had once helped her in the household. "Oh, it pleases me to hear you say that you teach your daughters what I once taught you," Grandmother told her.

"Hark! What is that noise in the street?" she asked while Mary was calling on her.

"Put on the new lounging robe that Cousin Angie brought you," we urged her. "It's wadded and warm. Here's a scarf for your head. Let us throw up your window. Listen to the City Band."

Delightedly she obeyed. After the serenade was over, she said she wanted to thank each member of the band. Into the house they filed, entering her room and receiving her thanks.

After she had gone happily to bed, the rest of us

forgathered again at Bessie's and had another sing. The children had been to the front the night before, but this night it was the old folks' turn. The day's events had stirred deeply old memories and emotions. Expression was necessary. Seated at the corner of the piano where Bessie's nimble fingers, or Zetta's, suggestively tinkled tunes at him or brought appropriate chords to his help, Gus shut his eyes and let the flood of songs pour out, while the rest of us came in, as we could, in a heavy thumping chorus. The old plantation songs he had learned in the sixties, the minstrel nonsense of the seventies, the Gilbert and Sullivan melodies of the eighties, the topical dialect ditties of the nineties, mimicry of Swede and German, Jew and Irish — out it all came, on and on it flowed.

How did he remember it all, I wondered. But as I looked around I saw that Charlie and Lizzie and Jennie seemed to know the words too, their eyes rapt with remembering, their lips moving, automatically, as they waited for the beat of the chorus and then came out strong. "Uncle Gus's got going," whispered the grandchildren, delightedly, while the great-grandchildren stared wonderingly. Often do we elders look at our offspring in startled fashion, seeing what we have produced, but not often do we catch them regarding us so curiously, bewildered by a sudden glimpse of our strange adult natures.

The first day of Grandmother's hundred and first year was Sunday, a day of peaceful, happy visiting. She sent her Bureau of Efficiency flowers to grace the pulpit of her church, and Dr. Goff, the minister, spoke appropriate words about their beauty and about herself that added to her sweet content. In the next days her birthday guests went their several ways, Lizzie hurrying with foreboding heart to the bedside of her stricken brother. "Tell him that I look forward to his coming this summer," said Grandmother cheerfully. "Tell him how we missed him and his dear family. Tell him all about our wonderful reunion."

But when Lizzie came again to Will she found that the stroke had robbed him of power to speak. Only his eyes showed that he understood what she said. When she spoke of the reunion, he covered his face and wept, unreconciled to having missed it. "There is no hope," wrote Lizzie. "Better tell Mother that it is now only a matter of days."

Grandmother took the news calmly, but with deep sadness. Easter day followed, and kind friends showered her with the thoughts and emblems of the Resurrection. She was comforted. To her, Sioux Falls and Fort Madison seemed but anterooms to Heaven. Then, again and again, we reminded her: "Will has lived a long and useful life. And he has been fortunate beyond the average man. How many have lived past fourscore years and had a mother every minute of that time? And *such* a mother as *you* have been?"

But it was a week of tension. Grandmother dreaded suffering for her son. Death she did not fear. The telegram was welcome that brought the news that Will had been released from pain and had passed on. The soft sound of "Rachel weeping for her children" was heard, but there was no passion, no rebellion in her cry. It was as if she too were released from strain and had found relief.

"From our earliest years we know that this must be

the end," she told us. "It is the carrying out of Nature's laws. Why should we be angry at God and rebel? But oh, I wanted to go first."

In the next days, her thoughts went back to the early years of her family. As we sat with her in the hours of the fair spring day when her first-born was being carried to his last resting place, she recalled his baby ways, his young manhood. "How pretty he was — my first baby! And how dear he was to mind. I can see him sitting at table on his father's knee, not touching a thing on Dan'l's plate because we had said, 'No! No!' And I can see him creeping across the floor to a basket of eggs in the corner, crazy to play with them, but drawing back, obediently, when told. Oh, my Willie was different from all my other children. They were all *good* to me, but Willie was always the first to think of something to do, if I were sick, the first to take hold and help. And he was always so good to my other babies. How he used to roll over and over on the floor, playing with Frank! Oh, I have been so glad to see how happy his own boy has made him, how devoted Knapp has been, especially since Carrie died."

At her bidding we opened a drawer in her cherry bureau where she kept specially prized pictures and brought her the latest photograph of her oldest son. On the cover of it she had pasted a flap in which she had inserted the Christmas card and letter he had sent her in 1922, the letter in which he had recalled to her the Christmas thrills of his boyhood, "when your family consisted of just two boys. It seems to me that, from September until after Christmas," he wrote, "I never opened my eyes and peeped into the sitting room from our trundle bed that you were not sitting in front of the old Franklin stove with candle or lard lamp suspended to the back of a chair, stitching, knitting, or darning. Santa Claus was a reality to us then, a reality brought home to us by your hard work and simple gifts. Plain molasses taffy; doughnuts cut out in the shape of a boy; a couple of oranges; wool mittens and stockings of your own knitting; perhaps twin suits of gray Kentucky jeans with little roundabouts and caps to match. Can't you just see how we used to look? In our own boy now we are greatly blessed. And his family is a continual joy to us. Ah, mother dear, the Lord only knows how many more Christmas holidays we shall be permitted to exchange greetings on this earth. Probably not many."

On the margin of the letter Grandmother had written: "There is nothing could give a mother more pleasure than a letter like this from a son eighty years old, who remembered the things his mother did to make Christmas merry when he was a boy."

With a groan, Grandmother handed letter and picture back to us, saying, "Put them away. He's gone! These things I shall send to his boy."

We saw her turn to her Bible. We knew she would read it again and again, and be comforted. And so we left her, knowing that she would meet each day of her second hundred years cheerfully and bravely, without repining, and that, like David, she would say, "While the child was yet alive, I fasted and wept: for I said, Who can tell whether God will be gracious to me, that the child may live? But now he is dead, wherefore should I fast? can I bring him back again? I shall go to him, but he shall not return to me."

EPILOGUE

Since the above was written, Grandmother Brown has slipped from the clasp of Time. On January 8, 1929, "contentedly weary of life," aged one hundred and one years and nine months, lacking only a day, she fell into her last sleep.

Toward the end her will to live weakened. Her body might have functioned longer, had her spirit so inclined. But when one has finished all one's tasks, when one has survived all one's contemporaries, what motive force is there to keep one going? It was partly because I saw this lagging of the spirit that I began to write this book. True, I wanted to put down in Grandmother's own speech for the benefit of her children's children her comments on the spectacle of life which she had witnessed; but, more than that, I wanted to set Grandmother herself a constructive task, to give her a new interest in life.

Between the birthday parties in celebration of the completion of her ninety-ninth and the completion of her hundredth year, I sent her chapter after chapter as I put them together from the notes I had taken down at her side, and she returned them to me with occasional corrections and additions. When she saw her own words typed, she had doubts about the propriety of having told so many intimate matters, but we reassured her.

I never showed her the account of the Centennial celebration. I feared that the sharp emotional contrast between that day and those that followed might have a depressing effect. The shock of Will's death turned her thoughts from herself and her early life to the existing situation in her family. She feared that Death would again approach her intimate circle. Her own physical condition was intrinsically good, but anxiety disturbed her digestion — at times very violently. "If only I did n't have to eat to live," she wrote whimsically that fall, after one of her "bad spells," "I might live on forever."

It was impossible to protect her from anxiety. Will had died and, though she controlled her grief and entered happily into the life about her, she was ill with apprehension whenever one of her dear ones was threatened. Blow after blow fell upon her in the next year. The first one descended at the end of the Thanksgiving Day that followed Will's death. She had spent it with Bessie. Lizzie was also there as a guest. Thankfully the four generations drew together. To Grandmother, with her New England background, the Thanksgiving festival had always seemed especially significant. For years she and her Dan'l had been wont to visit their farmer son at that time of the year, to survey with satisfaction his colorful fields and heavily laden table, giving spontaneous thanks to God for the beautiful earth and all the fullness thereof — for the turkeys and pumpkins and sweet cider that were the visible sign of His loving care. On this, her hundredth such day, she joined gayly in all the little festivities of Bessie's home; enjoyed the automobile drive going and coming; ate something of everything that was offered her; listened to the children sing; blessed them all by word and radiant presence. But that night came a telegram to say that Cousin Jennie was dying — Cousin Jennie, who had been to Grandmother like one of her own children, who had come all the way from Boston to be at the Centennial celebration. Grandmother was overwhelmed.

And then the cold Iowa winter closed in, taking its toll of the old and feeble. In the household of Grandmother's son, Charlie, there was sickness and sorrow for many months. His wife, Lyde, passed away; his daughter, Edna, lay for months at the point of death; his little grandson, Wayne, died suddenly. He himself was ill and broken. Knowledge of these events could not be kept from Grandmother. When Charlie recovered sufficiently to visit her, she gathered him to her as if he were still her baby boy. "Charlie spent the night," she wrote, "and, as the house was full, I had him sleep on the couch in my room." The comfort of it every mother knows — when she can stretch out her hand in the night and feel that her child is still there!

There came a few weeks of respite from anxiety, the hopefulness that comes when spring is in the air. She was in good health and spirits in April when the hundred and first anniversary of her natal day arrived, but, at her own request, there was no family reunion. She held to her resolution that after Death had once broken the family circle there should be no celebration that would emphasize the empty chair. She wrote Herbert that she would prefer him to postpone his visit until warmer weather. But the day sped happily, with kinsfolk and neighbors running in to visit her.

And so her last summer passed in fair contentment.

When fall came, she showed keen interest in the Presidential campaign. After her failing eyesight made reading impossible, she was accustomed to call on Bessie for information about current events. She discussed with Gus, too, the topics of the day when he came in to read her the evening paper. She voted for Hoover and manifested great pride in doing so, in the fact that she was probably the oldest woman in America to cast a vote.

What Grandmother dreaded especially was becoming a charge on those already sufficiently burdened. "I want to live, dear, as long as I am a pleasure to others," she told Bessie, "but when I can no longer wait on myself, then it is time for me to go." The feeble health of the son and the daughter-in-law with whom she made her home made her fear that her continued living added to their difficulties. To spare her dear ones she courageously exerted her strength to wait on herself as those who were with her all the time hardly realized she was doing. One day, in trying to swing herself from her roller chair to her rocker, she slipped and fell to the floor. When Gus picked her up she said she was not hurt at all, but in a few moments she sighed, "I believe I would like to put on my gown and go to bed." She never again had on her clothes. Each day she grew weaker, but she insisted that she had no need of a nurse. It was against her instinct to ask a stranger to wait on her — a monstrous expense besides! She consented only when Bessie came and reminded her gently that if she did not have a nurse her dear "Gussie" would be rushing to attend to each tiny want with his own hands — Uncle Gus whom the doctor had cautioned to keep very quiet; that Lizzie was confined to her bed with the flu and could not attend her; and that Bessie herself had sick children at home who could not spare their mother. And as for the expense — what of it? How absurd to consider it! Would Grandmother want to deny her children the precious privilege of making her a little love gift, especially at Christmas time? And so Grandmother was persuaded to welcome the wonderful nurse who was engaged to wait on her. In the three weeks of their companionship Grandmother became very fond of her. In other days she had known nurses — with "their caps and things " — whose failure to appreciate the Presbyterian Church and the Republican party had tried her. This one was "just perfect."

No one felt that the day of Grandmother's departure was inevitably at hand. She did not seem to suffer. So often before had her marvelous vitality asserted itself unbelievably and brought her back. But this time her will gave no support. Each morning she seemed disappointed when she opened her eyes on earthly things. Several times during her last week she said, "Well, Gussie, I guess it will be only a few days now," and seemed pleased with the thought.

Convinced as she was that she should leave them, she nevertheless never ceased to cling lovingly to those around her even while she stretched yearning hands towards those on the other shore. "Many times the nurse called me," relates Bessie, "saying that Grandmother wanted me on important business, and when I reached her bedside with an anxious, 'What is it, dear?' I would find that she wanted me only to hold her hand, to love her, to talk with her. It seemed to rest her as much as it inspired me."

To Bessie she gave minute directions about her little

legacies. Long since had she made fair division of her silver spoons, her brass candlesticks, her feather pillows. With every child of her blood she had been anxious to leave some specimen of her exquisite handiwork, and to that end had plied her needle diligently for years.

Many times during her last year had she talked over with Bessie the details of her funeral. It was a topic of conversation in which she took satisfaction. True to instinct, her mind leaped ahead to manage it all herself, that others might be spared trouble on her account and that every detail might be "just perfect." Lizzie was to comb her hair; Bessie was to dress her — in the black lace she had worn at her Centennial party; Dan'l's ring was to be taken from her finger after she was dead and given to Bessie's little girl, Jean — named for Jean Thomas, Dan'l's old Revolutionary pioneer grandmother; Dr. Goff was to be asked to read the Scriptures she had chosen — those which give promise of "everlasting life," of "many mansions" in the Father's house, of a "holy city" where "God shall wipe away all tears." She asked that Bessie's song, "Come, Thou Weary One,"[1] — for which she herself had been the inspiration, — be sung. Finally, "Let it be a plain funeral — without flowers," she said to Gus.

Not once during those last days was her mind clouded. On the evening of January 7 she seemed even brighter than usual, but about dawn the nurse noticed that, though she breathed regularly and appeared to be sleeping, her pulse had weakened to the vanishing point. Gus was summoned. "Mother!" he called, but there

[1] A sacred solo by Elizabeth Davis Soechtig. Lorenz Publishing Company, Dayton, Ohio.

was no response, though he took her hand and sat beside her, waiting. Her breath came regularly but pantingly. At eight-thirty it ceased entirely; her head fell back; she was gone. "Let Thy servant depart in peace" had been her fervent prayer, and it had been answered.

In one respect only were Grandmother's last directions disregarded; Gus let her friends and neighbors bring their costly hothouse roses and lilies and make of the room in which she lay in the majesty and beauty of her last sleep a fragrant place. It was fitting that they should do her homage. "It was the imprint of such characters as your mother upon the people of the early West," said Vice President Dawes in his message of condolence, "that has made for the establishment there of a great civilization. With her passing there is broken one of the last personal links between the heroic past in the West and the present day of fine fulfillment and continued promise."